THE
VANISHING
WHITE
MAN

THE VANISHING WHITE MAN

Stan Steiner

Drawings by Maria Garza

HARPER & ROW, PUBLISHERS

NEW YORK, HAGERSTOWN, SAN FRANCISCO, LONDON

1817

Portions of this work appeared in somewhat different form in *Natural History, Akwesasne Notes* of the Mohawk Nation, and *The Plains Truth* of the Northern Plains Resource Council.

FIRST EDITION

Designed by Sidney Feinberg

Library of Congress Cataloging in Publication Data

Steiner, Stanley.
  The vanishing white man.
  Includes index.
  1. Indians of North America.   2. Human ecology—
The West.   3. The West—Description and travel—
1951–   I. Title.
E77.S833 1976   970'.004'97   74–15854
ISBN 0–06–014078–X

---

76 77 78 79 10 9 8 7 6 5 4 3 2 1

For

   Clyde Warrior

and

   Larry Casuse

and

   Richard Oakes

Contents

THE
VANISHING
WHITE
MAN

The Prophecy of the Technological Hopi

🐾 TESTAMENT OF Alvin Dashee,
vice-chairman, Hopi Tribe

On the stones of the wind-honed mesa, amid the sagebrush and desert sands that blew down the streets of the old village, there stood an air-conditioned, wall-to-wall-carpeted, electric-heated, and fluorescent-lighted building. It looked like the suburban branch of a bank. But it was not. It was the tribal headquarters of the Hopi, one of the most traditional and religious tribes in the entire country.

In the mud-and-stone village it was an incongruous and unlikely sight. The one sign of Hopi influence was the larger-than-life kachinas, messengers to the gods, painted on the walls beside the glass doors.

Behind his corporate-size desk in his plasticized office sat a junior executive of the tribe. He had a civilian crew cut and a brusque manner of a veteran of the Marine Corps, which he was. The ex-Marine had "been away" for a decade, he said, and had recently come back to the village. In the "world outside" he had become an electronics technician. So he was as at home in his office as he was in his kiva, he said.

Alvin Dashee was the youngest man ever elected by the Hopi to tribal leadership. He was thirty-one. In the way of the Hopi he was still a boy.

"Let me tell you what I am thinking about," he said. "Why was I elected?

"I am in the Sun and Eagle Clan. So that is why I was elected, I think. The time has come for the Prophecy of the Elders to be fulfilled. And it is being fulfilled, I think. The people in the village streets feel we need warriors in tribal office. So the people elected me because I am in the Sun and Eagle Clan and I am a Marine. That was no accident, I think.

"So I was elected because of that. The chairman, who was elected with me, is in the Sun and Eagle Clan, too. Our clan are the enforcers of the law."

Was he telling me that he really believed in the prophecy? He was no old man. He wore no headband. He had seen the great cities of the world. He knew the importance of technological progress for his poor tribe. He was an electronics man.

"Yes," he said, and smiled. "But technology has not disproved the Prophecy. Technology has fulfilled, and speeded up, the coming of the Prophecy."

This is what he told me:

So they say the white man will come and go. They say that!

In our Hopi culture we have prophecies that tell us what will happen and what is happening. They say these are like checkpoints in history. They say these prophecies will happen because we lived in other worlds, in other high civilizations, where they happened before. They say these prophecies are the symptoms of history. So all they are really saying is that history repeats itself: the white man will come and go. I think that is what they say.

So I think I can make these correlations between what is happening now and what I think they are talking about. And I can understand this.

There is a prophecy that the roads will be built in the sky. And that has happened already. That is the route in the skies of the jets, the flight plans. I think that is what they are talking about. And I think the people in our village streets will agree to that.

There is a prophecy that the arrows are going to rain from

the sky. I think that meant the coming of the bombers. And that has happened.

There is a prophecy that our government, our leaders, will hang on a spiderweb. And I see our government hanging on a spiderweb right now. That is Watergate!

There is a prophecy that our leaders will betray their people. That a sign of this will be adultery, when the men betray the women, and then the women will betray the men. So that there will be no morality, only selfishness. And that is happening already. And I am afraid of that happening.

There is a prophecy of this energy crisis. It was maybe five years ago that our elders met and they said this: That we are going to run into this crisis. That we are going to run out of the white man's energy. That we are going to have a famine. That we are going to have to turn back to the soil. Mother Earth is going to have to be nursing us again.

So when this energy crisis was realized by President Nixon, it wasn't news to us.

And then there is a prophecy of the end of the world. . . .

There is a prophecy of Grandmother Spider. She is a clever old woman. She has two grandsons. They are like the two little war gods. They see that the world spins on its axis. One has the voice and one has the wind.

Well, the web of Grandmother Spider has provided the energy of this world. All the conveniences of life we have, they say, come from the web of Grandmother Spider. They say this web is the jets that fly overhead, the natural gases that are piped under our feet, the highways, the power-transmission lines of the electric grid systems, the communications systems, like television and radio waves—these are nothing but the web of Grandmother Spider. They say they looked into this hole and they saw this. It was like looking into a television screen. They say they looked again, and it was burning. They say the web of Grandmother Spider, all our energy, was burning up!

Whether the web was burning with actual flames, I don't know. That is a matter of interpretation. It may have been burning from within. Like a lot of human beings are burning from within. That may be what they were talking about. But I interpret this burning as a fire that is going to happen. That is how I see it. That is what this old Mother Earth is going to do. She is going to go in flames.

And when these things happen, it will mean the end of life on this world. In other worlds before, men have destroyed themselves and their civilizations. So we know these things have happened in the past.

So when they say that these things are going to happen, our elders probably heard of these things back in the 1600s, in the seventeenth century; but they were talking of the twentieth century. And the prophecies have been fulfilled. So I am not saying that our life will end tomorrow. No, in the Hopi way of time, and of thinking, this will be years. But this materialistic wealth is going to go. Money isn't going to buy anything. So the Hopi doesn't place money, the green stuff, with a high value. The Hopi doesn't value that.

There will be an end to all of it. This materialistic civilization is going to destroy itself. I think it is quite evident that we are going in that direction. And I am really worried about this.

So I think the Hopi knows something that we can offer. . . .

When you talk of prophecies, the elders say: You see! You see! For years and years the Hopi has been prophesying these things, but no one has listened. Now we are going to listen to the elders.

In our society we have many thinkers and philosophers who tell us these things. And this is not something they are making up. This is something they have known before we came to this planet, this world. This is something they knew in the other worlds. This is the pattern of life. This is history.

So I believe in the prophecy. I cannot turn my head around and say no. Far too many things in the prophecy have already happened.

We have prepared for it. If the trading posts and the supermarkets in the cities were to run out of groceries this week, it wouldn't hurt the Hopi. Because we are ready!

In the villages many of the families have enough food stored for two years. The elders say that when the crisis has come there may be no food in the stores, no energy in the electric wires, no fuel for our chariots, our cars. So we have been drying corn and squash and beans and fruit in the sun. In the old way. We have dehydrated foods and stored them away.

We learned the secrets of survival long ago. In this land we have maybe eight or ten inches of rain annually. So we have to be excellent farmers. We plant our crops at least eighteen inches deep and five or six paces apart. If we planted like the white man, our corn might come up straight as a soldier, but in a little while it would turn over and die. So we have learned to use every little runoff of rain from the mesas to get water. In the autumn we plow the fields. Then we put grass on the fields to hold the topsoil when the winds begin blowing. And when it snows, the grass holds the water. So in the spring the water is frozen in the soil, and when it thaws, there is water for the early summer months when the desert is hottest and there is no rain. So we can grow crops where no one else can.

So the energy crisis is not going to hurt us very much. Many of our people are not dependent on electricity or gas. We don't have big power lines running across our land. All we need is a small one to provide for our tribal administration building and Public Health hospital.

Most of our village people still use the traditional way of heating, by burning wood and coal in their fireplaces. And by using wood stoves. That's power. That's energy. That's heat. That's light. That's free.

It is true that our buggies depend on fuel. There are few of the old wagons left. But we still have our horses. In the Hopi prophecy they say that our chariots will soon be useless. They say that they were talking about the automobiles. We know that, we expect that.

So we have not gone all out for machinery, or industry, or technology, because that has a limit to what it can do.

Man will become so controlled by machinery, by the things his keen mind has developed, that these things will eventually dictate his way of life to him. And I think that is what they talk about when they talk about computers today. Computers can be good and computers can be bad. But I think we are coming to the time when the computers will dictate to us. Maybe it is too early to say. We are isolated from the outside world, so I don't know what kind of computers they've got out there. But this is what I think.

The people don't want industry outside their doorstep. Or near the villages. Or on the top of the mesas. We have no big industry on the reservation. In fact, we have none at all. That is because our tradition tells us that if we do that we will become dependent on the electronic world, the mechanized world. And we will become so dependent we will start losing our values.

And so we will respond only to those things that man has created himself!

And I think that is what the Hopi is talking about. We are not going to be able to use our own abilities any more. We are not going to be able to use the things the Creator gave us to use. He did give us a mind, a keen mind, to make decisions, but He did not say to do all these things that will eventually destroy us.

That is not the Hopi way!

In our way, the highest value is the human value, the value of the human being. That is priceless. That is something no one can weigh, as a value in dollars. No one can weigh what the human soul is, what human values are worth, what friendship is worth, what love is. That is the Hopi way.

All we are doing is trying to find ourselves, where we are. We are not going around and preaching. That is not our way. That is not going to change the prophecies. That is history.

And I think history is going to fulfill its role. There is no turning back. We are going to have to risk the consequences of what we've done, how we've lived.

THE ONE-THOUSAND-
YEAR-OLD MAN

NOWHERE on earth was there a place where the horizon was as endless. The sky was everywhere. One stood on the edge of a cliff and turned in a circle and all the horizon turned with you. There was no time. There was only space.

In all the land no people were so near to the sun. The villages of the Hopi were on the rim of the earth.

On the dry mud floor in the stone house of the one-thousand-year-old village of Shungopavi, in northern Arizona, the *kikmongwi* sat on wooden benches and bowed their heads as though in prayer. They were not praying. They were pondering the impact of statements of the white man's lack of energy on the villages. When the power plants and strip mines on Black Mesa darkened the sun and blackened the sky and drained the water of the cornfields, what will we do? these holy men asked one another. Where will we go?

"We have moved before," sighed an old man. "So if we have to, we will move again."

"That was one thousand years ago," I said.

"Ah, yes, it is true, we lived here maybe one thousand years," the old man said, and nodded. "Maybe longer."

Some said that the village of Oraibi on the nearby mesa was the oldest in the United States. It had been inhabited for a millennium. The old man politely disagreed. He remembered that his village of Shungopavi had been settled before that. "Maybe in the year of 800 my people came here. I remember something like that," the old man said.

"Remember? You remember?"

There was a puckish smile on his dried and aged lips. He delighted in telling the scholarly white men who visited him things the simplest child knew, and pretending it was wisdom.

"Man does not have the only memory. The stones remember. The earth remembers. If you know how to listen, they will tell you many things," he chided me.

The old man was not one thousand years old, though he seemed to be as ancient as the dried mud on the roof of his house. He was the *kikmongwi* of Shungopavi, the village chief. Claude Kuwanijuama was a man of enduring humor; he was bear-shaped, squat, and sturdy, and he wore a dignified headband on his long gray hair. He spoke with the authority of history. Everyone listened when he spoke, but he spoke seldom and softly.

He had come from the kiva to attend this energy conference. It was the time of the purification rites, for the village's Snake Dance. But the white man's need for energy had brought the bulldozers that were strip-mining the religious shrines on Black Mesa. And now this, too, was a matter of importance, needing purification.

Several of the clan headmen had come from the kiva with him. In the old house, beneath the low ceiling of century-old vigas, they sat in a circle and talked of what to do about the white man's energy crisis.

On Black Mesa the *bahana*, the white man, had dug the first of the many strip mines that were soon to unearth the coals of the West. It was to be "the largest power project in the world," the electric companies had boasted. Six power plants were planned, which would turn the energy of the sun and earth in the coal into fourteen million kilowatts of electricity. In the cities of Los Angeles and Phoenix and Las Vegas the *bahana* had no energy left. He had wasted it all. So he had come to the villages of the Hopi and demanded the coal that the people had been mining for so many hundreds of years. The old Tribal Council had given it to them.

Later, the holy men said the Tribal Council's signing of the government's strip-mining contract with the Peabody Coal Company was unlawful. Of eighteen seats on the council, seven were "empty." Some of the councilmen had never been "certified" by the village chiefs, as the Hopi constitution decreed. So there were only seven legal councilmen who had voted for the strip mining. But now it was too late.

In a small corner of the power project, known as Four Corners, the strip mines and electric plants were blackening the sun with more gray smog, sulfuric acid, and nitrogen oxides than plague Los Angeles and New York together. The man-made darkness was said to be the single man-made product that the astronauts could see from space.

"And when they do this thing the sun will darken," warned Herbert Talahaftewa, leader of the Bear Clan. "There will be no more sun. The sun will be black."

"It is prophesied," said David Monongye, a holy man of the village of Hotevilla. "Long ago we prophesied that the *bahana* would destroy the earth and destroy the air and destroy himself. So we have been expecting that."

In the plaza of the village the sun stood still, and it consumed the sky. It was late afternoon of a summer day on the high mesas. And the heat of the sun's energy was omnipotent: it filled the sky with space. In the one-thousand-year-old house there was no feeling of history, for when history was present everywhere, the past was the present. So the talk of the Hopi prophecy was as contemporary as the latest news of the energy crisis. The voices of the holy men were quiet, gentle, patient.

On the mud floor the grandchildren—or were they the great-grandchildren?—of the *kikmongwi* of Shungopavi had been playing beneath the bench on which he sat, in between his legs. He laughed with them.

All the time the holy men had talked of the Armageddon of energy they faced, the children ran and played at their feet. The children were respectful and quiet, uttering hardly a word. Nor had the elders said an angered word to the children, or told them to leave the room.

In one corner of the house, the women of the family were busy cooking a feast of beans and corn for the coming Snake Dance. They seemed to be chatting among themselves, but they were listening to the men with their eyes.

An elderly woman, her white hair thinned with age, sat upon a nearby bench nodding her approval, or disapproval, of the talk of the men. She never spoke. The opinions expressed by her nods were nonetheless watched carefully by the men with visible concern. She sat there as a grandmother might, or a matriarch.

One of the children began to cry. She had hurt her head on the bench. The old *kikmongwi* lifted her to his lap and comforted her. The talk of the holy men continued until the child, smiling again, crawled down and began to play.

The energies of the deserts and the mesas were matters of life and death in the villages. Was that why the entire family was included in the conference?

In the deserts the cycle of life was fragile. The delicate balance might be upset by one inch of water less than normal. And there might be famine. One error by the bulldozers and dragline cranes of these strip mines might affect the life of every Hopi. The *bahana* was merely worried about lowering the heat of his house by four degrees. Here, the villages might die.

And yet, when I tried to imagine as humane a conference in the executive suites of Peabody Coal, or in the offices of the Interior Department, where the strip-mine contracts had been written and approved, my imagination was not great enough. One Peabody executive had told me that when the company, a subsidiary of Kennecott Copper, negotiated the contract it had never occurred to them "that there were Indians out there."

In the coal-industry journal the strip miners were assured that there were merely "a few sheep, coyotes and Indians" to worry about.

"As we have known you white men, you have been cannibals," said Talahaftewa. "You have always been devouring everything on earth for yourselves. Even people. Even the animals. Even the earth. You have never respected anything, or anyone, on earth." The headman of the Bear Clan was stern and suspicious of me. He apologized for speaking so sharply.

"Why doesn't the *bahana* let us alone?" he asked.

That was why I had come to the Hopi, I said. Some good friends of mine were making a documentary film for television in which the Hopi, and the Navajo, too, would be able to tell the entire country what they thought of the strip miners on Black Mesa. It would be seen by millions of people. The National Science Foundation, National Educational Television, and the Ford Foundation were sponsoring the film. It may be important, I said.

That did not seem to impress the holy men of Shungopavi. Rarely, if ever, had they invited white men to film the villages.

"In the past the white man brought us his diseases. And then he brought us his hospitals to cure his diseases," Talahaftewa said sardonically. "Now the white man brings us his pollutions. And you come and say you will cure these pollutions you have brought us."

"We do not trust you!" said the Bear Clan headman accusingly. "Tell me, why should we believe a white man?

"I would like to trust you," he said, "but can I?"

The sun darkened in the sky. We had been talking for many hours. Still the holy men of the Hopi had not decided what to say. They knew that nothing they said would be listened to by the white man. It never was. We sat in silence.

Early that morning I had come to the village of New Oraibi to seek Thomas Banyacya, the interpreter and spokesman for the traditional chiefs, to request permission to make the film. Banyacya was not at home.

His wife came to the screen door. She smiled pleasantly and invited me in. She immediately turned her back to me, to work on the yucca basket she was weaving. On newspapers spread on her kitchen table were sheaves of long, thin yucca leaves. Her fingers deftly wove the fibrous plant, that had been dipped in water to soften its desert toughness, into a circle of beauty.

"Thomas has been expecting you," she said.

It was a curious remark. No one knew I was coming; I had told no one. The traditional Hopi had no telephones. And I had never met Banyacya.

Sitting at the kitchen table and sipping a cup of black coffee she had offered me, I told Mrs. Banyacya of the projected film for educational television. I told her I thought the film might be useful to the Hopi. I told her I thought the film director was a good man, for he knew nothing of Indians and he did not wish to "save" them. I told her he made films about eagles and coyotes, which he loved, but he knew very little about people. So he wouldn't be prejudiced by white myths.

Her laughter had turned her head to me. "That *is* a refreshing thought," she said.

So many ecologists, do-gooders, university students and professors, writers, friends of Indians, and sympathizers had come to help the Hopi that the Banyacyas had turned the house behind theirs into a "sort of dormitory" for "our visiting white friends." There was even a stove where these visitors could cook.

"Everyone says they want to help us," she said dryly.

On one side of the kitchen table sat an old, long-haired man. He said nothing while we talked. He was blind, I thought, for his eyes were clouded behind his thick glasses. But he was watching and judging me with all his senses. It was not until later that I learned the old man was David Monongye, one of the holy men of Hotevilla, where it was said that the sacred stones of the prophecy were secretly stored.

After an hour or so, the old man stood up.

"I will take you," he said.

"Where?"

"So you can see the *kikmongwi*. And you will tell him about this film project of your friends. And then we will see what we will do about it."

The old man led me by the hand, I did not lead him, into the courtyard, where my car was. "You drive," he said. "My eyes are not very good; my eyes are almost blind," he apologized. "But I know the way and I will give you direction."

In this way we drove to see the *kikmongwi* of Shungopavi. The old man knew the road up and down the mountain, but I was fearful.

The old man said, to reassure me, "I see the way. When I was young we came on horses."

On the cliffs, the thin line of asphalt clung uncannily to the edges of the mesas. The cliffs were two thousand feet high in some places. The road was manic. It rose to the sun, and vanished in space. Like Pegasus it then fell again.

In the canyons and deserts down below, the piñons and cotton-wood trees looked like no more than clumps of dry grass. What was it like to live upon the top of the world? In Tibet? In the Andes of the Incas? In the capsuled space of the astronauts? In the Hopi villages?

The mesas were fingers of a fist of rocks which extended from the palm of Black Mesa. And these fingers seemed to be reaching skyward, to the sun.

On the farthermost edge of the mesas stood the villages. It was as though the builders of one thousand years ago had sought to come as near to the sun as a man dared. Houses on these pin-nacles of rock were constructed of stone and mud. From the distance they looked like the earth itself, in perfect camouflage.

Once we came to Shungopavi, through the labyrinth of narrow alleys, between ancient houses, the word of our coming traveled quickly through the village. In moments the *kikmongwi* came running from the kiva. He was running, not walking, in the old way of the Hopi.

Like a jovial bear, the *kikmongwi* greeted us with a generous smile. He invited us to come into his house. And so the day-long energy conference had begun.

No one knew more about conserving the energy resources of the southwest desert than did the village chiefs and holy men of the Hopi. They had survived for centuries on their dry and arid mesas. In a land where the rainfall was barely six inches yearly, where no rivers flowed and where there were few springs, every ounce of energy in the water and the earth had to be used sparsely and wisely. In all the centuries that the people had mined the coals of Black Mesa, they had done no ecological damage to the earth.

"Our people were using coal hundreds of years before the Europeans," said Alvin Dashee. "If you go to the old ruins, where our people lived thousands of years ago, you will find they were already burning coal.

"In every village the people have their own coal mine, where they have always dug coal without strip-mining our mother the earth," Dashee said.

"We have good engineers in our clans. Maybe they could teach you something?"

And yet not once were these tribal miners asked their opinion by the *bahana* of the strip mines. No white man thought the Hopi knew anything, said the holy men.

"They seem to think we are dumb Indians," said Herbert Talahaftewa.

Once the elders had made a pilgrimage to the strip mine. The holy men had sprinkled corn meal around the bulldozers and draglines, to bring them into harmony with nature and halt them from doing evil. A mine foreman had said the sacred corn meal had "scared the hell out of the cat drivers." They thought the holy men were sprinkling blasting powder.

"Why doesn't the white man understand? He thinks we are trying to take away his energy, which he steals from us. He doesn't see we are trying to teach him the way to save his energy," the Bear Clan headman said.

"He is blind," said the old blind man. "So he destroys himself when he tries to save himself."

In frustration, the holy men had brought suit in federal court in Washington, D.C., seeking to halt the strip mining of the mother earth, and to restore the harmony of nature. They accused the Secretary of the Interior, Rogers C. B. Morton, and the Peabody Coal Company of violating the laws of God. "Carving up Black Mesa by the process known as strip mining is a desecration, a sacrilege, contrary to the instructions of the Great Spirit," stated the legal brief. These lands "are the spiritual center of the universe. It is prophesied that if [these] lands are ruined, the world will end."

The world will end! The world will end!

Nothing happened. The legal brief of the holy men was forgotten in the courts. The ecological lawyers were furious. The holy men of the Hopi shrugged.

It did not matter. Long ago the prophecy of the Hopi wise men had foretold the coming of the end of the white man. And when the time came, the web of gas pipelines and oil pipelines, roads and highways, electric transmission wires and jet streaks in the sky would begin to vanish, to be empty and useless. The energy crisis would come. And when the time came, the people would have to be nourished by the mother earth once again, for food in the stores would disappear. The return to nature would come.

"So we expected that," David Monongye said. "It was prophesied. It is coming true."

"So you think a documentary film will save the white man," said Talahaftewa. He laughed. "Who will produce the film? White men?"

"It may do some good, but it will probably not," he said.

At last it was decided. If it happened that the Hopi halted the strip mining on Black Mesa, in time so many ecologists, longhairs, and government officials would be coming to the villages to ask how they did this that it might be worse than the strip mining.

They thought it might be better if the film was a bad film. But if it was to be made by a white man, it probably would be. He would not know how to respect the mother earth. He would not understand the prophecy. He would not listen. He would not convince anyone. He would do no wrong and do no good. And if that was so, it might be interesting, perhaps, to let the film be made.

"Let them come and let them bring their cameras. And we will see what happens," said David Monongye. "That is how we have thought about it."

On the long road home from the Hopi to my house in Santa Fe, I wondered what I would tell the director and technicians of the television crew, who were waiting for the tribal elders' decision. I thought it wisest to try to tell them the truth.

Under the portal we gathered in the summer shade. Let me tell you what the *kikmongwi* have told me, I said, but before I do I must tell you why they have decided to say yes:

Because you will make a bad film.

Because it will do no good.

Because even if it is good no one will listen to it.

Because if they listen they will not understand.

Because the white man is ignorant of the meaning of life and does not respect the cycle of life, he will destroy his mother earth, which is sacred, which is his source of life, and he will destroy himself in trying to survive.

Because that is prophesied.

So you may bring your television cameras to the village and make your film. They will help you. This is what they say.

One man listened and looked up and shook his head. "Those damn Indians are nuts," he said.

And the television director was indignant. "We will show them they are wrong. I believe that the people will listen."

That was some years ago. In time the film was made and tens of millions watched it. No one listened to the holy men. Everything the *kikmongwi* and the clan headmen had said would happen did happen. The energy crisis came. The fuel crisis came. The gas crisis came. The food crisis came.

And what had happened upon Black Mesa was soon to happen to all the lands of the West; as the Hopi had prophesied.

Man Creates Nothing

❦ TESTAMENT OF Frank Di Luzio, former manager,
Los Alamos Scientific Labs,
Atomic Energy Commission

In the rugged mountains of northern New Mexico, on a remote and isolated high mesa surrounded by barbed-wire fences and armed security guards, the government established a secret laboratory for the manufacture of nuclear bombs, known as Los Alamos. The scientists had split the atom and had released in a warhead "more energy than mankind had ever known or possessed." Some thought that man had become almost godlike; he had the power of life and of death. With this "divine power," one editorialist wrote at the time, man could indeed destroy himself.

One of the young men assigned to Los Alamos was a self-styled humanist and lover of the "energy of life." He was a civil engineer, an enthusiast of scientific technology. Frank Di Luzio had never been on a desert mountain before. He had never known an Indian.

As a boy, he had wished to become a priest. Instead he had become a civil engineer in the U.S. Army Corps of Engineers.

The cross of God was laid aside for the slide rule of Mammon. Still, he would be troubled forever by man's "good and evil uses of energy" and the "morality of science."

In no time, this energetic young man became Director of Engineering and then Manager of the Atomic Energy Commission's operations at Los Alamos. A man of catholic knowledge, he soon distinguished himself as one of the country's scientific spokesmen and a policymaker in many fields: as Executive Director of the U.S. Senate Aeronautical and Space Committee, and Special Assistant to the ranking member of the Atomic Energy and Space committees, Senator Clinton Anderson; as Assistant Secretary of the Interior for water and environmental matters; as Staff Director for scientific studies on energy and natural resources for the Western Governors' Conference; and as consultant and science adviser to NASA, the AEC, to the State Department, and to governors and presidents.

Science was, and is, his life—"all of my life," he said. But the years had taught him to respect "how much man knows" and to doubt "how much man understands."

Now he was older, and maybe wiser. His sparse hair was gray, his intense face deeply lined and worn by a mixture of vitality and frustration. In his rapid-fire speech one of his favorite phrases had become: "It is a paradox."

What was a paradox? Life or science? He said, "Both!"

After a lifetime of devotion to science and technology, he had become "philosophical" about "human wisdom, or the lack of it." He had become a "red-blooded American maverick," he said, a "devil's advocate," a man who had "to tell the truth to those who don't want to hear the truth"—the scientists and technologists he worked with, and for, all his life.

"Someone has to," he said. "The pragmatists never care for a philosopher, you know."

If the specter of the dead of Hiroshima lingered over Frank Di Luzio's philosophical disquiet, he never talked to me about "The Bomb." No one liked to talk of it in Los Alamos.

In the old days the sheep of the Spanish farmers grazed on the grassy plateau of Los Alamos. The religious shrines of the nearby Pueblo Indians were hidden in the canyons. Some still are. The Poplars, which is what *Los Álamos* means in Spanish, was a quiet place. It was the site of nothing more destructive of the earth's energy than a dude ranch and boys' school for the sons of a few wealthy Eastern families, beneath the serene and wise sky of the mountains of the Indians.

Now the sheep were gone on the meadows of Los Alamos. But the mountains, the sky, the Indians had changed little.

Now, too, the secret laboratory was no longer secret. The atomic bomb was no longer worshiped as before. The "divine power" of man was no longer thought to have conquered nature. Even the wisdom of that thought was doubted.

And Di Luzio often wondered what the energies of science and technology had really accomplished for humanity. What good? What evil?

This is what he told me:

Man creates nothing.

Energy is not created by man. He uses it. He converts it from one form of energy to another. He is a form of energy himself. But he does not create energy and he cannot destroy it. Then why do some people think we manufacture energy?

We are arrogant.

It is the arrogance of technology, the arrogance of science, the arrogance of the Ph.D.s, and the arrogance of man.

If a man gets a Ph.D. and becomes an expert on the right leg of the bumblebee, what does he know about the left leg, or the wings, or the honey—or the flower? Nothing! So he is arrogant about what he knows about, and he is stupid about everything else.

If a man gets four Ph.D.s, he becomes four times as arrogant and four times as stupid.

One of the reasons we have this energy crisis is just that: We think we can do anything and everything we want. We think we can use up, and waste, all the energy we want and always manufacture more. But it takes energy to make energy. Sometimes we use up more energy in the process of energy production than we produce.

In the "Statement on Energy Policy" of the Western Governors' Conference we said this: "So much energy is used by man

and his machines to produce energy that a net loss might be in-
curred. Consideration should be given, as an example, to whether
construction of a natural gas pipeline from the Polar Cap to the
United States might not consume more petroleum-based energy
than the energy that would ultimately flow from the new
source."

One study shows that it may have taken more energy to dig
up the ore, to manufacture the steel, to make the pipe, and to
build the Alaskan pipeline than will flow through that pipeline
for the first two years that it is used. And that does not take into
account the energy used in pumping the oil during those two
years.

And that's stupid.

Man may have to change his whole approach to nature. We
see only the energy we get from nature. We do not look at the
energy we use up in strip mining and refining, in transporting
and using that energy; the energy not only needed to run the
machines, but the energy needed by the men—and their families
—who design, manufacture, and run the machines.

We have to begin to see the whole cycle. We have been intellectually arrogant. We have to stop and think about what we
have been doing.

All my life I have been involved with the administration of
science and technology. But I have always been aware that there
was too much awe of science and technology. There was not
enough concern for man, social concern.

Now when I look at what has happened to science and technology I see two things: Our lives have been changed without
our consent, and scientists and technologists have been placed
on a pedestal because of a mistaken understanding of their
capabilities.

Science and technology were credited with being able to solve
anything and everything. And man could be as careless, as care-
free, with nature and natural resources as he wished, because
science would always come to his assistance and by some magical
formula always bail him out.

I have the gut feeling that this is not so. Some things that man does to man and to the world, not even science, not even technology, will be able to help man change.

If man uses up "his" natural resources, if man pollutes his environment any more, then science and technology cannot bail him out. Nor can science and technology bail him out of his warlike attitudes, because science and technology have made war so attractive financially for the economy that I sometimes wonder what comes first, science or war.

So I have cautioned against things like the chemical engineering of the population. We are changing the environment of man to so chemical a state of environment that we may never be able to go back to a natural environment, to evolve into higher human beings. The invasion of our food chains, our biology, with chemicals may have changed our evolutionary patterns.

When I have spoken of this, I have been accused of using scare tactics. But these are things that worry me.

Man may go too far one of these days. Even if we know how to modify man, who the hell is going to set the standards? Who is going to say what the human being should be? Who is to say if biological engineering will be used for good, that it won't be used for evil?

Once we can change the make-up of man, and change the genetic inheritance, we are becoming godlike. I wonder who has the wisdom to set the guidelines for these experiments. There is a cry from the scientists in England to stop these experiments. Why? Because we may change the genetic characteristics of man to such an extent that there may come into being a whole new biology of man, new viruses, new diseases we know nothing about and cannot control.

To me the worst thing that could happen would be to saturate the government with scientists and technologists of this kind. Where the hell would you get your social concern! your morality! your philosophical input!

My feeling is that if God created man in His own image, He must have aspired for man to rise to the morality of God. He gave man a brain for that. So man must aspire toward that.

The irony is that Christianity gives man the privilege to make the right or wrong choice. He sometimes makes the wrong one. But if man is striving to be godlike—and I believe our potential is that great—then anything, even science, that defiles man and stifles his growth is wrong. There is no justification in the world for defiling mankind.

Therefore I dread the way scientists and technologists are making the matter of energy so abstract that man will be forgotten. There is an old Italian proverb that says, "No man can cry at every man's funeral." But man has to be concerned with man.

For me, man is the sole subject we should be concerned with. I have a deep, humanistic approach to science, which may be religious in a way.

Man cannot step out of nature. He is part of it. He has to be part of it.

And that is the reason I have become a great admirer of the philosophy of the American Indians versus the philosophy of Western Europeans. The Indian philosopher will listen to a bubbling brook and it will be gentle on his ears and he will talk about these beautiful sounds he hears. And he will listen to the wind whistling through the trees and describe it in beautiful words—and that will be his philosophy.

But the Westerner will look at the same bubbling brook and the first thing he will think of will be to put that damn water to work. He will want to build a dam there, and put in some power turbines.

Western man doesn't consider himself to be a part of nature. He has a religious arrogance. I have been accused of being sacrilegious for saying this, but I have found that some Jesuits and many Christian theologians are saying the same thing: that Christianity has made man arrogant toward nature because he feels that if, in fact, he has been made in the image of God and everything on earth has been placed at his disposal, it is his right to exploit it.

No Indian philosopher would exploit a stream, or a natural

resource, in this way. It may be that his philosophy stops him from utilizing nature. Now we are beginning to wonder if he is right and we are wrong.

Our feeling for the beauty of nature has been lost. In our philosophy we think that everything upon the face of the earth was placed here for our pleasure. We think nothing of putting it to work.

Strangely enough, when seeking to recapture the beauty that we have lost, when we retire from work, when we are old enough to be able to read a few books of philosophy, what do we do? We retreat into the woods, we buy a house in the country, we move to Florida, or California, or Oregon, to try to recapture the very things we destroyed in our own backyards.

It is a strange thing. It is a cycle of life.

THE SUN IS BECOMING DARKER

IN his hand a ring emerged from the piece of silver. On his finger it blossomed into a turquoise flower. Loloma, a Hopi artist and jewelrymaker, was sitting at his workbench. He waved at a sun-lit cliff across the canyon. "See the sun?" he said, pointing to the rock. "What do you see? Sometimes when I look, I see the sun in the rock, and I see the sun differently on different rocks on different days. And I try to see what the sun is saying.

"Sometimes they say the sun is not blind. The people are blind. The sun is not mute; it can talk to us. The people are deaf; they can't hear it."

Was he saying that the sun talked to him?

"It talks to everyone, but differently. Sometimes two people are sitting here on the workbench by each other, looking at the sun on the mesa, and they see different things. The sun sends messages in different ways. Why? Because the sun has more ener-gies than people know or understand. People cannot know all that the sun tells them. People cannot see all the things the sun sees."

The sun was wiser and older than the people. It was older

than the earth. The sun knew more than we knew because it had more wisdom, more energy, more power, more knowledge, more life, than we had. The sun told us things we were still too childish to see, or know, or understand. There was a great energy, as there was a great knowledge, stored in the sun.

Loloma suddenly asked me, "Why have you asked me this?"

Although we were good and old friends, we seldom saw each other, for we lived in different worlds. It was a long journey to his world on the mountain from my world in the river valley.

Loloma asked me, "Why have you come to see me?"

To see the sun. To see the mountains. To write these things, I told him.

"It is a good time for you to come," he said. "Every day I see more messages from the mountains, from the sun."

What did he see?

"The sun is becoming darker," Loloma said. "Every day there is less light."

And he told me this story. One day a few years ago, he had been invited to a Convocation of Indian Scholars at Princeton University. Everyone got up and made long academic speeches about the problems of the Indian people and the future of America. But he thought they were ignoring the true problem.

"I stood up. And all I had to say was seven words," Loloma remembered, with a smile.

Seven words?

" 'In the East, there is no sun!' I said. And sat down. First there was silence. Then they all applauded," Loloma told me, the shadow of a smile on his bright face. He knew the sun had darkened in the West, too.

On the sacred mountain of the Hopi, near Flagstaff, Arizona, there was a "15 percent decrease in sunlight," Dr. Melvin Goodwin, director of the State Health Planning Authority, had estimated. The darkness came from power plants hundreds of miles away, which were burning up the earth to create electricity for cities thousands of miles away. And so the sun grew dark.

Man had been darkening the sky for centuries. In one hundred years, from 1860 to 1960, the earth had been burned up so indiscriminately in furnace and factory by man in his quest for its energy that the carbon monoxide content of the air had thickened by almost 15 percent. Scientists of the climate such as Dr. Reid Bryson, of the University of Wisconsin, thought that the dirt and dust man spewed into the sky was blocking "more and more sunlight" from reaching the earth. The darkness might be disastrous. For if one percent less sunlight were to touch the earth, the climatologists thought a new Ice Age might descend upon humanity. Some thought it had already begun.

The earth was becoming not only darker but colder. Since the 1940s the global temperature had fallen by an estimated 2.7 degrees. On the North Pole, the Arctic icecap was becoming larger. One climatologist, Dr. George J. Kulka, of Columbia University's Geological Observatory, had discovered in his studies of satellite weather data that in the Northern Hemisphere, the region of snow and ice had increased by 12 percent since 1970. Year by year the earth seemed to be growing colder.

Some thought all this was due to sunspots. Some thought it was a cyclical weather pattern. But it was thought by others that man himself was darkening the sun and sky with the wasted energy he so recklessly spewed forth into the heavens.

In the old villages of the Hopi, where the scarce energies of the deserts were nourished and cherished as was life itself, these thoughts were sacrilege. The way man was darkening the sun was either "suicide" or "murder," said Loloma—"maybe both."

And yet the English physicist Freeman Dyson, of the Institute for Advanced Study, thought it a cosmic law: for everywhere he saw the universe to be "mindlessly burning up its reserves of energy"—inexorably drifting toward the state of final quiescence described imaginatively by Olaf Stapleton: "Presently nothing was left in the whole cosmos but darkness and dark whiffs of dust that were once galaxies." On earth the difference was that the darkness was not mindless. It was man-made.

On his mountain, morning by morning, Loloma had seen the darkening of the sun in the dimming colors of the dawn. His eyes had been measuring it as sensitively as a scientific instrument. The elders of the villages had seen it long ago. It was this darkness that they had foretold, hundreds of years before, in their Prophecy of the Elders.

It was coming now throughout the West. The desert sky of the Papago and the Apache was burnt darkly red and yellow by sulfur and copper. Soon the mountain sky of the Cheyenne in Montana, the Lakota of the golden prairie, the Wind River people of Wyoming, would be black with coal. In the sky of the white man the air of the city was already gray.

Once "the sun lay upon the earth," the Osage said, as a lover would, and in this way it brought "life from the earth." If the sky darkened, inch by inch, then would the earth be unloved and barren. Life on earth would wither and die. And the morning would never be reborn. That was why the dawn of each day was a "thing very mysterious," said Tahirussawichi, in the hako of the Pawnee, "although it happens every day." For it was "man's awakening, after that lapse into the 'nothingness' of chaos, which is sleep"; it was the miracle of a "daily" rebirth. In the words of the Navajo, the whole world was a "House made of dawn," in which the People lived; without the sun there would be no one, no thing, no world.

The day was created by the coming of the sun. So was life. In the deeply sacred ceremony of the Apache, when a girl becomes a woman in the rite of puberty, the "dawn boys" come with the morning sun to anoint the newborn woman with their light, which is their energy. And so the Apache sing to the rays of the sun: "They come wearing yellow shoes of sunlight. They come dancing upon streams of sunlight." The womb of woman, like the womb of earth, is made fertile by the energy of the sun, not by the energy of man. Man does not create life; he merely helps to birth what the sun has created. That concept of energy as the source of life is at once more humble and powerful, more simple and profound, than that of those men who believe they have created, or manufactured, the man-made energy of their self-made lives.

In the song of the Apache there is the knowledge that the sun's "light gives us [our] form and color" in a bodily "defined space" and a place in the cosmos of "fluid time." The energy of the sun is both beyond and within our beings, so, as Hartley Burr Alexander wrote in *The World's Rim*, this "reality of the primitive is no less than of an Einsteinian *physis*."

When a child was born, the Zuñi lifted the infant to the Father Sun, from whom the energy of its spirit had come. The Zuñi sang:

> Now this is the day,
> Our new child,
> When you go upright
> Into daylight.

"Some people say that we are sun worshipers. That is not so, in the way that they understand that," said Hopi tribal leader Alvin Dashee. "I think they say that because they think prayer to the sun is a philosophy of superstition. That is not so. The Hopi believes in the Creator who made the sun. And the sun is the most powerful and obvious of His creations. That we see. That we know. So we respect that and we have reverence for that. We know the sun is not God. The sun is the giver of light. The sun is the giver of life. When we pray to the sun, we pray to life. So that is not a superstition of the Hopi. That is the scientific truth."

It was true. For hundreds of years the worship of the sun had been ridiculed and romanticized as a "primitive" superstition of "prescientific" tribal people. The German philosopher Oswald Spengler had epitomized the European conceit when he denigrated the "primitive man," who like "a child" had no "real knowledge of history or nature," for he was "too intimately" part of the elements, like the sun. Egypt seemed a "mere incident" in history, he wrote.

Those nineteenth-century philosophical bureaucrats of the Bureau of Indian Affairs put it more moralistically and vulgarly. In 1882 an Indian agent named J. H. Fleming was sent to study the Hopi tribe, one of the first to do so. He wrote to Washington of the Hopi dancing to the sun: "The dark superstitions and unhallowed rites of heathenism as gross as that of India and Central Africa still infects them with its insidious poison, which unless replaced by Christian civilization, must sap their very life blood." That was one hundred years ago. He was wrong.

On the Pine Ridge Reservation of the Ogallala, that same year, the Indian agent V. T. McGullycuddy cursed the sun dances of the Lakota: "Dancing is diminishing, and the heathenish ceremony termed the Sun Dance will I trust soon be a thing of the past." He too was wrong.

In one way or another the tribes had learned to honor the energy of the sun. And how that energy flowed. The knowledge of the sources of life, in the green of a leaf, the black of the earth, a flower of grain, the light in a lover's eye, or the red blood of birth and death, had come from generations of observation and scientific thought. The tribal scholars and holy men were humbled by the sun in their knowledge, not in their superstition. The sun was worshiped not in ignorance, but in wisdom.

Still, it was wisely feared. The sun was not a heavenly gift to man, but, like fire, could be a force of life and of death. The Kwakiutl said: The sun has passed through the darkness of death, to become light. And the Witoto: Nothing is what we are made of.

If the sun was the source of life, then it had to be the source of death as well. On the earth, life was born of all that had died, in a leaf of grass or in an infant child. The Pawnee said: The dawn is "the child of the Spirit of Light and of Darkness." For life and death were as lovers. The concept of a negative and positive flow of energy in one being was surely as profound as any developed by modern physics.

As did many people, the Osage painted the bodies of their warriors "the red color shed by the Spirit of Day," so they would be "free of death." Red was the color of life, so red was the color of death. In many tribes the dead were painted red.

In the hako of the Osage it was said:

> Remember, remember,
> life of the great sun
> breathes life on earth.

So powerful is this energy of the sun that no man can know or imagine it. Scientists have estimated the radiation that is released by the sun's fires to be a "constant" 350 billion trillion kilowatts, a figure so vast it is meaningless: 350,000,000,000,000,000,-000,000. In one year the light of this burning sphere illuminates the earth with an equally incomprehensible 1,500,000,000,000,-000,000 horsepower-hours of energy. It is, as Luther Standing Bear had said, "the Great Mystery."

In the hako of the Osage it was also said:

> Remember, remember,
> winds of sacred fire
> create day and night.

The fires of the sun burn so furiously that some believe the scientists' figures are too timid and earthly. Felix Pasteur has said that the solar energy wasted on the wastelands of the Sahara in one year equals one thousand times as much power as man could obtain by burning *all* the earth's coal resources *at once!* In *Solar Energy*, the German science writer Hans Rau said of this: "If we covered only one-thousandth part of the Sahara with solar mirrors we can theoretically obtain enough solar energy to eliminate the need for coal."

By covering an area of desert in New Mexico merely sixty-five by one hundred miles with solar mirrors, with a minimal efficiency of 10 percent, enough power would be produced "to satiate the entire power requirements of the United States," said Rau. The strip mining of the West would cease. So would the destruction of wild mountains to obtain oil shale. So would the defacing of the land with gas and power plants. So would the darkening skies.

In the hako of the Pawnee it was said:

> Now, Mother Earth,
> Now, breathe life,
> Now, awaken night,
> Now, light is born.

Millennia before the scientists of Europe discovered that the sun, not man, was the center of our universe, the ancients knew. It was universal knowledge. Many hundreds of thousands of years of tribal societies had gathered a heritage of knowledge about the energy of the sun, its meanings and its uses. The solar science of the ancients was recorded in the sun calendars of the Maya and Aztec; the Andes observatories of the Inca, the astronomical stone scripts of the Egyptians and Assyrians; the calculated markings on Stonehenge, in England; the lunar calendar of the Medicine Wheel, in Sheridan, Wyoming; and the mysterious computation of the eclipses precisely recorded by the niches in the Great Kiva of the Chaco Canyon Pueblo, in New Mexico, which was abandoned in the fourteenth century. For as Hartley Burr Alexander has written: "Such conceptions belong to old Egypt and Babylon and Greece, to all tribal people, to Scandinavia and the Mongol world, no less to the people of America."

In ancient Egypt, when Pharaoh Tutankhamen had "restored the worship of Re-Aton, the Sun," during the Eighteenth Dynasty (he reigned from 1361 to 1352 B.C.), his priestly astronomers elaborated a sophisticated and intricate knowledge of the germinal power of the sun in the creation and growth of our solar system and our earth. They wrote of the effect of the sun's energy on the "movement of time" and the seasons of the year, the ebb and flow of the waters, and the volcanic rise and fall of the earth itself. They knew of the effect of the sun's energy on the greening of leaves and the growth of seeds, even in the womb: "Sun, you formed the children in women, and created the seed in men." A newborn infant, the Egyptians said, breathed the air created by the sun. They knew, as did the Zuñi, that all life came from light:

> On the day of birth,
> when a child comes
> from a mother's womb,
> Sun, you open its mouth
> and offer it life.

The sun was orgasmic. Its touch was as curative as an act

of love. In a song to Osiris, the Egyptians prayed to be bathed in the "flame spurts spewing from the prow of the Sun-boat":

> Oh, may I catch the spurts
> as a shrieking human
> catches the Sun!

In the land of Cleopatra, lovers sang to Isis, the goddess of golden light, who was the goddess of love as well. One Egyptian poet prayed to the sun: "I shall be cured at the sight of her. Let her open my eyes." The sun's light "is a better medicine than all of the medicines."

The healers of the Navajo, to this day, evoke the medicinal energy of the sun. And in the Wind Chant ceremony it is prescribed that the sick one have "his body painted with the sun on his breast." So, too, the medicinal power of the sun "purifies" and strengthens the spirits of the Sun Dancers of the Lakota, the Arapaho, and the Cheyenne.

"The Hymn to the Sun" in the tomb of the Pharaoh Ay, who succeeded Tutankhamen, sought to tell the origin of the sun's power as the astronomers of Egypt conceived it. And the story of creation that the sun worshipers told is revealing when compared scientifically to the story of Genesis in the Old Testament. The priestly astronomers wrote:

O living Sun, you who were the first to live . . .
Your rays embrace all lands to the furthest limit of all you created . . .
Sun, you created all earth by your own energy alone. . . .

On the tomb of the Pharaoh Ay the hieroglyphs had no signs for ions of positive and negative charges, units of energy and ultraviolet rays. But they may as well have had. The Egyptians knew that the energy coming from the sun had "millions of forms," beyond the knowledge and capability of human minds to know.

> Sun, when you rise in the form of the living Sun . . .
> You make millions of forms from your own form.

In the beginning the sun was not a male god at all, but was enwombed in the creative circle of Isis, the goddess of light, wrote one Egyptian astronomer. It was a "self-created sun." For Isis was depicted not simply as wife of Re-Aton, but as daughter and sister of the sun as well. It was a sexual relationship as complex as energy itself, confusing to the adherents of more simplistic religions, which have never doubted the maleness of their supreme God. But to those who believed in the energy of the sun it seemed clear that the source of life would embrace all of life within its own being.

So the sun was thought to embody both female and male spirits. It was mother and father of the earth. It was the "God of Duality" of the Aztec, who embraced all of creation, all of sex, all of the cosmic energies. The "old god" of the Aztec was *in Tonan, in Tota*—"our mother, our father"—and also *in Teteu inan, in Teteu ita*—"mother and father of the gods" in one creation.

In prayer after prayer the Aztec expressed this, as in a lament for a woman who died in childbirth:

> Arise, array yourself, stand on your feet,
> partake of the pleasure of the place of beauty,
> the home of your mother, your father, the Sun.

The Spanish inquisitor Juan de Torquemada, who was sent to Mexico to purge such blasphemies of the Indians, was understandably confused by this. "It might be said the Indians wanted the Divine Nature to be shared by two gods, who were man and wife," he wrote. In his *Aztec Thought and Culture*, Miguel León-Portilla referred to the concept as "the summit of abstract thought." The sun was not merely the "Inventor of Man," but it had invented itself. Ometeotl, who was the Creator of Life, "the dual god who dwells in ˙Omeyocan [the universe], the metaphysical place of duality, was self-invented." Then, if that was so, was not the sun a "unified masculine-feminine being" who had been born of its own inner energy?

"Light is born from light" is the way the tribes of Israel spoke of it in the Talmud. In New Zealand the wise men of the

Maori tribes said it this way: "From nothing comes begetting," as "From remembrance came desire," and when "the sun sprang forth," life began and "nothing" was "light." In the sun was the "chief Eye of Heaven," said the Maori. On the dry plains of India, it was written much more sensuously in the Rig-Veda (1500–1200 B.C.) that the sun was a "spirit like wine," and its "movements are the Law" of the earth: "So the sea swells with the sun's song. So the sun is the earth. So the sun is the pure air." In the beginning, there was nothing else save the one who "breathed breathless," of its own power. And from "desire," the fire of the sun, the *karma* of life was born.

In the Himalayas of Tibet, it was written in the *Bardo Thodol*, the Tibetan Book of the Dead, that a dazzling and perfect "Clear Light" became the "Divine Guru," the "tutelary deity" who was the "Guru Father-Mother." In death, the womb of rebirth was opened when "visions of males and females in union" appeared in the "Clear Light," that intense form of life's energy that was "beyond the Light of the Sun."

In the woods of Maine the Passamaquoddy tribe said it more simply, though the thought was as profound: Light gives us "our voice":

> So we sing with our light.
> So we are birds made of fire!

And in the *I Ching*, the old Chinese book of divination, it had been written: "That which is bright rises twice: The image is *fire!* Thus the great man, by perpetuating this brightness, illuminated the four quarters of the world" with the energy of light.

Man did not invent light. He was invented by it. He did not create energy. He was created by it.

In the beginning, this was universal knowledge. Every tribal people knew it, and had said it, in their own way. The decline of tribal life inevitably led to the decline of knowledge of the sun's energy as a source of life. This, too, was universal.

All this knowledge was to be forgotten. The rise of the Grecian philosophies of science and the Judeo-Christian religions eclipsed the sun worshipers. In the "rites of passage" to their city-states the tribes of Semites and Grecians, and many others elsewhere, began to abandon their belief in the creative power of the sun for faith in a manlike Creator. He was created in the image of man, and He created man in the image of Himself. After all, it was man who created the city, though he never created the sun. So in the city man became as a god. Zeus and Jehovah reigned in the heavens as omnipotent and autocratic rulers. And the universal and democratic power of the sun was dethroned.

"And God said, Let there be Light, and there was Light." In Isaiah, the Lord reiterated, "I form the light." And the sun was the servant of the man-god.

In the *physis* of Grecians, the sun was barely mentioned. Except as a myth. The universe of Aristotle was formed of the "four elements"—fire, earth, water, air—not of the "millions of forms" of the sun's energy the ancients knew. And man knew his diminished world through his "four senses," and "the causes named in *Physis*," which his mind observed. (In his melancholy, Saint Paul lamented, "In physis [there] are no gods.") If man had become the center of knowledge, so the earth became "the center of the universe," said Aristotle. The sun revolved about man. And what of the universe beyond? If the four senses of man could not observe, and know, the unknown ("We cannot name any beyond," Aristotle said), then the universe would be in darkness until man's knowledge "enlightened it."*

The Aristotelian "dark age" of feudal Europe followed, as night follows day. It was not until the dawn of the Renaissance that Europe rediscovered the sun, in the vision of Galileo and Copernicus and Kepler. Even then, it was centuries before the wisdom of the tribal scholars was comprehended in any but the simplest mechanistic way; if it ever was.

"In the heart of all sits the Sun," wrote Copernicus in his *Wybor pism w przekladzie polskim (De revolutionibus orbium*

* People in cities can "readily" believe "the sun stands still," the economist Stuart Chase wrote years ago. Because of the buildings, they never "see the sun rise and set."

coelestium). "It is rightly called the lantern of the universe by some, by others the soul, and by still others, the ruler. . . . Thus, verily, the Sun governs the stars that revolve about it. . . . And then, too, the Earth is fertilized by the Sun, and enriched by the annual harvest of light." All this, he thought, was merely "natural."

Copernicus might have been an Egyptian, or a Hopi. He seemed to have relearned more than a simple scientific fact that once had been clear to tribal astronomers. In his view of the universe, the greatness of the sun was evidence of the humility of mankind.

The "discovery" of America and the "rediscovery" of the sun were not a historic "coincidence," wrote Lewis Mumford in his essay "Return of the Sun God." In the Age of Exploration the sun became the Europeans' guiding star for the conquest of tribal life: "No longer was it a satellite or servant, but the master of human existence." As always in modern society, the sun became the symbol of empire. "When history is on the march, thanks to kings, heroes and empires, the sun is supreme," the classicist Mircea Eliade once had said.

On the sea, as on the land, the "Sun God's ascendancy" created not only a new "priesthood of science," but a "new ideology" of power. King Louis XIV of France named himself *le Roi Soleil*, the Sun King, and in the court of Elizabeth I, the idea of a "celestial majesty" was the most popular of "all Elizabethan commonplaces." In this century, the "Rising Sun" of Japan was but one of the empires that claimed the sun as its imperial conquest, and proclaimed, as had England, that upon its earthly domain the sun would never set.

Man had returned the sun to the heavens, but had ascended with it. He sought to recreate the sun in his own image, as he had God. If he could hold the power of the sun in his hand, would he not become as powerful as the sun? The "new religion of the sun," as Lewis Mumford named it, became a tool for man's mastery of his world. And the energy of man, not the energy of the sun, was deified. That energy was electricity, the word coming from the Greek *elektron*, the "gleaming of the sun." In the words of Matthew Boulton, in whose London factory the steam engine of James Watt was built, mankind progressed from being "steam mill–mad" to being "electricity-mad." "I sell here, Sir, what all the world desires—Power," Boulton said.

The Male Attitude, as perceived by Charles Ferguson (in his twentieth-century history of maleness), became more and more arrogant and egocentric. He wrote: "It is as if the Deity were seen in our day and our terms as a celestial Edison."

For man had done what the sun could not. He thought he had created eternal daylight. He thought he had abolished the darkness of night. If man could recreate and control the energy of the sun, in a machine or an equation, was he not as great as the sun? Soon he would be conqueror of the universe of space and time, as he had conquered light—he thought. The sun's energy had become "modern man's slave," wrote the scientist authors of *The Energy Crises*, Lawrence Rocks and Richard Runyon. It was "our mute and uncomplaining servant."

The sun had been dethroned from godhood to slavery. Man had become the slavemaster of the entire universe.

Now it was said that the white man had to learn to respect and conserve the energy of the sun. For he was burning up all that the sun had stored in the earth. There would soon be nothing. So he had learned to fear that; it was his "energy crisis."

Scientists now were saying that their power plants, where the energy of the sun and earth was burned to turn it into electricity, wasted more energy than they made. They created as much darkness as light. "We lose two-thirds of the energy content of our fuels when we convert them into electricity," said S. David Freeman, a former assistant director of the President's Office of Science and Technology for Energy. "The biggest waster of energy is the electric generating equipment" of the energy industry, said Frank Di Luzio, energy adviser to the governor of New Mexico and a former official of the Atomic Energy Commission. "Now, how can we conserve energy when we waste more energy than we make?" These were startling thoughts.

(Long ago, the power industry condemned its own wasteful-
ness. In an industry publication, *Gas Age Record*, the editor,
F. W. Parsons, wrote in disgust, more than forty years ago: "The
story of the development of life and industry in America is
the most amazing tale of the waste of wealth by a careless, im-
provident people that the world has ever known"; it had "robbed
our virgin acres of so much of their fertility that in many regions,
farming as a pursuit is about as obsolete as the spinning wheel."
That was written in the days before the men of industry began
to believe their own public relations.)

Once more men lifted their eyes to the sun—for salvation.
In the Ninety-third Congress there was a deluge of no less
than forty solar-energy bills. "The energy of the sun is forever.
And it is free!" said an advertisement of an energy company.
"EARTHLY ENERGY SHORTAGES SPUR RESEARCH TO COLLECT, USE SOLAR
RAYS," proclaimed a *Wall Street Journal* headline, subheaded:
"Old Dream of Putting Sun's Power To Work Gets Renewed
Attention."

Solar heaters, solar watches, solar honey, solar bread, solar
bath oil, solar perfume, solar lipstick, solar deodorant appeared
on supermarket shelves. On Madison Avenue, in New York, a
sporty men's shop offered an exclusive "Solar Watch," for five
hundred dollars, that was specially made "to be recharged under
a sun lamp."

So the Pawnee sang:

> O spirit of the sun, look upon us,
> Everything is awakened by light. . . .

To some, solar energy was regarded "with a religious feeling
like the Incas worshiping the sun god," said Dr. Robert Hirsch of
the Federal Energy Research and Development Administration
(ERDA). Not in Washington, D.C., though. Of the $100 to $300
million that ERDA said was needed for solar demonstration projects, Congress voted a mere $5 million in its Solar Heating and
Cooling Demonstration Act of 1975. And the Solar Research Institute, with its proposed budget of $48 million and staff of 630, was

diminished by the White House to a shadowy one-tenth of that: less than five one-thousandths of one percent of the national budget.

In the hope of cashing in on the selling of sunlight, the power companies established an Electric Power Research Institute. But its director, Pete Bos, was skeptical about the marketing of the sun. "Our program is: 'What can solar energy do for us?'" Bos said.

The selling of the energy of the sun was worse than sacrilegious. It was ludicrous. Still, it reflected the belief that the sun existed for man to use, rather than that man existed for the sun.

No sooner had men rediscovered the energy of the sun than they began to fight over who controlled it. Who "owned" the sunlight? It became at once a legal battle to be decided by the highest scientific authority. The "property rights to the sky," said a National Science Foundation report prepared by Daniel Dawes, of the School of Law at UCLA, were based on the "doctrine of ancient lights," in which it was written in 1189, in the reign of Richard I, that there "existed an enforcible right to light, air and view."

And in Roman law was it not written: *"Cujus est solum, ejus est usque soleum et ad inferos"*: "He who owns the soil also owns unto the heavens and the depths"?

That may have been well enough in the baths of ancient Rome, said William Thomas, of the American Bar Association; but was it legal in a world of condominiums and skyscrapers? "The law in the United States is well established that the surface owner has a right to receive light from that area of the sky directly above his property, but not to receive it across the land of his neighbors." To enjoy the energy of the sun "at an angle" might require new zoning codes and court decisions.

Man may "own" the right to the sun's light, but not the light itself. It was clearly a matter that the Supreme Court might have to decide.

In fear, the men of white science had begun to reexamine, redefine, and research the meaning of the sun. Yet they continued to know and see it only within their small minds—by what it did for them. Energy could be "best explained not so much by what it is as by what it does," declared a scientific report of the American Petroleum Institute. "And it can work." That is, "work" for man. In our society, energy "is precisely defined in terms of measurable units as the rate of flow of *useful* energy," wrote Dr. Howard Odum, a leading energy scientist, in *Environment, Power and Society.* That is, "useful" to man. "The word energy is defined in *Webster* as the capacity for performing work," wrote H. Landsberg and S. Schurr in *Energy in the United States,* a Resources for the Future study by a Johns Hopkins University group under the sponsorship of Laurance Rockefeller, Robert O. Anderson of Atlantic Richfield, and similar energymakers. That is, it "performs" for man.

The idea that energy was created by and for man was narrow-minded and unscientific. It was as senseless as the rhetorical conflict between those men who thought energy was most important and those who thought the environment was most important. It was an idea that did not exist in nature. Energy was the environment, and the environment was energy. Neither existed without the other. Man was part of the energy of the environment; whatever was done to one, by men, was done to the other; much as one could not drain blood from the body without draining blood from the mind.

So the energy of the earth *was* the earth. It could not be separated from the earth. No more than there was a conflict between the use of solar energy and the use of coal and oil; for coal and oil *were* solar energy.

Man recycled the energy of the earth and sun, and wasted most of it in the process. He nonetheless persisted in the egotistic belief that he "produced" it. He "developed" it. He "owned" it. For it was his to use in any way that he decided with his "energy policy."

And so man fought over energy as he had over gold. One of the Federal Energy Administrators proclaimed, in the language of those who came before and after him, that this nation could "develop its own energy" alone. He meant: "Let's dig domestic coal." In this way the "energy solution" would be "making energy more valuable as a commodity," so that there would be "energy independence."

From the White House to the smallest statehouse it was believed that man had the sublime power to do what he wished with the energies of life. The "profits and benefits of energy production" belong to us all, said Governor Jerry Apodaca, as chairman of the Western Governors' Regional Energy Policy Office; he demanded "a new national energy policy" to share the "energy production" the Eastern corporations were unearthing in the Western states.

The most primitive knowledge of how and why human energy was created seemed to be unknown to these promulgators of official beliefs regarding the sources of energy. Not the wisdom and profundity of the Egyptians and the Hopi, but the simplest understanding. It was not surprising that the corporations and politicians of energy often sounded so childish and ignorant when they pontificated about their need to "produce" more energy.

Believing their own myths as rewritten, the energy czars of technological societies would never solve the "energy crisis"; they merely deepened it. These policies were simply new attempts to unearth more of the energy of the sun and to waste more of the earth. None of the governments of the energy-"producing" or -"consuming" nations seemed to understand what energy was, where it came from, and why they had to give back to the earth the energy they had taken from it, not for the earth's survival, but for their own.

In a prophetic judgment, the great historian of the West H. H. Bancroft wrote fifty years ago: "We would clear off and appropriate the sun and moon and stars if we were able . . . [for] there is no limit to our greed."

On their mountains of the sun the Hopi elders laughed at that, though it saddened them. To them it seemed that the white man had not yet learned the meaning of the sun. Still he thought that he "created" the energy of the oil, gas, coal, and atoms of the earth in his power plants. He thought if only he could make more powerful machines, he could make more energy. He thought if only he could make more energy, he would be more powerful. That was his way.

"In his heart he knows it is not so, but the white man believes it anyway," an elder Hopi told me. "Because the white man believes he is the center of the universe. So he believes what he knows is not so.

"Galileo must have been a Hopi," he said. These men of white science did not seem to understand their own science.

If a man borrowed the energy of the sun, he had to give it back to the sun. So the Circle of Life would not be broken, he had to offer a gift of his own energy to repay this gift that sustained him. The energy of human beings was merely one form of the energy of the sun, the sky, the earth. Was that not why the Zuñi offered their newborn, in prayer, to the sun? Was that not the offering of bodily sacrifice of the Sun Dancers of the Lakota? Was that not why the runners of Taos Pueblo, in the Sun Races on San Geronimo Day, offered the energy of the running, their sweat, and their breath, to the sun: "So the sun can rise again."

But the white man never gave anything back. He did not know how. That was his real energy crisis.

Some of the white men, even now, thought the energy crisis was just the dubious "gas shortage." Once that had passed, *Time* magazine had pathetically declared: "The energy crisis is over."

"Why can't the white man learn anything he doesn't know?" a Hopi elder asked. "He maybe knows about the kilowatts, but he does not know about where the spirit of the sun comes from. He does not know that."

"Sometimes, it is said, the white man is like a child," said the Hopi traditionalist Banyacya. Is it not like a child to think that the whole world exists for him? To know nothing you cannot know? To see nothing you cannot see? In this way the white man is like a child, for he will not learn that the sun does not exist for him; he exists for the sun. "So we follow the spiritual circle," Banyacya said. "There is no end to it."

Man did not invent light. He was invented by it. He did not create energy. He was created by it.

The sun was the darkness. And the light. The sun was life. And death. The sun was the beginning of the earth. And it would be the end. So the elders of the Hopi said.

We Are Creating the Earth

❦ TESTAMENT OF Albert Caskey, foreman,
Big Sky, Colstrip, Montana

Not many have walked in the pit of a strip mine. I had never walked there before.

In the canyon of coal dug by the giant dragline crane the walls of earth were dead. The man-made canyon was lifeless and colorless. Unlike canyons made by nature, where the earth is rainbowed red and brown, it has walls that are either gray or black. On descending into an underground mine or cave, there is a feeling of fear and mystery, but a strip mine is more like an open tomb.

"Beauty!" he said proudly as he looked about the pit. "Isn't it a beauty of a cut?"

"Well," I said uneasily.

In his white hardhat, he was jaunty as a jockey. He drove like one. On the bottom of the pit the ground was rough with rock-sized lumps of coal. But he drove about as though this were his playground. The four-wheel-drive vehicle had come to a playful halt beside the gash in the mountainside, where the coal face was hidden underneath a fifty-foot overhang of rock.

On the edge of the cliff, above our heads, was a huge steam shovel. The machine seemed ominous when you stood beneath it, peering up at its gigantic gears.

"Come on," Albert Caskey had said. "If you want to see what

it's like to mine coal, you've got to go to the mountain. The mountain won't come to you."

So we stood in the pit. I tried to hide my unease.

He laughed. "It's safe." He patted the cliff with his hand, as he would a dog. In the coal pit he was at home.

Caskey tilted his steel hat back on his head. He was a small, compact man. He had the profile of an old Indian, with the eyes of a ferret. The skin around his eyes was wrinkled and scarred by the winds of Montana. He was foreman of the Peabody Coal Company Big Sky Mine, in Colstrip; a tough job in an "ecological war." And he was tight-mouthed about it.

It was said he did not like to talk much. But it wasn't that. "You can't dig coal with talk," he said.

Nonetheless, he loved to talk about mining coal. He talked about coal the way a sailor talks about his ship. He had been a coal miner since he was a young man.

On the road to the south of the Big Sky Mine was the Northern Cheyenne Reservation. It was said that a few of the tribesmen had been hired on as laborers, but they were not visible. Caskey did not mention them. He knew nothing about Indians, he said.

"I'm originally from Missouri," he explained. "They moved me up here in 1970, to the mining operation."

He was a newcomer to Montana. He knew little about the people or the land. He knew how to mine coal; that was all.

This is what he told me:

Is the strip mining hurting the earth? No, I don't think so.

We are creating the earth. We put the earth back better than it was before. Yes, better than it was—and flatter!

That's the truth!

See, in some of the places where the rock sticks out aboveground, we blast it. When we blast it, it becomes sand. You see, it's sand rock. Then we have a fine texture of sand instead of solid rock. We will have a finer soil here than before we began the stripping. So I think it will be better than it was before we blasted.

And we have reclamation, too. For seeding.

The people that see our reclamation are proud of it. But the people that criticize don't see it. I realize that they don't know exactly what we're doing. If they came out and looked at it, they'd agree the earth is a good deal better than it was.

See that fellow on the bulldozer? He's returning the contour of the hills just the way they were before we came. And he's planting seeds for reclamation.

I don't know what seeds we're planting. He knows that. Just seeds. Russian thistle? No, that just blows in. That's sagebrush, you know. That grows real well, up here anyway.

Now we have the reclamation law that's going to tell us exactly what we're going to do. To a certain extent we're being boxed in by the politicians. And they're regulating us to where we can't operate efficiently. Like we need to. I mean in the actual stripping, and the moving of the dirt. I think it's pressure by those environmentalists in the cities.

In the cities those people don't realize it's the environment that lights up their living rooms. Every time they turn on their lights they're burning up the environment. Will they live without electricity? I don't think so. They don't want to go back to candles. They don't want to live in the dark. They don't live here in the environment anyway.

So those people in the cities don't know what they are talking about.

The ranchers have nothing to gain from the strip mining. I can understand their feelings. Because it's the government, and the railroads who own the coal, who will profit. In this area of Montana the railroads have leased or sold the land and reserved the mineral rights. The rancher has no mineral rights. He just has to topsoil. He gets nothing.

It's the cities that get the coal. So the rancher gets nothing from that either.

Here at Big Sky we do about 180,000 tons of coal a month. That will come to about two million tons this year. We'll increase that next year. Now we can load a railroad train in about

two hours and twenty minutes, with our new front-loading system. A whole train. Every train has ten thousand tons and we're
shipping four trains a week.

That coal all is shipped to the cities.

I don't see that those people in the cities who complain so
much about strip mining have stopped using the coal. Someone
there is sure using it.

Do I worry about the national controversy over strip mining?
Not much.

We let the higher-ups take care of that. We just go on doing
our job. We dig coal.

THE SACRED
AND PROFANE EARTH — I

Earth, our Mother. Sky, our Father. Those were the two we
prayed to. And we followed their ways and we have survived.
From the beginning of our lives we depended most on the Earth.
For this reason we are crying about this destruction of our Mother.
The Earth. We say no! I say no! I talk that way about it!"
So said The Woman Who Had Squaw Dance.

The old women were wrapped in shawls, heads bent, watching
every word. And the old men were in shirtsleeves, ignoring the
cold room, sitting as young men might, taut, suspicious, listening
for the words no one said: words of beauty and harmony. But
there were none.

On that wintry evening the old sheepherders of the Female
Mountain, known to white men as Black Mesa, had gathered in
the chapter house of the tribe to talk of those who had come to
dig up the Mother Earth. These men had the name "Peabody"
on their hardhats. Some said they were "strip miners"; but at that

time few really knew what that meant. The Old People came to hear what was happening. In the beginning, few spoke. They sat silently. They were sitting on three-quarters of a billion dollars' worth of coal, but they did not believe that.

None of the Old People knew, or could have known, that the earth of the Female Mountain was but the skin of a great body of coal that lay beneath the west of the continent, all the way to the Arctic Circle; it was a dark womb of fossil fuel underneath these canyons and prairies, from the deserts of the Southwest to Hudson Bay. Some said it was the largest body of coal on earth.

"The Persian Gulf of Coal" it was hopefully named by *Fortune*. In the business magazine a "New Age of Coal" in the West was heralded, which the financial prophets thought might be worth not tens, but hundreds of billions of dollars. That, too, was unbelievable.

In the snow on the Female Mountain it was so cold that night that they said the trees shivered, the stars were frozen. The coyotes were howling at the growls of the strange new animals—the bulldozers.

The Widow of the Late Mr. Lokasikai spoke the thoughts of many: "We get the feeling no one is really concerned about our situation." That was always so. No one knew, then, of the sorrows of the Old People; for no one knew, then, of the "energy crisis." It was the fourteenth of February in 1970 when these things began to happen on the Female Mountain.

Some of the talk was sad. And some was becoming angered, even then.

The old man Yazzie remembered how he had fought the bulldozer with his fists. The road to the strip mine was being dug through his hogan, wide as an interstate highway. "Some time back I found red flags in front of my house," he said. "That was to be the road." The old man asked politely that they build the road somewhere else. No one listened. One morning he was awakened by the bulldozer. It was coming right at his hogan. He rushed outside. And he stood there and waved his fists at the huge machine, the old man said, until it turned away.

"I still wonder," he said, "if I did not say anything, what would have happened!"

Many said that the bones of the dead were dug up by the bulldozers. Said the woman Crank, "I know one grave that was disturbed." It was then that the archaeologists came from the university. They had a "research grant" from the coal company. They gathered up the bones of the dead and took them away in plastic bags. One archaeologist had a boyish beard and friendly eyes. I asked him, "Is it true you follow the bulldozers with plastic bags?" He was insulted and walked away sulking. Later a book of "Archaeological Finds" was published by the scientists.

"My mother's grave is no more," an old woman told me. "Her bones are gone."

On the Female Mountain there was an old woman. Her name was known as Kee Shelton's Mother. That was not her name. She said: "In Navajo my name is Asa Bazhonoondah, The Woman Who Had Squaw Dance. I am eighty-three years old. I am originally from Black Mesa, the Female Mountain. I was born and raised there. My parents and grandparents were all from the same place. I was born in a hogan which was still standing the last time I saw it. But now I do not know, maybe they have torn it down. They tell me my parents used to live right at the mining site at the time my mother was pregnant with me. Then when she was going to give birth to me they moved eastward. My mother died and was buried there."

The Woman Who Had Squaw Dance said: "Even when we were small, our cradle is made from the things given to us from the Mother Earth. When we die we go back to the Mother Earth."

The Woman Who Had Squaw Dance said: "The Earth is our Mother. The White Man is ruining our Mother."

In sorrow, the old woman said this to the white men of the Committee on Interior and Insular Affairs of the U.S. Senate of the Ninety-second Congress, before the hearings on the "Environmental Problems Associated with the Production of Electrical Power by Coal-Fired Plants in the Four Corners Region of the Southwest, U.S.," held on May 28, 1971. Senator Paul Fannin, of Arizona, was the sole member of the committee who was there. He listened to her attentively. But the old woman wondered if he knew that the Mother Earth was his mother, too. She gently tried to teach the senator, as a grandmother should, things he ought to know.

The Woman Who Had Squaw Dance said: "Everything is our prayer. Everything is our song to the mountain. We were living a good life, but this summer we really had it bad. Everything is wrong.

An old hogan of one family was bulldozed to the earth. So was a religious sweat house. The earth reservoir of one man, which he had built by his hands, was flattened. None of the People were ever "consulted" by the "bulldozer people," Cecil Yazzie said. "We were just ignored. We have no one to listen."

Ni hideneetaa! Our People have been deceived, said Calvin Atcitty. "We consented to have the land surveyed," but no mining was to begin until the People were asked. "This never happened. So we never consented to the actual mining," Atcitty said. They have robbed us, as they always do: *Da ni iih yee!*

And the Old People said: In ignorance the white man will devour the Earth. *Ni hideesnaa,* the Earth trembles. The *bila-gaana,* the white ones, are like hungry animals, *da niighaa dichin!* They are unearthing the *chiidii,* the Spirits of the Dead.

Once it had been a serene and peaceful place. It was *hodiyin,* a sacred mountain, and many Medicine People lived up there. In those days no whites lived there and few came, any more than atheists went on pilgrimages to Jerusalem.

None of the hardhats of Peabody knew, then, what it meant. A young Navajo war veteran from Vietnam, Robert Salabye, tried to tell them: "Black Mesa is our sacred mountain. I am sure the dominant society would not like to have their Independence Hall, or the White House, strip-mined. Black Mesa to the Navajos is just as sacred and holy as Mount Calvary or Saint Peter's Square is to the Christians." But the hardhats could not hear him.

In a few years the Old People who sat in the chapter house that evening would all be bulldozed from their lands. Their hogans gone. Their pastures gone. Their sheep pens gone. And the families of the old man Yazzie, the woman Crank, Calvin Atcitty, Cecil Yazzie, and many more had signed a petition that accused the Peabody Coal Company of "the rape of our Mother Earth."

The quiet and incredulous sheepherders said: "It is a fact that Peabody likes to dig where people live. We, the American Indians, are landlords of the land, and demand respect from the white people who are on our land." But their proud words came too late. On the Female Mountain not even sheep had "a peaceful sleep" now that the bulldozers had come.

It was not their fault, said the president of Peabody Coal, Ed Phelps. The Old People "have their homes on coal deposits," and his company would "reimburse the tribe" for the "removal" of the sheepherders. My Lord! Were a few sheep to stand in the path of the nation's need for energy?

The conflict was romantically reported in the newspapers. Some twenty television and film companies asked the tribe for permission to film the exotic battle: the quaint old Navajos fighting the huge equipment of the largest strip-mining company in the country. In *The New York Times*, a story that I was asked to write was headlined: "THE NAVAJOS VS. THE BULLDOZERS." And yet that was not the conflict; it was a confrontation between two ways of life and of death that were facing one another on the Female Mountain.

One of those years some tribal leaders had asked me to put out a "Fact Sheet" on what was happening. "That publicity will help us," said Peter MacDonald, who was later to become the Navajo tribal chairman. So that is what I did. In one of those "Fact Sheets" I wrote of "colonialism" in the government, which treated the People like children and acted without their consent or knowledge.

No! That is not what we want to say! the Medicine People on the Female Mountain told me. That is all right to say, but this is what we think: Beauty and harmony are the heart of the Navajo way of life. It is believed that this comes from the eternal and natural balance of the Female Mountain (Black Mesa) and the Male Mountain (Lukachukai). If these mountains are disturbed, the balance of beauty and harmony of the Navajo way may die.

So that is what I wrote. It was not ecology, but life itself, that was threatened.

That winter there were many strange deaths. Several of the People died by "accidents." The chairman of an electric company died in his sleep the night before he was to talk to me. One teacher in Rough Rock, at the foot of the Female Mountain, hanged himself. He was not Navajo. But he had fought the strip mine. And he had lost.

"People have said to me that your strip mine is responsible for these deaths," I told William Stockton, a vice-president of Peabody. A soft-eyed, white-haired, and grandfatherly man, he seemed startled. "I am not accusing you of murder," I told him, "but this is what the People have told me."

In his executive office, he hunched behind an oversize desk, as though weighed down by thought. This was not the kind of corporate problem he was accustomed to.

"All my life I have been in the coal business," he said. "For forty years. That's all I know. When we signed that contract to strip-mine Black Mesa, we signed a coal contract. Not an Indian contract. Not an ecology contract. Not a religious contract. And the Interior Department assured us the Indians and the Tribal Council had all agreed.

"Tell me," he said sadly. "Hasn't the Tribal Council got any influence? If we had known what we were getting into, maybe we would not have done this. Lord knows, we don't want to hurt anyone."

Mining men denied that there was a morality of mining. It was a job they had to do, so they did their job. Maybe the energy crisis created a sense of national urgency in the country, but the digging of coal was still simply hard work, done with sweat and skill.

In the days when mining men were more moralistic, those who stood in the path of their diggings were thought to be immoral. The righteous tone of the Victorian era was voiced, in the 1880s, by Congressman James Belford, of Colorado, when he berated the Ute People of his state for their opposition to mining their land. Miners were heralds of "the swelling tide [of] civilization," cried the congressman; "the idle and shiftless savages cannot be permitted to guard the treasure vaults of the nation."

That moral tone no longer was fashionable. And yet in the attitude of the government and the corporations there was an unspoken echo of that self-righteousness. It never occurred to the white men that these native People might say no.

In the shadow of the sacred Shiprock, the People of the Navajo community of Burnham were twice to vote their opposition to two massive coal-gasification plants the government, the corporations, and tribal officials wished to build on their lands. But the democratic vote was rejected. Another vote was ordered. And for the third time, in the spring of 1975, the community voted—114 to 14—to reject these plants they called the "monsters." Still the decision of the People was ignored.

"The probable disintegration of Navajo culture" would be a by-product of the plants, said the Environmental Impact Statement of El Paso Natural Gas, one of the gasification-plant builders. And the corporate report detailed a "wide range of detrimental effects," such as the "possibility of emission-related diseases" and destruction of family life through "increased rates of alcoholism."

And yet, even though the Burnham community, as had the nearby Nenahnezad and Shiprock tribal chapters, voted to oppose the endangering of their homes, they were no more heeded than a rural white community in the path of an interstate highway. "The problem is to get [their] land," said a corporate officer of WESCO, one of the coal-gasification conglomerates.

The Woman Who Had Squaw Dance said: "Our Mother wanted us to live longer, but the white man is shortening our lives by destroying the Female Mountain, making it into a coal mine. We have so many grandchildren. How are they going to live?"

On the Female Mountain, the Old People knew a *lahgo e en-neh,* a metamorphosis, had begun. The body of the earth had been opened so the white people could take the energy away. And they would place nothing in the wound. The earth would be empty, for the white people will have devoured all its energy. *Iidodiil,* they will make it extinct.

The Woman Who Had Squaw Dance said: "Peabody ruined it because they were hungry for the coal."

It may be the Old People knew more than they knew. The fifty years from 1920 to 1970 had seen the consumption of the earth's energy by the whites increase by 3,040 percent, from 57.5 billion to 1.648 trillion kilowatts. And that meant that the whites were devouring the energy of America three and a half times as fast as they were being born.

These whites had been on their way to the Female Mountain for a long time. Some of the Old People remembered when they first came.

It was during the deathly blizzard of 1949. Snow had fallen on the desert like a blinding sandstorm. The sheep were lost in the drifts. Everywhere in the hogans there was starvation. And in the remote villages, without logs for fires, the children were freezing to death.

Some may remember it was the time of the Berlin airlift, when food was parachuted to the starving Germans. Few remember it was the year, as well, of the Navajo and Hopi "haylift," when straw was parachuted to starving Indians. Of the two events, the first has receded into history, while the second has just begun to reemerge from history to haunt the country.

To appease the Act of God of that winter, an Act of Congress was offered. Congress had grieved, once more, for the poor Indians: it enacted a Long Range Navajo and Hopi Rehabilitation Act of 1950, which seemed to give $88,570,000 to "rehabilitate" the tribes. Of this, $500,000 was designated by Congress for "Surveys and Studies of Timber, Coal, Minerals." The government advised the Navajos to give $197,000 of this to the College of Mines of the University of Arizona and New Mexico's Institute of Mining and Technology, in 1952 to 1954, for "Mineral Resources Surveys." It was then that these surveyors learned what the Old People had known for hundreds of years. The Female Mountain was called Black Mesa because it was full of coal.

I remember a tribal official telling me at the time, half elated, half amused: "They say we have more coal than the state of Pennsylvania." He was not exaggerating.

The "energy crisis" came to the People that winter. In the guise of helping the starving Indians, a white "coal rush" was begun. "Almost simultaneously with the passage of the Act private industry began to extract subsoil riches from the reservation," noted Lawrence Kelly in *The Navajo Indians and Federal Policy.* So it was that in 1951 the Navajo Tribal Mining Department was established at the "suggestion" of the government. Its paradoxical aims were said to be to "protect Navajo mineral resources," and to "promote mining"—which it undertook to do by giving "free drilling permits"! In a few years mining operations by the *bilagaana*, the whites, had increased from 3 to 133 yearly.

It was an act of charitable avarice. Even the feeding of the starved People had been made conditional upon the Act of Congress that decreed they give up to the federal government protection of their earth and its coal before they would be fed. "All Indians within the tribal or allotted lands of the Navajo and Hopi reservations shall be subject to the laws of the State wherein such lands are located," said the Fernandez Amendment; for if the states could tax the Indian lands, they might soon foreclose on their coal and oil resources.

Though their People were starving, the Navajo Tribal Council voted 26 to 19 that President Truman veto the "aid" Act. Said Tom Lincoln, a councilman at the time: to get that congressional money it was necessary to trade "our bodies, our souls, and our blood." He voted no.

An old councilman said: "We were hungry, but we were not *that* hungry."

(Curiously, twenty-five years later, when the coal companies were after the mining rights on the Northern Cheyenne Reservation, one company offered the tribe a "million-dollar" hospital. The tribe had no hospital at all. "No," said the Cheyenne chairman, Alan Rowland. "We would rather be sick!")

In "one fell swoop" the earth and water rights of the People might fall into the hands of the state courts, said President Truman in vetoing the Act. He insisted that Congress eliminate the strings to its "aid."

No sooner had the word of the coal discovery reached the East than men with attaché cases began quietly to appear on the Female Mountain. They came, most often, led by guides from the Interior Department's Bureau of Indian Affairs. And few of the Old People knew why they had come.

One day in the early fifties, a stranger came to the Female Mountain. He was T. C. Mullens, then president of Peabody. Later he was to tell the Senate's Interior Committee: "Black Mesa is no stranger to me. I first arrived in the early 1950s to inspect the old coal workings on the reservation." To his dismay, he found some insurmountable obstacles. It would be the richest coal contract his company "ever negotiated," he said, if only that coal could be profitably shipped to the markets "over 1,000 miles away"; but it could not.

One day in the late fifties, I was invited to the home of an old friend, John McPhee, who was the administrative assistant to the Chairman of the Navajo. He was not a Navajo. He was not an Indian. He was a former officer of the Arizona Mining Association, and he was determined to get that coal. And as the friend of the People, he, too, wanted to aid them before he died.

The Woman Who Had Squaw Dance said: "Even though I'm old, I think about this every day and night. The white man ruined the air. They are the ones who are hurting us. They are making our life line short."

Some days before, at the meeting of the tribal Advisory Committee, I had jokingly been asked if I was writing another *Laugh-*

ing Boy, the romantic novel about the Navajos by Oliver La Farge. One tribal leader had pointed his finger at McPhee, the sole white man in the room besides myself, and said, sardonically, "He's the only Laughing Boy we have around here."

McPhee was no romantic. He was angry. He told me that he had pleaded with an executive of the Santa Fe Railroad to lay a track up to the Female Mountain to get the coal out. The cagey old railroad man had scoffed: "I would not touch that coal. No one will touch it with a ten-foot pole."

That evening at dinner, I asked McPhee: Did the People know he was negotiating privately to mine their coal deposits? Would he do the same to white ranchers? He merely smiled. Perhaps he knew the coal was of a low grade and would create fumes so dangerous that it could not be burned in many cities, by local ordinances, even then, twenty years ago. The coal was so poor it crumbled in the hand.

There was an old saying: "It's difficult to know if it's cheap coal or rich dirt."

Years ago we would break off handfuls of coal and burn it in our campfires. The People had done that for centuries.

One of the myths about Western coal was that it was "low-sulfur" coal. And safer to burn. It was not. The coal was so weak in heat that more of it had to be burned, and it ended up poisoning the air with as much sulfur as better coal or much more.

Some way had to be found to burn the coal where it was, and keep the sulfur in the West, away from the cities of the East. Let the Indians be poisoned by the smog! Once that was done, the energy not merely of the Female Mountain but of the entire Western continent would be opened for the people of the cities to feast upon with oblivious and blind eyes.

And then the men with attaché cases would come like locusts. They already have.

None of these men had ever lived on the Female Mountain. And many of them had never been there. "If you see one of these mountains, you've seen them all," an engineer for one of the strip-mine companies once said to me. "The coal is the only thing that is different." He was paraphrasing the old myth men told one another about women.

In the days when he was Secretary of the Interior, Walter Hickel told of a trip that he had taken to the West with one of the White House's "top energy men." Their plane was fogged in, or fogged out, of an airport where it was to land. Instead it landed in a nearby state, a mishap the secretary apologized for to his White House guest.

"Oh . . ." The man who influenced national policy toward the West shrugged. "What difference does it make?"

These men knew little of the land, but for those studies and statistics they read. And they never held its energy within their hands or tasted the dust of its loneliness or embraced the warmth of its soils. In ignorance they had to believe what their computers told them: the Mother Earth had become a computer print-out.

One year recently, the computers of the United States Geological Survey simply "lost" one-third to one-half of the nation's energy resources. The "new data" in these computers estimated the oil reserve to be one-third and the "undiscovered oil" to be less than one-half of what the old data thought it was just one year before. In dismay, the head of the President's Energy Resources Council announced that the newest truth of the revised computer print-out "hangs over the nation like a thundercloud."

In some ways, the estrangement of these men from the mother earth was pathetic. Soon after I had issued those Black Mesa "Fact Sheets," a letter appeared in the *Navajo Times* calling me a liar. One of the reasons I was wrong in my apprehensions about the strip mines, said Ed Phelps, then the executive vice-president of Peabody Coal, was that in the mining gashes "natural lakes" would form to beautify the desert. Unbelievingly, I asked one friend, who was then an executive of Peabody Coal, how these miraculous "natural lakes" would come about in a desert where in dry years the rainfall was at times no more than six inches. Well, he said, Ed Phelps is not too familiar with Black Mesa.

And so it was wisely decided to have some scientists study the Female Mountain. In a little museum in the town of Flagstaff, a group of benefactors (the strip-mining company was among them) financed expeditions to catalogue the flora and fauna on the Female Mountain before the bulldozers and dragline cranes replaced the bobcats and hawks. The director of the funereal expeditions was an eager and friendly young environmental scientist from New York. He loved the West.

One day I said to him: What have you found out?

"The eagles will fly away or they will die," he said. "So will the mountain lions and coyotes and squirrels and rattlesnakes. They will all leave. They can't live on coal slag heaps."

And the People?

"They will adapt," said the young scientist.

The Woman Who Had Squaw Dance said: "Soon the Navajos will resemble the Anasazi ruin. The wind took them away, because they misused the earth."

The Woman Who Had Squaw Dance said: "The white men wish that nothing will be left of us after this is over. They want us to be like the Anasazi."

Who Owns the Sunset?

TESTAMENT OF Walter Hickel, former Governor
of Alaska, and former Secretary of the Interior

"All around was the wilderness, a no-man's land of mountains
or of cragged islands, and southward the wide, the limitless
Pacific Ocean," wrote Rockwell Kent of his year, 1913, on the
Island of the Fox, off the Alaskan coast. "We came to this new
land entirely on a dreamer's search; having had vision of a
Northern Paradise, we came to find it."

That vision is still in the eyes of the true Alaskans, native
and white.

In the minds of men who saw Alaska as a mine of resources
waiting to be mined, exploited, drilled, and piped, it was the
"Last Frontier." To people who had opposed this, and lost, it was
the "Lost Frontier"; it had suffered the Manifest Destiny of the
West.

In the eyes of Walter Hickel this was blasphemy.

Never "confuse the destiny of Alaska with the destiny of the
West," he said. If a man wants "to know Alaska he must know
the mountains and the sky." And then he will know why Alaskans
are not, and will never be, like the "Lower 48." "We are a different
breed," he said. "We are honest. Even if it hurts us."

An ornery, honest, direct, intense, blunt-spoken, romantic,
and at times bullheaded man, the former governor of Alaska
thought of himself as a rugged man of the West. He loved the

West. He loved the riches of the West as well. And he had
prospered in both his loves. Some called him an "environmental
entrepreneur"; he was as "hypocritical as a land developer." But
Walter Hickel was not defensive. He had the instincts of the
ex-prize fighter that he was.

He remembered his youth: "In 1938 I won the Kansas Welter-
weight Golden Gloves championship. There was a tournament in
Hobbs, New Mexico. Well, that was really a rough little town in
those days. I went there, and went through four fights, clear
to the finals. And I lost the finals. And I think the reason I lost
was that I met a pretty little girl the night before the fight and
I didn't get too much sleep."

The Kansas farm boy had a small-town humanness about
him. In the cabinet meetings of the Nixon administration, his
openness and straightforward way of talking, as Secretary of the
Interior, were ill-placed in a world of Madison Avenue "newspeak" and political paranoia, disguised as policy.

Soon enough he had been fired. Not simply, he said, because
of his fatherly letter of compassion for the nation's rebellious
youth. But because he had spoken out against the petroleum companies, who at the time favored what he said was "dependence
on cheap crude oil from abroad," which at the time they owned.

And so he was to return to the mountains and the skies of
his beloved Alaska. But even the mountains and the skies of
Alaska were changing. So were the people. In his attempt to be
elected governor again, he lost again. The founding father often
has been forsaken by his children.

Was he bitter?

This is what he told me:

Never shall bulldozers level the Tetons, never change the
Grand Canyon. In a minuscule way the land might alter at the
moment, but nature will bring it back. More than that, there's
a spiritual, religious influence of the land upon the people.
That's why the Indian worshiped the gods he did. And that's

why the white man came. The West challenges man, as the Pacific Ocean challenges man. And the vastness of the West, in my opinion, brought out the best in man.

The real meaning of the founding fathers of this country wasn't realized until they broke open the West. When the West was broken open, the vestiges of the European establishment were truly broken. The great freedom of the individual to which the early visionaries aspired became a reality. In the West the people want their lives to be their own. They don't want to be *told*. That's the independence of the West.

The West had a greater influence on the East than the East ever had on the West. The East's influence was a monetary, materialistic one. The West's was religious and philosophical; and that will endure long after the material gain of the moment.

The West will not only influence the people of this continent; it will influence the people of the world. There is no more unique piece of real estate than America. The uniqueness of America is its West. . . . The land will always influence man by the very ruggedness of its nature.

The settler and the Indian knew the goodness of nature. But they also knew the cruelty of nature, the cruelty of a tornado, a flash flood, hunger, cold. Yes, nature can be cruel. It can also be kind. The true environmentalist is one who understands that there is a balance in that. The balance of kill or be killed. The balance of use, but not destruction. They are both there in nature.

Nature isn't all merely the pleasantry of God; nature is the real God.

The whole question of the environment is not how to isolate man from nature, but how to make him compatible with nature. The Indian understood that. The Indian respected the land. By the same token, God wanted the Indian to use the land. The Indian and many of the early settlers really understood the environment. That understanding is a far cry from the protectionist who only looks at nature on a TV set.

I deeply respect the American Indian's philosophy of nature.

I can understand his feeling and sympathize with it. He is content to live with nature. He does not feel the need to conquer or destroy nature, the way we do, and have done.

But that may be why the Indian has not made as much progress as he could have. I do not know if we could live the "Indian way" and still have the progress that we want.

It is something we have not learned how to do.

That's why I think that the energy crisis may be a blessing in disguise. We will have to tighten our belts. We will have to rethink our purpose, as individuals and as a nation. It might make us respect what we have. It might make the scientific community face the fact that we do not have to waste the energy we have.

More than any people on earth, the American people are proud of their private-ownership system. They should be. But we are largely unaware of our public obligations.

Free enterprise if allowed to run totally free will destroy itself. I am a product of the free-enterprise system. And I know we have to make money. We have to compete against one another. But without any regulations whatsoever we will literally gobble each other up.

This country was founded as a free society. At the turn of the century, when we went from an agricultural to an industrial society, we confused free enterprise with free society. Freedom ends when it infringes on another person's rights. So what I am saying is that government should not itself get involved in business, but should set down those regulations that will keep free enterprise free.

I believe it is the obligation of government to represent the total public needs. Not merely to meet our physical needs, but to respect the environment of the heart, the mind, and the soul.

The President is really the president of the largest corporation in America. The smallest child has as much stock interest in the continental shelf as the president of any large company. The great rivers belong to the smallest child. So do the lakes. And so do those millions of acres that stretch from Cape Cod to the Pacific Ocean. These are not for anyone's private exploitation.

But that does not mean you cannot use them privately. It means you cannot abuse them privately. That means that the government should be concerned, it should care, it should plan. I'm sure you remember Abe Lincoln's old phrase: The government should only do those things that the individual cannot do, or do as well.

And what of the controversy over energy in America? I, for one, believe we are getting a confused, somewhat false picture. There is a crisis of energy, but it is not what you might think it is. We are not running out of natural resources. If we are running out of anything, it is imagination and leadership. The crisis is really a crisis of management, of control.

Environmental needs touch the whole of the living of life. What is the environment? It is not just rolling beaches and the rolling prairies. It is the area in which you live. It could be a junkyard across the street. Poverty, for example, is a bad environment. So is the lack of energy. I think it is time that we quit playing politics with the energy crisis. The so-called energy crisis has become a popular cause and a political bandwagon.

I do not accept the idea that we have to reduce our pollution standards to produce the energy the nation needs. Nor that we should back away from the environmental challenge. America is greater than that.

And the development of the West requires that we look at its best and highest use. To do that we have to understand what's there. It's the lack of understanding that has led to desecration and waste.

And the development of the West can never be out of the hands of the West. Even when the outsider moves in, finally he becomes a Westerner or he leaves. Problems arise only when they try to push the influence of other areas on the West. Today's development doesn't necessarily have to mean strip mining, denuding forests, and fouling the wastershed. Development can be the planting of a tree as well as the cutting of a tree.

The natural resources man needs to exist are more abundant in the West than they have been in the East, and always will be.

But there's also the spiritual inspiration that will always be here. You can always look at Mount McKinley, or the vastness of the Wrangell Mountain Range, or the Teton forests, or the Pacific Ocean. They will never change. What we have to be sure of is that we do not develop the West for artificial reasons. And then the West can help the East become a real society, not just a plastic society.

Ask yourself: What is the value of a sunset? Or the beauty of a mountain? Or the lonely stretch of beach? Or just the chance to renew one's spirits? Who owns our great rivers? Who owns all the waters that run down the mountains to the seas? Who owns the sunset?

These are things no one can buy on the New York Stock Exchange.

Find men of conscience in the West, and they will develop the West in the finest way. The West knows the balance of nature. It's time that the rest of the world and the nation listened.

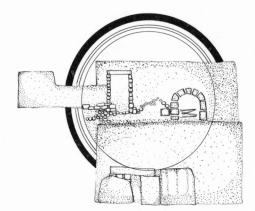

THE SACRED
AND PROFANE EARTH – II

In a sedate mansion near Embassy Row in Washington, D.C., a group of distinguished energy executives and government officials, scientists and technicians, had for many years been prophesying and planning for the needed exploitation of the energy of the West. They may not have known where the Female Mountain was, but they had known for a generation that within its womb was the energy the white man needed for survival.

Man had an "insatiable hunger" for the energy of his mother, the earth, they said. In the past, "scarcity, no doubt, characterized many relatively primitive societies," but the "civilized society" of "Western Man" needed ever greater and greater amounts of "resource abundance." So it was survival, not malice, that compelled "Western Man" to demand the energy of the "primitive societies," said the scientists.

The Woman Who Had Squaw Dance said: "I don't know the white man's ways. But to us the Earth, the Air, the Water, these

*are Holy Elements. That is why I don't like it [the mining]. The
whites have neglected and misused the Earth."*

The manufacturers of the recycled energy of the earth, led by
Laurance Rockefeller, of Standard Oil, and Robert O. Anderson,
of Atlantic Richfield, had founded Resources for the Future,
RFF, in 1952: "for research and education in the development,
conservation and use of natural resources." It then had begun
the monumental task of compiling the "detailed projections to the
year 2000 for the demand and supply of energy."

One of RFF's prompt conclusions was that America was on a
collision course with the earth. It was contentedly devouring itself.

"In using fossil fuels, vast as the reserves may be, the people
are living off capital." Soon the earth would be hollow as a dead
star: "it is simply a matter of time."

*The Woman Who Had Squaw Dance said: "The dust of coal
that contaminates the water is killing our animals. Many of the
sheep of my children were killed. I have some cows that started
dying off. And now it happens too often. Almost every day.
Wooded areas are being cut down. Now the air is becoming bad.
The air is not working. The herbs taken from the Mother Earth
and given to a woman in childbirth no longer grow. The land
looks burned."*

*The Woman Who Had Squaw Dance said: "I see the cedar
trees beside the ponds turned red. The grasses are dying."*

*The Woman Who Had Squaw Dance said: "Even though I
am old I think about it every day and every night, how they're
destroying my land."*

In the mountains of the West there was at least a moment
of solace from the "energy crisis" of the whites' cities. The RFF
study *Energy in the United States* forecast that the "low quality
coalfields of the mountain states [will come] into sharp focus"
when the "cost reducing" technology of strip mining was developed. Now that "important development of coal production [in
the West seemed] about to unfold." That was in 1960.

Not long ago, when the country had hardly heard the words "energy crisis," RFF was defining the future problem. They had to. As President Nixon's Secretary of the Interior, Rogers C. B. Morton, casually remarked, "The energy crunch really began after World War II."

Someone had to plan for everyone else's "future shock." RFF did so, quietly at first. It was in 1952 that *Resources for Freedom,* the government's first comprehensive worldwide energy resources study, was issued by President Eisenhower's Material Policy Commission. The chairman of that body was William Paley, who became the first chairman of RFF that same year.

That was the year, it may be remembered, when the "extensive investigation" of the coal on the Holy Land of the People began. And so what was to happen to the sheepherders upon the Female Mountain was indirectly the first step in the fulfillment of a national policy. In this sense, it was not unknown, nor unplanned.

So it was that the new "energy crisis," that was so to shock the country that it is still in a trauma, was neither new nor surprising to the energy technocrats. Some seemed to welcome its challenges and to profit from them.

Conquest of the West begun in the Eisenhower years was greatly accelerated during the presidency of John Kennedy, when his Secretary of the Interior, Stewart Udall, encouraged and signed the coal-mining leases on the Female Mountain and the power projects at Four Corners. (He later "regretted" this in a public *mea culpa.* Perhaps, he said, "I did not do enough for the Indians"; but the country's "need" for energy seemed to be more demanding.)

The need for energy was to reach its zenith with the ascendancy of Richard Nixon to the Oval Office, and with his choice of John Ehrlichman as the director of the White House's "domestic" policy desk—a position of power in deciding the fate of the lands, the resources, and the peoples of the West.

In the old tradition of political spoils, the President nominated a supporter, Walter Hickel, governor of Alaska, as Secretary of

the Interior. But it was not to be. In his book *Who Owns America?*
the unreconstructed Alaskan told of an incident that was to fore-
tell his future, and the country's.

Soon after his nomination, but before this had been made
public, there was a Republican Governors' Conference in Palm
Springs, California. That day under the desert palms, the flam-
boyant lobbyist for ITT, Dita Beard, held one of her famous parties
"to celebrate the impending nomination" of Rogers Morton as
Secretary of the Interior. "Dita and her friends [in ITT] were
excited about the prospect," Hickel puckishly recalled. The lobbyist was not mistaken, merely premature, in her celebration. In
an unexpectedly short time the outspoken Alaskan would be fired
by President Nixon, not for the reasons given, he insisted—that
was a "cover-up"—but because he opposed the White House's
plans "for the country to be stripped nude" by what he called
"the administration's wasteful energy policy."

And who was nominated to succeed Walter Hickel but Rogers
Morton. They wanted an "Easterner," said the Alaskan.

It was in those years that ITT had offered to finance the President's renominating convention. And Rogers Morton, who had
been the chief fund raiser for Nixon's presidential campaign
of 1968, was expert at soliciting political contributions from em-
ployees of the energy industries. At one political fund-raising
dinner, sponsored by the American Petroleum Institute, in Hous-
ton, Texas, five million dollars were raised. Rogers Morton was
the guest of honor. The oil producers, who owned some of the
largest coal producers, were at the time buying up leases to millions of acres of coal and oil reserves in federal lands in the West,
administered by the Interior Department.

"The name of 'the game,' " said Rogers Morton's Under Secretary of the Interior, Hollis Dole, "is profit."

Once more the reconquest of the West was about to begin.
The reign of Rogers Morton as master of the vast empire of resources and lands of the Interior fiefdoms, together with John
Ehrlichman as the policymaker at the White House's "domestic"
desk, was to change the face of America. As Stewart Udall would

say: "The Nixon administration . . . developed a *sudden* coal bias."
Within a year it was announced that the country faced an "energy
crisis"—because of its dependence on "foreign" energy. And that
the strip mining of the West had become almost a patriotic
"necessity." Project Independence was born. That was ironic, for
one of Walter Hickel's blunders had been that he "was a minority
of one" in warning, in 1969, against the dependence on foreign
oil.

It may be forgotten that one of President Nixon's first acts on
taking office had been to appoint Maurice Stans, chairman of the
giant Western Bancorporation, as Secretary of Commerce. And
one of Stans's first acts was to appoint his administrative secretary
as chairman of the strip-mine and power-plant complex known
as the Four Corners Regional Commission, on the lands of the old
sheepherders.

This all seemed so far from the elusive Female Mountain, but
it was not.

When the huge coal-gasification plants were to be built in the
shadow of the sacred Shiprock years later, an official of El Paso
Natural Gas spoke of the plants as "pilot" projects: the "models"
for the future. Navajo tribal councilman Fred Johnson responded
angrily: "The gasification process on such a massive scale has never
been perfected anywhere in the world. But now they're going to
try it out on us. Are we going to be guinea pigs and sacrificial
lambs for the white man again . . . so the white kids on the West
Coast can have electric toothbrushes?"

Once again the treatment of the Indian would be the "model"
for what the white men would later do to their fellow whites.
And thinking: Lo, pity the poor Indians, the whites would not
suspect that they would be the next victims.

On the old sheepherders' land the first large-scale power projects and strip mines in the West were to be built. The Peabody
Coal executive T. C. Mullens said it clearly: the strip mining of
the Female Mountain "will stand as a 'model' for other groups of
companies, who must necessarily follow our path in the future."
Whatever happened on the Holy Land of the People, if their

"model" worked, would soon happen on the ranch lands and mountain ranges throughout the West.

The "Navajo plant" was to be another such "model" of things to come. "How well this plant is accepted," said William Gould, a senior vice-president of Southern California Edison, "will give a direct indication as to whether the Kaiparowitz project [a vastly larger complex] will ever become a reality." Ecologists "could destroy its economic advantages" and "could provide an impenetrable barrier to the successful completion of the project." But the "Navajo plant," on Indian land, was built, and the Kaiparowitz plant, on the whites' land, was not.

Here was to be the "model" for the awesome phalanx of "250 major new coal mines" and the "150 major coal-fired power plants" that were to become crucial to the national "energy crisis" policies of Nixon's chosen successor, Gerald Ford, in his "State of the Union" message of 1975. No one had known, or if they knew they did not say, that the "model" on the pastures of the Old People on the Female Mountain would lead to that.

"Rog Morton's marching orders," President Ford told a joint session of Congress, had been to "promptly [begin] utilizing our coal resources"—so that by 1980 coal would replace oil in the production, that is, the recycling, of electricity. The Secretary of the Interior was logically charged with the task because most of the coal lay beneath the public lands and the Indian reservations that he alone managed.

"No one cares about smog" on Indian lands, said a Los Angeles newspaper.

The Woman Who Had Squaw Dance said: "When I first realized I had eyes, I saw that the air was clear. Now it is becoming hazy and gray. The coal mine is causing it. Because of the bad air, animals are not well. They don't feel well. They know what is happening and are dying. The animals are worrying and so they are dying."

The Woman Who Had Squaw Dance said: "I'm pleading with you. Why are you destroying them this way?"

In her words there was a sorrow too silent to be heard. No one listened.

A Navajo tribal official lamented: "So maybe that's why they chose our land for their model. On Indian land they get away with doing so many things they could not get away with doing on privately owned lands. So we were sitting ducks. They know the government would do whatever they wanted. And we could not do, or say, anything without government approval. And if we did, the government would veto anything we did.

"So we were guinea pigs for you," he said.

There was still another good reason for beginning the quest for energy in the midst of the deserts of the isolated and remote lands of the People. At the time, it was thought that the People were powerless and almost extinct. Self-determination was unheard of then; it had been government policy to convince the tribes to vote for their own "termination," as Congress had decreed in 1953. One government expert, Allen Harper, the "head of government service to the Navajo," had said in 1951 that the lands had "a resource base which even if fully developed" would barely support 30,000. So he recommended "relocation" of the poor Indians from their poor lands into the city. Twenty years later that "resource base" had become one of the richest in the country, and 125,000 People lived on the land.

For more than a century the People were accustomed to having their lives planned for them by men whom they had never met, who lived thousands of miles away. They ignored that. Even their tribal councils had been set up by white men in the Bureau of Indian Affairs to deal with other white men. They were used to that.

Sometimes it seemed as if the Bureau was a "home for all bureaucrats who couldn't succeed elsewhere" and who had a "perverted urge for power" because, "unable to deal successfully within his own culture, the typical Bureau employee attempted to rule people of another culture." That was the psychological explanation of Peter MacDonald, chairman of the Navajo Nation. "The Bureau officials regard the Indian people and Indian governments much in the way an overbearing parent regards a recalcitrant child," he said.

When the Tribal Council passed a resolution, it had to be approved or disapproved by the Bureau, said MacDonald. To accomplish this, the bureaucrats had three stamps: "If the 'A' stamp is used, it means the resolution must go to Washington for approval. If the 'B' stamp is used, the approval of the Area Director is required. If the 'C' stamp is affixed, then no Bureau approval is required.

"No government department that I have ever dealt with has ever evolved such a complex system of saying no," said MacDonald.

Not everyone remembered it that way. The Bureau's director of resource developments on the People's land in the sixties, James Canan, seemed to blame the tribal leaders. "The tribes were pressuring hard to get in on the proposed developments," Canan said, "and in fact, pushed the Bureau further than we felt was desirable."

Still, the Bureau official admitted, "The principal role of the Bureau [is] in working up the sale." Former Commissioner of Indian Affairs Marvin Franklin put it succinctly: "In administrating to Indians, traditionally the federal government has concentrated on lands and property—and neglected people."

In solemn meetings of tribal councils, eloquent orations were given and ritual votes taken on matters everyone knew had been decided long ago, and far away, by white men. The disdain, if not contempt, for democracy among the People could be seen in the vote of the Navajo Tribal Council in September 1969, when the Salt River Project had requested formal permission to build its power plant at Page, Arizona. For it was known that the company had ordered from General Electric turbine generators for the power plant, costing over $100 million, in December 1967— *two years before* the tribe was asked for its ritual votes of approval.

The ritual votes of the tribal councils were meaningless. By government regulation these votes had to be taken—but the government, time after time, made certain the matters had been decided long before the tribal councils were given a chance to even discuss them. One blatant instance of this was the leasing of tribal land to the Utah Construction and Mining Company for strip-mining the coal of the Four Corners region, which the unknowing tribal councilmen duly voted on and granted in 1957, though the company had been given the right to 139,000 acre-feet of water for the yet unpermitted strip mine and power plants of the region by the government in 1955—*two years before* the tribal council voted its permission.

Remembering how the strip-mining contract on the Female Mountain had been approved, Navajo councilman Keith Smith said, "The council never had good discussion on it. We were asked, in effect, to say yes, or no, to the proposal."

One elder of the tribe remembered: "Some of us thought it would be something like the oil drillers who come and drill little holes in the ground. That was all. We had seen that. We'd never seen strip mines. So we did not know that this hole would be maybe miles long. No one ever told us that."

(In Montana, the Cheyenne said the same thing: "In the beginning, the old fellows on the council did not understand coal leases," tribal chairman Alan Rowland said. "They had knowledge of oil and gas companies who came to us for leases, dug a few holes, gave us a big bonus, and left. No one explained to us that strip mining wasn't like drilling a few holes. And the Bureau gave us the wrong advice. They always do. They think we are just dumb Indians. They try to fool us, to intimidate us, to bribe us. They are arrogant bastards.")

Many thought it did not matter. Every year, year after year, the men came from Washington with documents, studies, reports, programs, projects, resolutions, congressional bills, and presidential orders and leases. The People would talk of them, and vote on them, and nothing ever happened. That was the way of the white man. He had to be humored.

One day in the summer of 1970 I was visiting the tribal office of the Hopi. One tribal leader was methodically reading documents.

"What are you reading?" I asked him.

"The coal contracts," he said, sighing.

"But you signed them so long ago. Why read them now?"

"The tribal chairman said to me, 'You better read them thoroughly. We signed them, but no one read them thoroughly.'"

Not that it would have mattered too much. The "energy crisis" was not up to the People. And no one asked them for their solutions.

Some thought the leases were not that bad. The People would at least get coal royalties and a few jobs. Clarence Hamilton, the Hopi chairman who had signed the leases, had said, "They are not only giving us economic development; it also gives us employment."

In the past, "coal, uranium, oil, and gas were just literally given away," said Peter MacDonald. Now "we're trying to balance everything on how much money we get."

The Woman Who Had Squaw Dance said: "How much would you ask if your Mother had been harmed? There is no way we can be repaid for the damages done to our Mother. No amount of money can repay."

The Woman Who Had Squaw Dance said: "Money cannot give birth to anything."

No one said it, but everyone knew it. These new leases were like the old treaties that the government had used not to give land to the tribes, as they said, but to take it away. In the nation's history there had never been a treaty that took land from a white man and gave it to an Indian. Even those treaties that protected the reservation lands did so at the expense of much larger lands that the People had to give up for the privilege of being protected.

It was an old story. The People were given a little of what was theirs, and the whites took the rest in exchange.

The Woman Who Had Squaw Dance said: "The government told us at Fort Sumner [in 1868] they weren't going to hurt us any more. But they lied. We signed a treaty at Fort Sumner and they told us they weren't going to bother us any more, but they broke the treaty so many times that my People are hurting from it. Why are they doing this to us?"

Some now said the mining leases were illegal. The government had been knowingly violating its own laws, they said.

Some now said that the new mining leases were worse than the old treaties. In the government's treaties of the past, no matter how much land was taken away, there was some land left for the People. But in the strip mines and the power plants the earth was devoured, the rivers were consumed, the sky was polluted and a way of life vanished. All that would remain would be a few years of money, until that too would be gone.

Even worse, unlike the old treaties which the government always broke after signing them, in the new mining leases the government broke its own laws—just by signing them. The Secretary of the Interior had said so.

In Montana, the angry Northern Cheyenne threatened to go into court and accuse the government of willful "fraud" and "deceit" in negotiating the mining leases. Fearful that the People might establish a legal precedent for more democratic and open leasing practices by the government, the Interior Department sought to head off a confrontation in court. Some insignificant and obscure technicality had to be discovered by which the government could benevolently allow the Northern Cheyenne the right to cancel the leases—which covered half of their land, 213,000 of 432,000 acres—without denying the authority of the Great White Father in Washington to make the decision for them.

And so the Great White Father found a technicality. The Secretary of the Interior, Rogers Morton, withdrew his approval of his own department's coal leases, because, he said, it was suddenly discovered that they violated "long-standing" laws and regulations (CFR 25, Sec. 171.9). These newfound but old laws prohibited leasing of more than 2,650 acres of tribal land for coal mining unless a waiver was obtained from the Commissioner of Indian Affairs. Since there was "no evidence [of] an explicit waiver," said the Secretary, his approval of the leases was now "denied." Of course, this was a singular case, and did not apply to any other mining leases.

But what about these leases on other tribal lands that held one-third of the coal resources of the nation? The Secretary preferred not to discuss it.

Were all these leases really illegal? It seemed likely. The government leases on the Reservations of the West almost all exceeded the acreage limitations and almost all were negotiated without the needed "waiver."

Several Indian experts and expert Indians were asked what they thought of the "long-standing" law. None had ever heard of it. Embarrassed by their disclosures of their violations of their own laws, a high-ranking official of the Bureau wrote in a "Confidential Memo": Someone had indeed ignored the law. It was "an outmoded provision which should have been removed from the regulations but had not been, due to department inertia." So it was still the law. Not merely that, but the limitation applied to "oil and gas and all other minerals." He thought it had been written in the 1950s, after the Congress had passed the Termination Act of the tribes. And it had been hoped the Reservations might be divided up and leased.

Still, no action was taken on these apparent illegalities. The Department of Interior was accustomed to operating within its own laws or without them.

The People had no voice in its decisions. None of the men of the Interior Department's vast and powerful bureaus were elected; they governed the domestic affairs of the nation by authoritarian decree, much as the Pentagon did overseas. In this, the Interior Department was the Pentagon of our land. But unlike the policies of the military, the programs of the baronial bureaus of Interior were seldom open to public scrutiny or press investigation. In the era of Vietnam the public's eye was elsewhere.

An understandably perturbed vice-president of Peabody Coal complained to me: "We are not quite sure what the ramifications are." He needn't have worried. There were no ramifications.

It was nothing new for the government to violate its own treaties, or now leases, with the People. In one generation, or two, somebody would write *Bury My Heart in the Interior Department*.

In the beginning, Peter MacDonald had said, "I am not opposed to strip mining." Even then he had been troubled. As a young boy he had been trained to be a medicine man, but he had become a civil engineer instead. As chairman of the tribe, he was the man in the middle.

"The Navajo people are in no position to judge which side, if either, is wholly right," he said.

Still, he was fearful. "I do not want to tell my children why the legendary Window Rock has been blackened with fly ash, why the sheep are dying from sulfur oxide poisoning [or] why parts of the Navajo Reservation must be abandoned."

In time, some tribal leaders did listen to the cries of the Old People. "Our people appear to be doomed to breathe polluted air," said Wilbur Atcitty, executive administrator of the Navajo Nation. "No longer will we allow this monster the freedom it has enjoyed in the past. We will make certain that our Navajo people will not have to pay with their lungs for year-round heated swimming pools" in Los Angeles.

The Woman Who Had Squaw Dance said: "Sweet talk! Whenever we elect somebody who says he's going to really help us, after he's elected he doesn't keep his word. It's like that all the time. Whatever the white man says, that person that was elected just falls for that. He forgets his People, forgets us, starts selling our land. They just sign whatever papers the white man puts in front of them. But we don't want anything to do with that. We want our land back."

"Nowadays some of these leaders don't just talk with two tongues. They talk with two mouths," said a young activist. "They say one thing to the white people and another thing to our people. And the funny thing is they defend 'Indian rights' and say 'preserve our culture' to the whites, but they say 'white is right' and we have to give up our culture—for 'jobs'—to our people.

"Why? Because they have been bought by the media. And the whites," he said.

Once native land could be "leased" for the gift of a few blankets. Thus the Dutch, in 1654, claimed possession of the beaches of Coney Island, in New York, after giving Guttaquoh, a headman of the People of Manahaming, the gift of "two guns, three pounds of powder," and a bit of cloth. That was typical. In later years, a pickup truck and a few cases of whiskey may have helped convince a tribal leader to sign a minor government contract. Now it was said that a Swiss bank account may have replaced the blanket.

"These new energy leases are worth billions. On the reservations we have never seen so much money," said one nationally known leader. "And we have never seen so much corruption. But it is worse than your kind of corruption. Where there has never been any money, then money does more than corrupt. It destroys. It is destroying our best leaders."

As the "coal rush" swept upon the West, there were more and more rumors of "gifts" to local officials. There was talk of secret FBI investigations, of defrauding the People, and of larceny involving energy resources. Still there has not been, as of now, any public report of grand jury findings. Nor, as yet, have there been any indictments.

In many colonial countries it had become a reluctant business practice to offer generous "gifts" to the national leaders for favorable attention to leases of energy resources. The executives of several multinationals have confessed to giving gifts of millions in the hearings of the Senate Committee on Multinational Corporations. And some of these same corporations hold extensive leases on energy resources in tribal and public lands in the West.

In the West these gifts have taken the form of government and corporate grants, excess (government) property, and just plain cash offered to tribal governments; they are labeled "development funds." In the Southwest, this benevolence has been coordinated by the states of Colorado, Utah, Arizona, and New Mexico, with the assistance of the federal government, through the ubiquitous Four Corners Regional Commission. Its stated goal of "the development of a depressed, but beautiful, area of this country" hardly hinted at its enormous power as the donor of tens of millions, not only to the rural and tribal poor, but to the local municipalities, counties, universities, and institutions.

Among the recipients of the Four Corners Regional Commission were those local tribes whose earth was rich with energy. In one year alone, the offices and enterprises of the Navajo Nation received gifts of $3,398,889.61 in equipment and funds. That year, 1972, the Bureau of Indian Affairs received gifts valued at $2,269,908.45 from the generous commissioners.

All in all, some $4.5 million yearly in gifts has been given to tribal governments. These gifts have not noticeably increased the tribal officials' desire to publicly criticize "energy development" in the Four Corners region.

"Some tribal chairmen are not dedicated to their people," Wendell Chino, chairman of the Mescalero Apache Nation, said. "They are dedicated to their job. Instead of serving their people, they serve themselves. They are interested in power."

Chino was sometimes said to be the "conscience of tribal leaders"; he was president of the National Tribal Chairmen's Association, and he talked with severity of the growing corruption of the leaders. "It isn't just that these tribal chairmen go after women, drink, and all that. That isn't something I would say something about. That is their business. But what I do criticize is that they do not work at their jobs, for their people. That's not what a leader of the Indian people should be. He should be a strong leader for his people, or he should not be a leader. He should resign."

On the Female Mountain, the damage had been done. The "model" strip mine and energy-consuming power plant had given birth to a brood of what the People called the "monsters," which were spreading throughout the entire West. On the sacred land of the Navajo Four Corners alone there were plans for as many as seven huge coal-gasification plants, which would cost billions of dollars, on the land of the old sheepherders.

There was talk of building a city. Some said that it would be a new city of 25,000. Some said 75,000. Actually, the Westinghouse Corporation, at the request of the Four Corners Commission, had long ago drawn up plans for "an ultramodern city of 250,000"! It was to become "A Model City for Indians," *U.S. News & World Report* said, describing it, in 1969—a "testing ground" to "benefit" people by urbanizing them. "Our idea is to bring the twentieth century to the Indian," said a city planner.

"And if you build Pittsburgh here, we will not have to go to Pittsburgh to die," said a tribal official. "That will be the end of our way of beauty and harmony.

"Everyone talks of self-determination for Indians," he said. "And what do they do? They offer us self-destruction of our resources and religion. I say this is not economic development. This is the economic termination of the reservation."

The Woman Who Had Squaw Dance said: "Even now our herbs are vanishing. Three times I have gone looking for herbs. I could not recognize the place where to find them. I couldn't find my way around the mountain because it was so ruined. Our prayers and healing have been tampered with and they do not work as good any more. That's why our values of things are no good any more. They are taking the Holy Element from her veins. Our Mother is hurt. Our Mother is scarred."

More in anger than hope, John Redhouse and Gerry Wilkinson, of the National Indian Youth Council, in nearby Albuquerque, issued a challenge to tribal officials and the government. "It appears that the Indian people will have to pay with their land, their culture, and their sacred religion to maintain heated swimming pools in Los Angeles," they said. "It is perhaps ridiculous for Indian people to challenge a multibillion-dollar industrial operation, but if our right to an existence as a People is threatened by corporate greed, we have nothing to lose."

And yet these mountains were merely wounded. They had not died. They had suffered worse destruction in the past and they had survived in many worlds. Some things died and some things lived. In one hundred years would the power plants or the Female Mountain still be alive?

The Woman Who Had Squaw Dance said: "A long time ago the earth was placed here for us, the People, the Navajo; it gives us corn and we consider it our mother. We make prayers for all the blessings of Mother Earth, asking that we may use her legs, her body, and her spirit to make ourselves stronger, and more enduring."

The Woman Who Had Squaw Dance said: "How can we give some things of value to Mother Earth to repay the damages the mining has done to her?"

The White Man's Suicide

❦ TESTAMENT OF Frank Tenorio, secretary,
All-Indian Pueblo Council

"Personal penance" was what he called it.

It was soon after he had been convicted of criminal conspiracy in the Watergate cover-up that John Ehrlichman, former domestic policy adviser to former President Richard Nixon, announced that rather than go to prison he would like to work with the Pueblos of New Mexico—to do "penance."

Life on Indian reservations "is no easy life," Ehrlichman's lawyer, Ira Lowe, had told Judge John Sirica. His client would, however, sacrifice the comforts of a prison cell to go into the "remote" mountains of northern New Mexico to "help" the poor Indians. "We have talked to the Pueblos and found out what their needs were," Lowe said. Ehrlichman could help them solve their land and water problems; he was a "land use lawyer," and he was "sympathetic" to Indians.

The director of the Northern Pueblo Council, Herman Agoyo, listened politely but with surprise to the unsolicited offer. He did not say no and Ehrlichman's lawyer took that to mean yes.

Governor Lucario Padilla of Santa Clara Pueblo, who was chairman of the council, replied that they did indeed have some water problems. "We could certainly use some plumbers in our struggle to establish our water rights." Though he thought perhaps Ehrlichman "would be more useful in providing community service in the form of ditch [digging] work, as spring is at hand."

That might be of more help to him than he could be of help to them, Governor Padilla said. "Being compassionate people, we would be pleased to assist in the rehabilitation of a felon, but we do question whether Mr. Ehrlichman's offer of legal assistance is all that appropriate," the governor said, "at this point in time."

And then the governors of the eight pueblos met and unanimously "denied Mr. John Ehrlichman's request."

"This trial just ended before Judge Sirica has focused attention of the non-Indian community in this country on lack of credibility insofar as political institutions are concerned. We needed no Watergate to be made aware of the fact that the government agencies are not above verbal duplicity," Governor Padilla said.

"One can only wonder what sort of assistance Ehrlichman contemplates when he offers to help the Pueblo Indians of New Mexico."

The pretense of penance was poorly timed. It came at an uncharitable moment.

On the sun-baked plazas of the Pueblos there was already a surfeit of government lawyers who the people wished would go home. The State of New Mexico had launched another of its endless court cases to destroy Pueblo self-government, this time by denying their age-old water rights. And the federal government had sent some uninvited lawyers to "defend" the Pueblos. "The fox is protecting us against the other foxes," said Frank Tenorio, from the San Felipe Pueblo.

An eloquent and scholarly man, Tenorio was secretary of the All-Indian Pueblo Council. His sense of justice was not, however, recognized by the courts.

For thousands of years his Pueblo, like most of those in the valley of the Rio Grande, had been building their homes and farming their fields along the river. Now the newcomers in the growing cities and agribusinesses of New Mexico needed, and were determined to take away, the ancestral water rights of the villagers. The state engineer, Steve Reynolds, had filed suit claiming the water belonged to the state. Pojoaque, Nambe, Tesuque, and San Ildefonso Pueblos had contested this, in a landmark case known as *New Mexico* v. *Aamodt*. The case was a "mess," Tenorio said.

If the water was taken, the people would "shrivel," Tenorio said. "Water is the blood of the people." And the Pueblos "were shocked by a statement by Vearle Payne, Chief Judge of the U.S. District Court of New Mexico, that 'Pueblo Indians are not considered by Congress to have any reserved water rights. . . .' This decision," said Tenorio, put the Pueblos "firmly under the thumb of the states."

And so the Pueblos wished to fire the government lawyers and hire their own. Their right to hire their own lawyers was denied them by Judge Payne, a ruling later overturned by a higher court. Still, they feared "the government was getting ready to 'throw' the case."

In the spring of 1976 the United States Supreme Court ruled that the State of New Mexico did indeed have jurisdiction over the Indians' water rights, reversing one hundred years of moral promises and legal decisions.

One day that autumn, the Pueblo leader journeyed north to Shiprock to ask for the aid of the Navajos, the traditional enemies of the Pueblos. The old enemies were no longer enemies, Tenorio said, for now they had common enemies, who wished to take away the water of all the Indian people.

This is what he said:

My name is Frank Tenorio. I am a Pueblo Indian from San Felipe Pueblo in New Mexico. I have been involved in the fight to save our people's water for many years. Against us we have arrayed the forces of federal, state, and local governments, as well as private interests of powerful corporations and individuals. In our fight we stand alone against the combined interests of the most powerful country the world has ever known.

In a way I might be termed a hematologist. This is a medical doctor who concerns himself with problems of the blood. For water is the blood of the Pueblo people.

There has been a lot said about the sacredness of our land, which is our body; and the value of our culture, which is our soul; but if the blood of the people stops its life-giving flow, or becomes polluted, all else will die and many thousands of years of our communal existence will come to an end.

Surely the Great Spirit did not intend for us to shrivel up and die and our bones to be scattered, only to be remembered in anthropology textbooks.

If a Pueblo who died twenty thousand years ago should return to live with his relatives today, he would be perfectly at home. We have kept our relationship with nature and now we as a people see that we are one of the few custodians of this kind of knowledge left. Maybe this kind of knowledge is what the world will need to survive.

Our old enemies, the Anglos and the Spanish, have now settled among us. They will not give back to us what they have stolen, but we have survived. We have survived the Spanish, the Anglos, and the technological revolution. But now we face our greatest enemies. They do not go by the name of Coronado, or Cortez, or Custer, but by the name of the Army Corps of Engineers, San Juan–Chama Diversion Project, Salt River Project, and so forth.

In facing these new adversaries who threaten our existence, I know now how my Pueblo brothers who have passed on felt when they stood on the rooftops of their pueblos and saw for the first time these people with white skins, with shining armor, shooting fire out of sticks and logs, which were killing their people and destroying their homes.

We learned their powers and we survived them. We will also learn the ways of all our adversaries who hide behind such initials as BIA [Bureau of Indian Affairs] or BLM [Bureau of Land Management], and we will survive them, too.

Basic to our problem is the conflict of interest in the federal government regarding Indian affairs. The Department of the Interior is charged with the protection and preservation of natural resources for the public good. It is also charged with the protection and development of Indian lands. . . . When there is a conflict between public interest and Indian interest, the Indian loses.

Our present situation is analogous to a farmer who has his chickens and his foxes in the same coop and who is charged both with feeding the foxes and keeping the chickens alive. We all know the results to be expected from this kind of setup.

Our water, our sacred water, is a good example of what is happening to us.

It must be remembered that with the ever-expanding and wasteful urbanization of Indian country, we Indian people of the Southwest find ourselves with the last good land and the last good water left. As the white man wastes his resources, he casts a covetous eye on what we have preserved for our own needs. We have not wasted our resources.

There is something suicidal in the non-Indian's belief in ever-expanding development and his belief in his ability to be able to continually reform nature through technology. The Southwest, in terms of water supply, can only support a limited number of people; that is a fact of life. The fact is that the Great Spirit put only so much water on this earth, and that is a fact the white man refuses to confront.

We Pueblo Indians are rapidly approaching an Armageddon —a final, decisive battle between our right to survive and the prolongation of the white man's suicide.

Our first line of defense has been and should be the Winters Doctrine. This doctrine was enunciated by the Supreme Court in 1908. It states that land reserved for the Indians by law or treaty—that is, Indian reservations—is entitled to use water rising or flowing on this land, to develop it now and in the future, whether or not Indians are now using the water. This doctrine is in direct conflict with the prior-appropriation laws used in most states.

The law is on our side, but might is not.

As you recall, the Supreme Court in the early 1800s ruled that the Cherokee tribe could not be removed from their ancestral homes in Georgia. President Andrew Jackson said, "The Supreme Court has made its decision; now let them enforce it." The Cherokees were removed. History seems to be repeating itself with the Pueblo Indians today.

People in power have always stolen from Indian People. But I must hand it to the present United States government; never has any government gone to so much expense and into so much detail in order to steal something from somebody. I guess that is the American Way.

The fact is that our water is being taken and our whole way of life is threatened.

We Indian people do not always understand the laws, largely because they are numerous, complex, and ever-changing. But we do understand fairness. Fairness is the right to exist as a people. . . . Fairness is living up to one's solemn agreements and contracts. . . . And fairness is having enough water to raise one's corn and feed one's family. . . .

My people back home do not fully understand what is happening to them. We grow up believing that people will do the right thing, if they know what the right thing is. This is our belief in America. It is up to this nation as a whole to prove us right or wrong.

THE HOLY WATER

MANY years ago there was no rain upon the earth. The earth became very dry. Many plants and animals died of thirst. The people had very little to eat. Rabbits and squirrels, prairie dogs and antelope, were all they had to eat. And many of these animals were dying. There were no crops of food because there was no rain.

So the story of the Rain Ceremony of the Navajo begins, the way some tell it.

In the Navajo Curriculum Center of the Rough Rock School the ancient story was told in a textbook for young children, *Grandfather Stories of the Navajos*. So the young would not "walk away" from the People's "path of beauty and harmony," it was printed in the textbook, said John Dick of the Tachii Nii clan, a member of the Board of Education; it was the guide "to the future" of the past, he said.

And what had happened was this:

In fear, the Earth People asked the animals why this had happened to them. The Gopher wished to help. And he dug deep until he came to the damp earth. And then Hummingbird came and he pecked in the damp earth until he came to Frog. And Frog said: The Earth People have become dishonest. They have forgotten to respect the earth and the sacred things. So the rains have been taken away from them. They have to go to the Water Ox, in The Place Where the Rivers Meet, for advice.

And so after many difficulties the Earth People did go to The Place Where the Rivers Meet to see the Water Ox. The Water Ox was understanding. Everything will be all right, he told them, if they did these things: "He told them to go home and mend their ways of living. He told them to respect their sacred things and ceremonies. He told them not to do things that were wrong—and dangerous. He told them to be kind to each other—and not to be selfish."

And so the Earth People went home. They did these things he told them. They respected the earth and the sacred things.

And so the rains came for twelve days. The rivers flowed. The seeds sprouted. The crops grew. The harvests were abundant. And the Earth People had learned the lesson of the ecology of water: When the earth is abused, the water will dry up, for the rain rises from the earth before it falls from the sky. The earth is the mother of the rain.

In the mountains of New Mexico, where the little river of Los Piños and the great San Juan River come together, there is The Place Where the Rivers Meet. It is an actual place. Where the Water Ox lived is the precise spot where the Bureau of Reclamation of the Interior Department had built the towering Navajo Dam, to feed water into the power plants and strip mines and coal-gasification projects of the Four Corners Commission's energy-consuming complex.

One day in the autumn of the year, I was going to a Water Resources Conference in the town of Farmington, sponsored by the Navajo Nation. Not knowing the road too well, I found myself driving on the very top of the Navajo Dam. In the water hundreds of feet below I could see the place where the Earth People had asked the Water Ox for rain so long ago.

Beyond the dam was the lake, crowded with sailboats and cruisers. On the roadside there was a litter of beer cans. The water had become a favored place of the electrical engineers and strip miners, who came there on weekends to enjoy nature and to get drunk. And to escape from the smog of the power plants, where they worked, in Farmington.

I doubt that they ever asked the Water Ox how to respect the earth and sacred things. They knew nothing of the story of ancient ecology.

The People who had lived in the valley of the rivers always drank the water sparsely and reverently. It was Holy Water in the desert. Whoever wasted it wasted life. Not only the People, but the earth itself, would die if the water of the rivers dried up.

For hundreds of years, the People in the great city of Pueblo Bonito in Chaco Canyon, and in the river bottoms, built few industries and irrigated few fields. They knew there was little water in the rivers and they could not use more water than there was. No one who lived in the deserts would be so foolish; it would be like quenching your thirst by drinking your own blood.

In the nineteenth century the white ranchers came to the valley. "We pushed the Navajo out of the good bottom land, pushed 'em back up the dry mesa, where they couldn't hardly grow a thing," remembered San Juan County Sheriff Dan Sullivan. That was in the 1880s, when his grandfather had been sheriff. Still, the ranchers knew to respect the water; their lives and their ranches depended on it.

But the new townspeople knew none of that. Many of them had come to the West from the cities, when the oil discoveries of the 1950s turned these sleeping ranch towns into "boom" towns; to them water was something that came out of a faucet.

Men who did not know what water was thought they could use it as they wished. It was needed for the "production of energy." As it had been needed to turn waterwheels of the early mills and for steam engines. But they did not understand that water *was* energy. It was full of many chemical energies that fed and enriched the fish and animals. the earth and sky. The energy within water was so strong it moved mountains, dug canyons, and shaped the continents. "Oh, how many cities, how many lands, it has consumed," cried Leonardo da Vinci; its "raging and seething" was so powerful "no human resource" was equal to it. It was a Holy Element, said the Old People.

On earth three-quarters of the space was water. In the sky there was a vast sea of water that would cover the entire earth more than an inch deep if it fell every day. Even a small thunderstorm of rain released more energy than a 120-kiloton nuclear bomb. There were more than 10,000 thunderstorms each day. And so it could be said that the energy of 3,650,000 nuclear bombs rained upon the earth every year.

Now the earth seemed to be growing dryer. In ancient times, during the Pleistocene age, the Southwestern deserts were tropical seas and marshes. Once one-fifth of North America had been covered by lakes, but now less than half of these lakes existed. And everywhere there was less water.

The new townspeople of Farmington knew none of that. They knew nothing of water.

In the Holiday Inn of Farmington, the conference had already begun when I arrived. The representatives of the Navajo, Ute, Apache, and Pueblo people were smiling, for the town's Rotary Club was meeting in a nearby room and their singing could be heard through the walls:

> Oh, give me a home where the buffalo roam . . .
> and the skies are not cloudy all day.

The smog over the town was said by the astronauts to be the worst "man-made" pollution on earth. In the hills beyond the town was the largest strip mine on earth. And now there were plans to build the greatest complex of coal-gasification plants on earth, near the town.

And the white businessmen of the town now sang the plaintive refrain "Where the skies are not cloudy all day," like happy children who knew nothing of the meaning of their song. They were mostly advocates of the coal-gasification plants; to them it meant growth and money.

"For the benefit of distant metropolitan areas that want electricity, men of immense power want to make a slave state of this part of the country," intoned the keynote speaker at the conference, William Veeder. "Colonialism," he called it. It would be the "genocide" of the People.

The Indian People would be the "first victims" because it was their water, their land, their coal, and their energy, but they would not be the last. He believed the entire West was becoming a "slave state" of the "water and energy thirst" of the government. The people of the West, Indian and white, were being "bled dry." And so they would die, said Veeder.

Had not the Four Corners Commission itself said: "The Region, in many respects, resembles a number of less developed countries in the other parts of the world"?

Who was William Veeder? He was an intense little man, with a flushed face and quick angers. Not many years ago he had been the government's leading "expert" on Indian water resources and he had headed the Bureau's office in Washington. But he had been too outspoken in defense of water rights and the Department of the Interior had sought to banish him. So after a lifetime as a lawyer in the Justice and Interior departments, he had been exiled to an office without a title, and a desk without a position.

"I have been instructed to say that I do not speak for Justice or Interior," he said, laughing. "Nor do I speak for the Secretary of the Interior."

That way he had the freedom to speak honestly, he said. "I don't believe we can mince words any longer. You're being planned out of existence by the Department of the Interior," he told the People. "The plan is to plan the American Indians out of existence." It was the "most concerted and vicious attack on Indian water rights I've ever seen."

Why was he so furious? "There simply is not enough water for both the People and the energy industry," he said. "So we have to choose. It's as simple as that."

More water than existed in the rivers had been offered by the government to the energy industry. "The river is overcommitted. It is a bankrupt river," said Veeder, for if all the water allocated was taken out, "there could be zero flow" by the time it reached the People.

Physicist Charles Hyder, of NASA's Goddard Space Flight Center, agreed. So "recklessly high" were the allocations of the river that the Department of the Interior was "open to charges of embezzling water from the San Juan." The flow of the river had been "steadily decreasing" for many years. By the 1980s, if the depletions had not been halted, there might be "a dry riverbed." Even the reservoir behind the Navajo Dam might run "dry for extended periods. . . . We can expect a drought."

The prophecy of drought should have surprised no one. In the early 1960s, the Select Committee on National Water Resources of the United States Senate had declared that the demand for water by the projected power plants would be greater than the flow of the rivers by 1980. And by 2000, the demands would "exceed estimated maximum supply" by 40 percent. No one explained then, or has since, just how one could use 40 percent more water than there was.

"Nature will not supply enough water to support the apportionment made," the Upper Colorado River Commission had warned in 1965. Who would? There was not enough water in the rivers for "present uses and new developments." So it seemed logical to the commission that any further projects "would be unwise."

Even the Department of the Interior's own Energy Management Team had forecast "significant shortages [of water] occurring in all states, except Wyoming, by year 2000." In the Colorado River Basin they had "assumed" there were 5,820,000 acre-feet of water, of which they planned to allocate 6,200,000 acre-feet for future use.

Still, the government was offering more water than there was in the rivers. The coal-gasification plants at Four Corners were promised 2,744,280,000 cubic feet of water, the power plants

2,787,840,000 cubic feet and the cities on the Rio Grande about 7,187,400,000 cubic feet. Even this would not be enough, some planners said; though this water and that promised to the People for farming was a third more water than existed during a good year.

"It's all done with mirrors," Veeder said. "It's very scientific. It's just a refinement on how to rip off a river. On my desk every morning there is a new computer print-out of the water in the river, done by a computer analyst who's never got his feet wet. It's a spooky numbers game.

"Computers will do whatever you tell them to," he said. Except for one thing; you cannot get any water out of a computer.

And the computers of the United States Geological Survey mindlessly predicted that in twenty-five years, by the year 2000, the water "need" of the country would "double." The computers did not say where double the water would come from.

Now there were more "computations" than waters, said a report by Senators George McGovern and James Abourezk of South Dakota, and Representatives Patricia Schroeder and Frank Evans of Colorado. A study of the Interior Department's own water estimates took "no calculator to come up with a total that exceeds the water," said the congressional report. If this nonsense did not cease, the result "could be disastrous."

That reminded me of the meetings we had had in the county courthouse a few years ago to discuss plans of an East Coast real estate developer to build an "El Dorado" in the deserts. There wasn't enough water for a project like that, said the local ranchers. Indignantly, a New York lawyer for the developers got up and yelled, "I tell you, we got ten million dollars to prove there is water!" The laughter that greeted his remarks seemed to confuse him.

An old farmer seated in front of me half turned around and said, "Well, I heard of turning water into wine and wine into water. But with dollar bills?"

In the old days, when words meant what they said, no one was ashamed to call the desert a desert. On the maps of the nineteenth century, the Great American West was known as the Great American Desert, from the Mexican to the Canadian border; for the rains on the plains of Montana were, and still are, almost the same as on the deserts of New Mexico.

Nowadays, the real estate developers have changed the name of the desert, but the desert has not changed. If anything, it is a greater desert than ever. There is less grass. There is less water. "Most of this region is arid or semiarid," said the RFF study *Natural Resources for U.S. Growth* in 1964. Though more than half of the land in the lower forty-eight states is in the West, the water resources are one-fifth those of the East. And the runoff of useful water is less than 16 percent of the national average— barely 2.3 inches of water yearly.

In the deserts, for many years, the water level has been falling. The pumping of ground water "is greatly exceeding recharge" —that is, rainfall—noted Leopold Luna of the Geological Survey as long ago as 1959. "In those places, continuation of withdrawals [of water] at present rates, in time, [will] lead to exhaustion of the supply," wrote Luna. And the waters might be so deep that any wells would be "in excess of the limits of economic feasibility." That was years before the cities of Denver and Phoenix, and the majestic power plants, had risen from the deserts to their towering heights of folly.

Once I asked the former Southwestern regional director of the Bureau of Land Management, Eastburn Smith, what he thought the building of the cities in the desert meant to the water resources. He told me that at the time the city of Phoenix was built he had had "more than three hundred" requests for deep-well permits on his desk. Since his hydrologists advised him not to sign them, he refused to do so. The ground water might become exhausted in twenty-five years, they thought. But the Secretary of the Interior had insisted that he sign the permits. So he did so.

"What does that mean?" I asked him.

"Let's see." He chuckled. "That was fifteen years ago. So they have ten years left."

In the dim days before the light of the "energy crisis" exposed the diminishing waters to the eyes of the nation, the politicos of New Mexico simply gave its scarce water away to the power and mining corporations. One gift, of about six *billion* cubic feet of water from the San Juan River, was given to a strip-mining company, Utah Construction and Mining, for a simple fee "permit" of seven hundred dollars; the water was worth, at today's rates, as much as fifty million dollars.

Learning of this, Representative John Mershon asked the state engineer whether the mining company had not actually been given "this water virtually free."

"That's right," the official, Steve Reynolds, replied.

In disbelief, the skeptical Mershon noted the "permit" was "predated" February 1955; for a few months later, in June, the Interstate Streams Commission was to "reserve" all the water in the San Juan Basin. There were hints of conflicts of interest, and of bribery, when it was discovered that a commission member, later its chairman, was a businessman from the San Juan River Basin. Mershon said, "I can read a lot of other interesting relationships into this."

But the gifts of water to the strip-mining and energy companies were never investigated. They never have been. Somehow the theft of the energy of the nation and its water have never been questioned.

So great was the quantity of water consumed by the technology of taking energy from the earth that a relatively minor source, oil shale, "would take all the water in the Colorado River to cool the equipment needed to get the oil from the shale," said a senior technical specialist of Hercules Inc., Billings Brown. And the gasification plants would use geometrically larger amounts; water was a main ingredient of the process by which the energy of the coal was formed into the usable gas. No one even knew for sure how much water would have to be wasted. The process was too new.

One thing *was* sure: the water used in gasification was lost forever. It never could be used again.

"There simply is not enough water in the western states to

permit the enormous congregation of coal-fired generating, gasification and liquidization plants envisioned in recent years by
utilities and oil companies," declared a comprehensive study issued by the National Academy of Sciences in 1974. And if the
plants were built, the strip mines needed to feed their furnaces
could wound the earth beyond healing, especially where there
was a desert rain of less than ten inches a year. Scientists suggested that these vast regions be written off as "National Sacrifice Areas."

And yet if the earth was wounded, it would heal, though it
might take a hundred years. The death of a river, and the drying
up of springs beneath the earth, were more difficult to atone for;
it might take a millennium, if it could ever be undone. Can a dead
river be "reclaimed"? Is a desert such as the Sahara forever?

Maybe that kind of thinking was unthinkable. In times past,
many peoples who did not heed the hard truths of the desert
dried up like dead seas. Once the sands of Death Valley lay beneath a sea that was 180 feet deep. The animals, or humans, who
may have bathed in its water have disappeared without a trace.

One way the technicians thought of preserving the water was
to build huge dams and reservoirs. But in the desert, massive
structures such as these might someday seem as puzzling as the
pyramids of Egypt.

The sun in those cloudless skies of mountain deserts burned
so intensely that water in the reservoirs and lakes of the West
evaporated so quickly that more water was being lost in one day
than all the cities in the country used in one year. That made some
of the People ask: Did the dams of the U.S. Army Corps of Engineers, and the Bureau of Land Management, which had built the
Navajo Dam, actually decrease, rather than increase, the water
supply? I had often wondered why the ancient peoples of the
deserts, with their intricate systems of irrigation, so seldom
seemed to have built dams. Perhaps they knew better.

It was a perversity of history, perhaps, but the Navajo Dam
had been built by the government supposedly to preserve the
water of the People, who had been "pushed out" of the river

valley by the whites. That, at least, was what the Act of Congress had said. Some remembered that Congress had been reluctant to appropriate money for the dam until Senator Clinton Anderson of New Mexico convinced them it would "aid the Indians" by making farmers of them; it was benevolently named the Navajo Irrigation Project.

And it was true, the water had been mainly reserved for the People in the Colorado River Storage Act of 1962. More than 22 billion cubic feet of water (508,000 acre-feet) was set aside for irrigating the crops of the would-be Navajo farmers. The Secretary of the Interior was forbidden to "enter into contracts for a total amount of water beyond that which, in his judgement . . . will result in a reasonable amount being available . . . for the Navajo Irrigation Project."

Once the dam was built, the congressional promise was forgotten. In the spring of 1966, as soon as the Navajo Tribal Council granted the coal company its "drilling and exploration contract" on their Female Mountain, the then Secretary of the Interior, Stewart Udall, "in his judgement," suggested "cutting back" on the Navajo Irrigation Project by almost 40 percent (198,000 acre-feet). The water would go to the power companies. Since that time the government had been "cutting back" on the Act of Congress so insidiously that less than half the water "reserved" for the People was still promised them.

At the very beginning of the dam-building, the editor of the *Navajo Times*, Chet MacRorie, had suspected the tribe was being used falsely. The conduits taking water away from the People's lands were vastly larger than those for bringing water to it. He wondered if the government had ever intended that the Navajo Irrigation Project become a reality. "A BIG WATER GRAB," the tribal newspaper had headlined the exposé a decade ago. It had editorialized: "Water is liquid gold. Powerful interests will leave no stone unturned to obtain water."

In the summer of 1976, the Navajo Irrigation Project had finally begun, but most of the water was devoured by the power plants. "The most efficient use of water is industrial," said Bill

Grant, a manager of the strip mines at the Four Corners. And as the Interior Department had long ago decreed, water for both agriculture and industry "will not be available."

"We have been 'skinned' many times, and we are getting 'skinned' again, and we do not like it," said tribal councilman Carl Todacheene.

Some of the People, too, were tired of being "skinned." They voted Carl Todacheene out of office and replaced him with Fred Johnson, a young tribal lawyer who fought to preserve the little water that was left in the river and who opposed the energy-consuming power plants. In anger, Johnson wrote to the then Secretary of the Interior, Rogers Morton: "What happens when most of the San Juan River is depleted 10 years from now? *Who gets the water when the river goes dry!*" The Interior Secretary had no answer—because there was none.

On the northern plains the story was as absurd. The great rivers were being drained on the basis of computers' promises. And the ranchers and Indians were being "skinned" to supply nonexistent water to the energy-consuming plants. In Montana these industries had filed requests for more water than existed in the Yellowstone River in most of the dry years, which were many—more water than all the ranches and towns had used for generations. And in Wyoming, the water in the Green and Powder and Tongue and Bighorn rivers was "reserved" for the energy companies. One coal-gasification plant had to be canceled, after the Interior Department had approved it, when someone discovered more water had been appropriated for it than there was in the rivers. While in New Mexico they went on appropriating water on paper. And then arguing whether it existed or not. The absurdity was accentuated by Dr. John Clark, director of the state's Water Resources Institute, who declared: "New Mexico's water is almost fully appropriated and utilized," but people were still seeking "more uses for water."

Some states attempted to halt the water charade. Or was it a mirage? In Montana, legislators at the request of Governor Thomas Judge declared a three-year moratorium on large water withdrawals for nonfarm use from the Yellowstone Basin. But in most states the computers could not be stopped. They went on giving away water when there was no water.

The situation grew desperate. Soon state was fighting state, cities were fighting rural counties, for water that no longer existed except on paper. And everyone was fighting the native People. "Water is so precious in the arid West that men have been shot in disputes over it," the editor of the *High Country News* reminded his readers. When Senator Abourezk suggested a moratorium on the use of all tribal water, he "made no friends among Western senators," said a New Mexico newspaper. It literally told him to go back where he came from—South Dakota. And it warned that if the "downtrodden Indians" take control of their water right, "the West may no longer control its own economic destiny." A "water war" had begun. . . .

All across the country the People faced "seizure of their water rights for non-Indian projects," Ernest Stephens, who had been an administrator of the Bureau, told the Senate hearings on water rights. So did the ranches and farms, cities and towns, of those white Westerners who were too fascinated by the computer print-outs to notice that their wells were running dry.

"These water rights problems and situations are kind of a spider web in the network of problems that affects all tribes no matter where they live and no matter the amount of water they do have," the president of the National Congress of American Indians, Mel Tonasket, told the hearings. "Almost every day we find a tribe is fighting a life and death struggle just to keep control of his land, let alone the blood of the land, his water."

Said Wendell Chino, long-time chairman of the Mescalero Apache Nation and president as well of the National Tribal Chairmen's Association: "Even though the Indians are legally entitled to waters that arise, border, or traverse their lands [there is] a scheme and design to take away Indian waters. Who are the instigators of this scheme?" It was, he said, "the country of the eagle." If these "raids" on their waters did not halt, there might be a "catastrophic upheaval for the Indian people."

Leaning on the podium at the Holiday Inn, William Veeder looked back somewhat cynically at the government's promises of water for farming. "I don't believe the projects *ever* really took the Indians into consideration," he said. The law simply was "suppressed and ignored" by the government.

"I am very ashamed. I am ashamed of what my community, the white man, has done to the Indian people," he said.

The river of the water belonged to the People, Veeder said. It had been inscribed in our laws by the Supreme Court, in 1908, by the "Winters Doctrine," which stated: Water that arises on, or flows through, an Indian reservation belongs to the People, whether they use it or not. "The power of the government [was] to reserve the water [for the Indians] and exempt them from appropriation under the state laws"; for the People had a "prior" right to the water that was historical and irrefutable. They had been here first.

If "one tribe" were to enforce the U.S. Supreme Court's Winters Doctrine, "all current developments . . . in the Southwest Energy complex would have to end," said the report of Senators McGovern and Abourezk, but the "court decision has been totally ignored." Even though the native people had "prior and paramount" rights to the water, they said, "Indian water rights have *never* been taken into account."

And yet the President's National Water Commission had, as recently as 1973, affirmed these water rights to mean that the Indians' "water rights may even be said to have existed from time immemorial."

"That is good and reassuring to hear," said Peterson Zah, of the Navajo legal services, DNA, "that we have legal rights to the waters. However, one cannot drink such an abstract word like rights. We know we have rights to the water, but we have no water."

"Let me tell you this," Veeder said. "It's easy for me to sit here—a white man—and tell Indians what to do. I *don't* tell the Indians what to do. But I would urge the Navajos to insist on their water rights. To be aggressive."

Zah eyed him sadly. "Being aggressive is not the Navajo way," he said. "I do not always understand the way of your white society." That the whites take away the water of the Indians— that was easy to understand. That was to be expected. That the whites take away the water of the whites, so the whites will have no water to drink—that was more difficult to understand. Zah lifted a paper cup of water on the table. "Let's say I have a cup of water. And everybody in the room is thirsty. And so I say everybody can have a drink of my water," Zah said, indicating the roomful of whites and Indians. "And a man walks into the room from outside, whom nobody knows. And he takes my cup of water. And he drinks it all. And no one else can drink.

"I don't understand that man," Zah said.

In the eyes of a young man at the end of the conference table, a "militant" leader of the People, there were tears.

Once the river "ran both ways, up and down," the People of the Penobscot Nation told Henry Thoreau in the 1840s, but "since the white man came it all runs down," they said. He seemed to believe them, for he wrote in his *Journal:* "Now they must laboriously pole their canoes against the stream."

That may have seemed an ancient myth. Of course, it was the truth.

Progress Is Not a Holy Grail

⚜ TESTAMENT OF Thomas Bell, Oregon home-
steader and publisher of *High Country News*,
Lander, Wyoming

One day he and his family just pulled up stakes and headed
west for a homestead in the mountain valleys of Oregon. It was
beautiful but raw land, without so much as a pump for water or a
fence post. He had to dig the well and irrigation ditches, set in the
fence posts, assemble a wood-burning stove, saw logs for fire-
wood, and plant the crops.

"I have rediscovered my hands," he said.

To homestead late in life and late in the twentieth century
was not easy. Some thought old Tom Bell had "gone crazier than
ever."

"My hands were the soft, manicured hands of an editor," he
mused. He had been the publisher of the "conscience of the
Rockies," the *High Country News*, an environmentalist and
ranching newspaper, back in Lander, Wyoming.

And he had decided it was time to practice the "love of the
earth" he had preached.

His hands were now scarred and bruised. One bone was
broken in his left hand. For a time he was "in desperation because both hands hurt so badly and I still had so much to
do": to milk the cows, to butcher and cure the meat, to build the
barn, to midwife the calves, to plant the garden, to tend the
orchard, to pick the apples, to squeeze the cider, to put up the
hay, to grind the grain.

A man has to learn once more to use his hands, he said; for his peace of mind.

Some said he had caused more trouble for the banks and mining companies than the "Hole in the Wall" gang of Butch Cassidy ever did. Some said he was the "Henry Thoreau of the West." Some said he was "touched."

Actually, the homesteading of the West was not new to the Bell family. Old Man Bell, his grandfather, had been one of the first white ranchers to settle on the rolling green hills of western Wyoming. The family had been ranching for three generations. And Tom Bell was well known and respected in his home town, a solid citizen.

That seemed so long, long ago. He had sold the family ranch to finance the *High Country News* and to fight to preserve ranch life and wild life.

"I became pessimistic," he said. So he packed up and left the valley where his family had lived for three generations. If he could, perhaps he would have gone by Conestoga wagon, but he drove westward, to Oregon.

On his homestead he began to "preach radical environmentalism." By that he meant: "If we were really created in God's image, how is it that we could so treat that which is God's?" for if we sin against life, we sin "upon ourselves." He feared that the environmentalist movement might become too intellectual and arrogant. If there was "arrogance in our own right," he said, "that *would* lead to the downfall of mankind on earth." And so, though it might make him "a pariah even among my own friends," he began to call for humility and frugality—"Yes, even the penuriousness of our Pilgrim forefathers."

"God, help me forsake any power which might breed arrogance or contempt. Keep me humble and honest," he prayed.

This is what he told me:

On the way home from school when I was a boy, I would lie on the bank of the stream and watch the ground trout spawning. In the spring I would go off in the hills and know where the sage grouse nested and where their young were and where the old hen took the chicks and what happened to them and if the coyotes got some. And I would watch an eagle and a hawk get one of them.

And that would make me wonder about life: what it meant.

Probably I had as many ties to the sage grass and the hills as I did to my friends in school. This was a mystery to them, because I had good friends, and yet I didn't.

My great-grandfather came to the valley as one of the earliest settlers. I was not born there, but I was raised there, on a small ranch outside of town. My character was built on that ranch. I went to high school there and on to college and then off to war and to a varied sort of life.

As did many young people, I had a goal. I trained myself to go and do one thing. But I learned soon enough that you can become greatly disappointed by what life holds in store for you. The politics of bureaucracy in federal and state government is intolerable; at least it was for me. I had to get out.

Then I came home.

In those days my wife and I had three sons. Then we adopted three more children. But I can't really say it was because I loved children, though I love my children, or I loved people. I'm not really sure I love people all that much.

Often I would rather be by myself than be with people. I am not the gregarious sort. I can go off and hike into the mountains and be by myself for weeks and never miss a human being. I think I could be happy in the hardwoods of the East, or along the Maine Coast, or the coast of Oregon, or in Alaska, where I spent some time as a young man.

So my love is for the land. My love is for the earth itself.

And yet, though I love the mountains to the west, the Wind River Mountains, where I have hiked through them and spent days in them and I am tied to them in a way, yet I am not. Because I see them changing. The mountains are going to be changed by what is happening here.

So the kids that come after won't possibly know the things I did. If enough people come here, the elk will be displaced animals, the beautiful pronghorn sheep will be gone, the stream where I lay to watch the trout spawn will not be the same. The children are the ones who are being sold short. By us! All I want is for my three sons, and now my grandchildren, to be able to live as simple and happy a life as I did, without having to worry about grasping for money or the things that only money can buy.

Money cannot buy sunsets. Money cannot buy the bugle of an elk that I heard a few days ago in the woods. Money cannot buy the natural beauty of life people may find if they know what they are looking, or listening, for. So many people don't know what they are looking, or listening, for that they will never find it. And they think they can buy it.

That's not true for me. I never had a hankering for a million dollars.

And I see many of the young people are coming to realize that there are ways of life money cannot buy. And even though they have been raised in an age of materialism, in good families, with all that money their parents never had, they rejected all that. And they are beginning to go back, back to the simple life, the life I lived as a boy. The sort of life where we can see the sunsets at night and hear the sound of a stream when it is rolling the boulders and experience the things of the earth that have always been here and will be here when man is gone.

That does not mean we ought to go back to the caves. It does mean that as a society we ought to begin to realize that progress is not the Holy Grail. That there are better things on this earth than progress.

America is many things. It is a great country of cities and countryside. There are people who like to live in cities. Who would not like to live where I live. Who like to see the world in museums. But you cannot put nature in the museums.

America is many things. It is the forests, both hardwood and pine, where you can still hear the elk bugle and see the grizzly bear and walk in the forest without fear of rampant crime and you can feel yourself going back to the good earth.

To kneel down on the earth that you get under your fingernails when you dig in it and plant vegetables in it, to play on it and walk on it and love it—that is America. There is a finiteness to the earth. We do not understand the earth any more. We cannot use it up without someday coming to realize we have used up our great country—used it up! If we've learned anything from our space explorations, I hope it is the knowledge that our earth is, after all, only a small ball in the universe.

I am not really deeply religious. And yet maybe I am, in a way—religious about life.

I am Tom Bell of Lander, Wyoming. And I am a member of the human race.

THE CIRCLE OF LIFE

Within and around the earth,
Within and around the hills,
Within and around the mountains,
Your power returns to you.
Pueblo Prayer

SEVEN men stood around a mud puddle. The whole world was in that mud puddle.

In the spring sun, snow on the roof of Tesuque Pueblo's community center had begun to melt. The puddle grew larger. An old man squatted by the water; he took a twig and dug a little ditch so that the water flowed like a miniature river across the courtyard. "Now," he said, "the water is free."

One of the younger men dug the heel of his boot into the mud. His heel dammed the rivulet so that merely a trickle of water passed his foot.

"You damn Indians need a dam," he said gruffly.

"Who are you," the older man asked, "to tell us what we need?"

"I'm from the Corps of Army Engineers," said the young man. He tilted his black cowboy hat, with its dangling feathers and bright beads, jauntily back on his head. "We'll build a hydroelectric dam and a power plant. Here!" he said, as he dug his heel deeper into the mud.

The older man was angry. He said, "Why?"

"Nature is the obstacle to growth," said the young man. "It has to be rooted out. That is what the Corps of Army Engineers is all about. We dam the rivers, we stop nature. So mankind can grow. That's like pulling up the weeds to make room for the flowers."

"That's just the beginning of things we're going to do for you damned Indians," said a second young man. And he bulldozed a clump of grass with his shoe. "I am the Secretary of the Interior," he announced with a toss of his shoulder-length hair; "and I'm going to help you dumb Indians to get smart, by leasing your land for a golf course and subdivision for white suburbanites. Here!" he said, and stomped the grass. "We'll build a drive-in for hamburgers and a movie drive-in and a money drive-in and a liquor take-out. And then you will become as civilized as whites."

"And you will be able to enter the mainstream of white society," said a third young man, as he tossed a fistful of pebbles into the mud puddle. They sank into the turgid water, out of sight.

The older man squatted by the puddle and he sighed sadly.

The older man was a holy man. Coyote was his name. All these men were from the White Roots of Peace of Akwesasne in the Mohawk Nation. But they were not all Mohawk. One was an Algonquin, from the north, in Canada. One was an Aztec. One was a Pueblo. And the older man was from California. And they were all brothers, they said. Even to the mud puddle.

In the plaza of Tesuque Pueblo they waited for the dancing to begin. So they performed the drama of the little mud puddle as they waited. Year after year they journeyed from People to People seeking the meanings of the earth, the water, the sky, the spirit of America. And telling what they learned, in dances and in words, about the Sacred Circle.

One thing they had learned was this: "In the Circle of Life every being is no more, or less, than any other. We are all Sisters and Brothers," they said. And so their lives were shared with the "bird, bear, insects, plants, mountains, clouds, stars, sun. To be in harmony with the natural world, one must live within the cycles of life."

This was their message. So they had come to the little Pueblo of Tesuque, in New Mexico, to say this: *Whatever the People did to the earth they did to themselves.*

In the hills of Tesuque the earth was hard, it was dried and wrinkled as an old man's hand. The hills were as still as the Pojoaque River, which was mostly sand. A desert village of a few hundred People had existed here for many hundreds of years. It was like the Promised Land of Israel. Once the People had known how to live in the desert and had been independent. No one had dreamed of breaking the Circle of Life.

"People did not think it was possible to get something for nothing," said a young woman of Tesuque, "from the earth."

Now there was a nervousness in the village. Few farmed the earth. The People went away every morning to work as maids in the motels of Santa Fe and as janitors in the scientific laboratories of Los Alamos. And the earth would soon be dug up, like graves.

A few hundred feet away was Colonias de Santa Fe. It was to be a subdivision of more than fifteen thousand white suburbanites in a pueblo of less than three hundred, which "land developers" and government officials of the Department of the Interior's Bureau of Indian Affairs had talked the Tribal Council of Tesuque into leasing to them for ninety-nine years. The "developers" of the land were a group of statehouse politicians, a local judge, the campaign manager of a United States senator (the same United States senator who had introduced the bill to grant the developers a ninety-nine-year lease on the Tesuque land), three business partners of the governor, and a real estate promoter with Mafia connections—the usual crowd, who proposed to offer the desert land for as much as thirty thousand dollars a half acre.

There were some routine public scandals and customary lawsuits. After that, the somewhat embarrassed federal government ordered a "suspension" of land sales, in the face of charges of fraud, or deceiving the Pueblo People, and dubious legalities such as the government's oversight in not issuing an environmental-impact statement—a lapse which a law-abiding group of Pueblo People, the Tewa Tesuque, said had made the lease illegal, though apparently not invalid. And so the original land "developers" had quietly stepped aside, to be replaced by another group of white men who the government hoped would be less of an embarrassment.

Colonias de Santa Fe had been begun because some cronies in the statehouse needed a private golf course. The eager government, always willing to help a tribal People to "develop" the land, obligingly hired an economic and management consultants firm for thirty thousand dollars that same year (1967)—it did not ask the Pueblo People for their opinion until later—to plan a subdivision for "non-Indian housing" on the Tesuque land. And, of course, the golf course.

The "traditional importance of land to the Pueblo way of life" was "non-economic," said the consultants' report. It had been spiritual. But that was a "stagnant" way of looking at life, the experts said. And so they suggested some "broader considerations": "It is recommended that all six Pueblos . . . develop suitable parcels which can be subdivided into estate sized lots and leased to interested parties"—that is, white men. And since so little of the land was farmed by the People, it, too, should be leased to the "outside interests"—that is, white men.

No "housing for Pueblo residents" was even "discussed" in the government report. "Land resources are defined very narrowly to include only [white] residential land," the report explained, "to serve the expanding [white] population."

"The impact may be one strong enough to eventually threaten the Indians' traditional way of life," a later government study said. So much so that religion might be forced "underground."

Still, these things were not "clearly understood" by the government, said the government.

Some of the people of Tesuque Pueblo began to talk so loudly against the development that the government offered to listen to them at public hearings. A dozen Tewa women and one Tewa man came to speak.

One old grandmother, who spoke no English, spoke in Tewa. Her words were translated: "She said all she wants now is her land back. She wants no money."

There was a very old woman who said: "I am not giving my land. No! That's all I want to say!"

And a young mother from Tesuque wept: "My Indian religion, my culture, is more important to me than those houses [of the development]. What are they saying to the Tewa? They are our brothers, but they don't help us. They don't care."

She wept: "I have a three-year-old daughter. She asks me questions. What will I tell her?"

She wept: "Where is your heart, BIA?"

An old grandmother said: "I am speaking with the help of my faith, for those that are to be born. There are people of our tribe who are coming [in the future] who need that land."

Another old grandmother said: "When I was a young girl, a wise man told me the time would come when the ants would come over the hills. You white people are the ants."

The superintendent of the BIA sat with glazed eyes. He hid his expression. He was a man of some sensitivity, who was pained by the words of these women. In the back row sat the tribal chairman of Tesuque and two of the Tesuque councilmen. These men could not look at their grandmothers. The tribal chairman held his head in his hands.

An old woman of Tesuque told me: "It has come to this. Will our men follow the whites' government? And ruin our land? Or will our men follow their women? And save our land?"

Man was the "master" of the earth, the white man said. And his mastery was not merely the gift of his God; it was his duty unto his God. Had not God "created all things for man's sake"? asked John Calvin in the sixteenth century.

Of man's conceits, none were as egotistical and self-serving. The Calvinist belief was that God in His wisdom had taken one week to create the universe "before He fashioned man," because He wished to prepare "Everything He foresaw would be useful and salutory for him"—for man. Man was not the mere master of the earth. He was as a god on earth, for God served him as he served God—a self-centered idea of religion that denied the Circle of Life and reshaped it as a halo about man's godhead.

These conceits of Calvin were no greater than those of the Catholic humanists of the Renaissance who had given birth to them. In the words of the philosopher and humanist, Bishop Pico della Mirandola: "It was to man alone . . . at the moment of his creation that God had bequeathed the seeds laden with all potentialities—the germs of every form of life. . . . *O Adam, I have set you at the very center of the world!*" exulted the Bishop, in the name of God. The myth of masculine dominance would never be more religiously voiced.

And such ideas of man's omnipotence upon earth inspired the courage and imagination of the seafarers and scientists of the Renaissance. They may be said to have launched the ages of enlightenment and colonialism upon the sea of this new religion of man.

That sanctifying of man led to the profaning of nature. If man was as a god on earth, it was not merely his right, but it was his duty to rule the world. And nature was to become a romantic pleasure, at its best, and the obstacle to man's reign, at its worst. As the English chemist Robert Boyle, a founder of modern science, said with some disgust: "The veneration [for] what they call nature has been a discouraging impediment to the empire of man over the inferior creatures of God." And he made it clear that all the creatures were "inferior" to man.

"Nature is not sacred," the Catholic theologian Charles Davis declared flatly, "to the Christian." In this belief science and religion were "in conformity," he said.

And so, armed with these twin weapons of God and science, the Europeans set forth to conquer the earth. In the Plymoth colony, John Winthrop, in 1629, echoed the Renaissance belief that was to be reechoed throughout the conquest of America: the land was "the Lord's garden," and the white men were "the Lord's men," sent by "God's will" to cultivate it. "Why should we then stand starving" while idle infidels let the earth "lie waste without improvement"? Surely it was "the original plan of the benevolent Deity" that the earth "be under a state of cultivation," said another of these founding fathers. As Cotton Mather, reverend of Salem, intoned: "What is not useful is vicious."

In the colonial *History of New York*, written in 1809, Washington Irving set forth the morality by which this new religion of man was to justify the imposing of "God's will," and man's, upon the land. The creator of Rip Van Winkle was sardonic, but accurate:

"Whereas it has most unquestionably been shown that heaven intended the earth should be plowed and sown and manured and laid out into cities and towns and farms and county seats and pleasure grounds and public gardens, all of which the Indians knew nothing about, therefore they had no right to the soil . . . therefore they deserve to be exterminated."

And in time "God's will" was to be Manifest Destiny. In justifying the "Trail of Tears," President Andrew Jackson said: "What good man would prefer a country covered with forests, and ranged by a few thousand savages, to our extensive Republic, studded with cities, towns, and prosperous farms?"

The flesh and bones of these "dead Savages . . . must fatten the corn hills of a more civilized race," said the Vermont lawyer Thomas Farnham on a tour of the new frontiers in 1843, for "the Indians' bones must enrich the soil before the plough of civilized man can open it." For the native people and the native earth were one; "Thou earth!" Prospero had cursed Caliban. The judgment of Jehovah was no less severe. Man had indeed become as a god, if he was white.

Man's desire to conquer the earth was not mere greed. The

idea of man as a god upon the earth may be derived from Genesis itself, according to the modern theologian Harvey Cox. In *The Secular City* he wrote: "Just after his creation man [was] given the responsibility of naming the animals. He is their master and commander. . . . It is his task to subdue the earth." If man was the father, then it was his fatherly duty to care for his children, it was his "Christian obligation." He conquered the earth not in hate, but in love, for their sake.

In the recent United Nations Conference on Human Environment, faith in man's "stewardship" upon earth was reaffirmed by hundreds of leading international wise men of science from fifty-eight nations. It was man's responsibility to the earth to "manage it" with love. "Is it not worth our love?" asked the scientists. As if man might choose, as a father might, the way to love the earth, or whether to love it at all. Man had come from the earth. He was its child. But no longer. "Man makes himself," the scientists said; he had begun to "draw away from his ancestors," for he had begun to "control life," not on earth alone, but in its sources in the universe. Now "he comes to conquer for himself the blinding, death-dealing energies of the sun." The white man's science and religion were agreed. Man was chosen.

"*Coming:* The control of life. All of life, including human life. With man himself at the control." These words were written by the president of the Council for the Advancement of Science Writing. He prophesied: "Also coming: a new Genesis, The Second Genesis. The creator, this time around—man." The rhapsodic, and somewhat incoherent, newspeak heralded nothing less than the new biomedical "creation myth" of "Genesis II," in which man would create life itself in the scientific laboratory. In a "glass womb."

In the "creation myths" of modern science the religious belief in the godhead of man had reached a sublime limit. Man no longer merely ruled the earth. He "created" it. For as farm "cropland can be 'created' where it does not exist," by use of chemical fertilizers, so the energy of the sun within the earth was "created" by man. So wrote the scientist authors of *Natural Resources for*

U.S. Growth, published by Resources for the Future. Once energy had been made into "attractive commercial ventures" by man, it became real. "In this way reserves of ore are 'created,'" said the scientists, "just as fertile land is 'created.'"

The earth was the child of man. He was its loving father. Man had not "emerged" from the earth, its child, as the tribal People remembered; he was its creator. And interestingly, in this new religion of creation woman was no longer needed, or even mentioned; the earth mother had vanished. She no longer existed. In the womb of earth as in the "glass womb" of the scientific laboratory, man, by himself, thought he had become the creator of life in his own image.

Man no longer needed the Circle of Life. He had created his own. He had broken the Sacred Circle.

The omnipotence of these men had become awesome. In the hope of learning the secret of the new "creation myths," I had wished to talk to Laurance Rockefeller, a man whose vision had guided man's endeavors to harness and control the resources of life, and a founder of Resources for the Future. But he did not wish to talk about it. His private secretary offered a curious apology: "Because of the importance of the subject with which you are dealing, he [Rockefeller] regrets he must ask to be excused."

"Of course," a young native American scholar said. "How can you talk to God?"

And yet man's conquest of life on earth had made him a stranger in his own land. It had brought him no peace, and little grace.

In the "Ascent of Man" he had triumphed over the "inferior creatures of God," but in doing so he had to abandon the Circle of Life and leave his place in the natural and eternal harmonies of ecology. The wisdom and companionship of a leaf of grass, of a tree, of a flower, of a stone, were no longer necessities for him. He studied them. And he might still admire them. But he was not awed by them. He did not love them as a sister and brother, born of the same mother, the earth.

Once Spinoza had asked: Can a stone think? His descendants had forgotten the question. And so they could not imagine the answer.

If the earth no longer was sacred to man, the womb of his spirit, then he no longer had to respect it. He could do to it anything he needed or wished to do. It was simply dirt, which had no more meaning than he, as its master, gave to it: a piece of paper, a lease, a suburban utopia. The reign of the white man gave him a sense of power and wealth. It gave him a deeper feeling of "aloneness" than man had ever known. He created a new word for it: alienation.

Man was alone. In that heaven of his own creation he knew the loneliness of a god. Lamented the scientific prophet of *The Second Genesis*: "If each of us is 'forever a stranger' how much more strange, how much more alone" is man in the new world of his making. Where he is "free" of the family of man and the Circle of Life. Where no one "belongs" to anyone, or anything, beyond himself.

In the cities it seemed as if man were God, for he was their architect. He designed, built, and demolished them as he willed. The creation myths of the white man were the reality of the cement mountains of buildings and cement valleys of freeways, where everything was man-made. And the very seasons of the earth and the Circle of Life were controlled by man in shopping centers and on playing fields, Astrodomes with plastic grass and fiberglass skies. In these cities a leaf of grass, a tree, a flower, a stone, were memories or affectations. The earth no longer seemed necessary for survival.

And most white men lived in the cities. So did most of the native People. Even they had become alienated in their own lands. The loneliness that man's mastery of the earth had created when the Circle of Life was broken by the new creation myths of the white man had begun slowly to alienate everyone and everything. In the *Navajo Times*, one of the People wrote, as Everyman:

Our Dine [people] are afflicted by a feeling of loneliness. . . .

Our Youth wander about the reservation . . . seeking relief from it. . . . Parents cry themselves to sleep. . . .

The feeling of loneliness is much like: the mournful cry of the coyote . . . the sad cooing of a dove . . . it is as real as the winter. . . .

Even when surrounded by loved ones, the feeling lingers. . . . People laugh, but cry inside . . . alcohol only adds depression. . . . Everyone talks but nobody listens. Why? What to do? When?

Corn pollens lie about unused. . . . Prayers, of all faiths, do not come from the heart. . . . The counsel of the elderly, filled with much wisdom and experience, is unheeded.

All Mankind claim divine creation, inherent in everybody is: a longing to be spiritual, to be happy, to do right.

Not only had the white man done this to the native People; he had done it to himself. What the white man had done to the native land he had done to all the land of America. And by that mighty act he had made himself a stranger, an endangered species. The conquest of the earth enabled man to feed on its energies and resources. Man was devouring his conquest. So much so that he no longer remembered, or needed to know, the way to feed himself. In the nations of farms he was starving, and in the cities his acts of love had turned against him. Of all the beings on earth, man had become the most vulnerable. Now he consumed enormous amounts of energy to perform the simplest acts. He had developed the appetite of a dinosaur, which had trampled its food in search of its food.

Once, long ago, the chief Seathe, of the Suguamish Nation, said: "This we know. The earth does not belong to man. Man belongs to the earth. This we know. All things are connected as the blood that unites a family."

Earth is not sacred in the way a church is. Not as a holy relic or the plaster statue of a saint. The earth is sacred as a source of life, and it was the spirit of life within it that the People worshiped, the native people said. In the flesh of the earth, as in the flesh of the body, there was this spirit. They were one.

In the hills of Montana, the Crow wise man Curley said it

this way: "The soil you see is not ordinary soil—it is the dust of the blood, the flesh and the bones of our ancestors. *The land as it is, is my blood and my dead;* it is consecrated; and I do not want to give up any portion of it."

Once the Old People, as did all people, knew that life had emerged from the earth, as the energy of life came from the sun. They did not believe in the creation myths of the white man's religion. They remembered that the emergence of humans from the earth had come in many forms, through many worlds, whether in the Four Worlds of the Navajos, or under the Four Suns of the Aztecs. In the memory of the origins of tribal life, evolution was no theory; it was the memory, uncanny in its accuracy and detail, of the Circle of Life.

Once the Circle of Life had been known to all people. It was the learning and knowledge and wisdom that had been gathered not only by men and women but by the stones and the trees and the insects and the elements, through millions of years of existence upon earth. There was no religious mystery in the Sacred Circle; its power was in the wisdom it held. No one would ever know the millions of shepherds and farmers, holy people and philosophers, who had given of their learning and experience, remembered through all the ages of human life, to strengthen this living library of knowledge.

If a flower was outside the Circle of Life, or a stone, or an animal, what would happen to it? It would die. But that was impossible. It was too wise.

Once a wise woman of the Tulalip People, Yetsi Blue, who was known as Janet McCloud, told me she thought she knew why the white man believed in his creation myths. The knowledge of the Circle of Life had been lost by him; he was afraid that he was going to die all alone. She told me:

"People are like a tree. The leaves of the tree are our thoughts. The branches are our limbs. The trunk is our body. The roots are our veins, where our blood flows from the earth. If you cut the root of the tree, it will die. So the People will die if you cut their roots from the earth.

"And when we die, our body goes back to the earth. And then our body will feed the roots of the trees. And then we become part of the trees. And we feed the worms. And the worms feed the birds. And we become part of all that. So all of that, that's part of me. That's what I am.

"We are children of the earth."

She told me: "That may be why the white man is becoming weak. He has cut his root to the earth."

The loneliness of these white men may have made them fearful, she thought. "So that may be why he feels he has to conquer the earth. Because he feels he is alone, and he will die alone. Because he has left the Sacred Circle. Because he has become an orphan. Because he has abandoned his Mother's love. And he fears the Mother Earth will not comfort him any more. He may be right."

Some of the philosophers of the Old People sensed this unease in the white man more than a hundred years ago, when they first met him. He seemed possessed by a frenzy of activity and, at the same time, a loneliness. The Lakota thinker known as Luther Standing Bear had commented many years ago on the strange nervousness he had seen in the conquerors of the West: "The white man does not understand America. He is too far removed from its formative process. The roots of the tree of his life have not yet grasped the rock and soil."

In America the white man was "still troubled by primitive fears," Standing Bear said. "Only to the white man was nature a 'wilderness' and only to him was the land 'infested' with 'wild' animals and 'savage' people. To us it was tame. Earth was bountiful and we were surrounded with the blessings of the Great Mystery. Not until the hairy man from the East came was it 'wild' to us. When the very animals of the forest began fleeing his approach, then it was that for us the Wild West began." And that explained why "The man from Europe is still a foreigner—and alien.

"Men must be born and reborn to belong," said Standing Bear. "Their bodies must be formed in the dust."

Not in one generation, or in two, but in time, the meaning of
these words began to become known to the white man. It was
not that he came to understand the wisdom of the Old People,
but that he began to doubt his own creations.

Year after year when he was Secretary of the Interior, Stewart
Udall approved leases for the damming of rivers, the strip mining
of mountains, and the building of power plants that devoured the
earth. Now he wondered if he had not been mistaken. For the
"Indian way" had taught him that the Circle of Life had to be
restored. And it was time "to call a halt to decisionmaking by dis-
credited technological superoptimists" and "arrogant engineers."

Man's "arrogance" was a "self-deception" and a "fallacy," said
Udall; for he was not as a god upon earth. And more and more
white men began to doubt their conceits.

"There is a connectedness in nature we never used to recognize," wrote scientist Lewis Thomas, president of the eminent
Sloan-Kettering Cancer Center and author of *The Lives of a Cell*.
And the humility of his words had a foolish sound, but the simple
thought voiced a deep unease. "Our definition of 'life' is under-
going a profound reappraisal. So are many other notions about
ourselves, and the world in which we live," observed *Scientific
American*.

And so a small migration back into the Circle of Life began.
It was not, as some have thought, the migration of city people
back to the earth. That was but a small part of it. Nor was it a
quixotic tilting at windmills, seeking "clean air" in a sky whose
darkness was beyond man's reach. That, too, was but a small part
of it. Man was beginning to rediscover the nature of life—its
cycles, its ecology, its harmony, its discords—and his place on
earth.

To some the pilgrimage went no farther than the nearest
empty lot. In Berkeley, California, in the late 1960s, students
cultivated a "Power to the People Park" on university land. When
they were asked to leave, they issued a leaflet with a photograph
of Geronimo, though none were native People, which said: "Your
land title is covered with blood. Your people ripped off the land

from the Indians. If you want it back now, you will have to fight for it." The return to the Circle of Life had taken a political turn, but the People Park vanished.

And then there were pilgrims like Anthony Rousellot. For eleven years he had been a broker on the floor of the New York Stock Exchange, but he had sold his home in the city and his country estate. Crossing the country, he had "taken up residence among the Indians, Chicanos and hippies," in Taos, New Mexico, where he was searching for "the spirit" of the land.

The "Call of the Wild," as an acerbic editorialist of the *Wall Street Journal* called it, was being heard even within the canyons of finance. In the late 1960s and early 1970s, a "growing number of affluent persons [were] rejecting what might best be called corporate America" to "get back to nature," much as "Daniel Boone come to visit the 20th century." This was "naïve" and "disquieting" to the newspaper of Wall Street, for it was occurring in a time of economic prosperity.

Still, urban and suburban life had "degenerated into a screeching, mind-rattling endurance test." In these "rotting" conditions, "almost all of us are bound to hear the call of the wild at one time or another and plainly more people are heeding it," the newspaper concluded, then added, with Job-like despair: "What price material riches?"

Out of the migrations from the cities a new environmental movement was to arise. Born not of nostalgias of the older conservationists, but of the "future shock" of the newer technologists, it had as its aim not to conserve what God had created but to recreate what man had destroyed. These new environmentalists were more likely to be scientists than woodsmen. "Can science restore the integrity of science?" was the question Barry Commoner asked. And he replied: "Scientific knowledge is our best guide to *controlling* natural forces." If man merely was more scientific, he not only could "control" the Circle of Life, but could turn it back to more human ways of living. In this way, the creation myth of the environmentalists differed from that of the technologists only in its aims, not in its conceits.

That may be why environmental-impact statements have become so popular; for they encourage the self-importance of technologists in using technology to estimate the technological power of man. More important, they imply that man's impact on the environment is the crucial act.

Man had to plan to control his environment more wisely and to maintain the balance of nature. Once he had learned to do that he could rule as a benevolent man-god. And he would mend the broken Circle of Life. That was somewhat like asking a rapist to oversee the convalescence of his victim.

The new seekers for the Circle of Life seemed ill equipped for their journey, both spiritually and intellectually. They, too, were arrogant. Much like missionaries of the new creation myth of ecology, they came singly and in communes to learn the "Indian ways" of living in harmony with the conditions of rural poverty and government bureaucracy. They were the technocrats of *Mother Earth* magazine. It was a strange encounter.

"The ecologists are replacing the anthropologists on the reservation," said Russell Means, of AIM (the American Indian Movement). "It's the ologists who tell the white man they can make him into God. They can't. They have not made man into a God. They have put man into a cage. To be free a man has to be free of the ologists. He has to become the sister and brother to his sisters and brothers in nature. He has to learn how to listen to what his sisters and brothers, the eagle, the prairie dog, the fish, the horse, and the grasshopper have to teach him. And that's what this ecology movement should be all about. It isn't.

"Man is the weakest of all the animals. He is weaker than the grasshopper, and could not survive by himself as well as a grasshopper. He has been taught all he knows by his sisters and brothers in nature. He calls that 'science.' And if he does not learn to listen to his older sisters and brothers, he will become dumb." Still, the "ologists" did not listen. They began to teach before they learned.

One of the nation's most widely acclaimed media ecologists

was filming a documentary in defense of the Sacred Lands of a tribe. He became angered by the way the People "overgrazed" their pastures. Theirs was a desert land. And for hundreds of years they had miraculously survived there, with little grass and less water.

The white ecologist was not impressed. He fumed: "They knew nothing about scientific land management." So he talked of offering a tribal youth, whom he had chosen, ten thousand dollars, to "run for tribal chairman."

"Not even the government interferes in tribal politics like that," I told him.

He replied, "These people don't know what they're doing to their land. Someone has to tell them."

In the Tesuque Pueblo, an environmental group had become so annoyed at what they thought was the inability of the Tribal Council to deal with the subdividers that they offered their own lawsuit, in the name of the People. They even tried to "overthrow the Pueblo's government." They wrote and circulated a petition calling for a tribal government of their own creation. Sadly, one Pueblo woman said of them, "They are no different than the subdividers."

And on Black Mesa years ago, some ecologists had begun nationwide publicity to "save the Sacred Land of the Navajo and Hopi from strip mining." I remembered asking them if they had spoken to the tribal leaders before beginning the campaign to save them. They didn't know the tribal leaders, they said. So I gave them the telephone numbers. They never called.

Years after that, these white ecological saviors published full-page advertisements in several newspapers appealing for funds to help the Indians. They did very well. By that time the Navajos had their own Save Black Mesa Committee, which was penniless. They visited their saviors to ask for a contribution.

A young Navajo woman came from that meeting in tears. She was studying for her master's degree at the university. Even the thought of asking a white man for help was a humiliation to her.

"They wouldn't give us a cent. They treated us like children. And they raised all that money to help *us*. . . . These people are no better than missionaries!"

One of the cruelest battles between the environmentalists and the People occurred in the deep canyons where the Havasupia live. In a narrow cleft of the Grand Canyon, the People had been "confined" by governmental decree. Their land was so inaccessible that it could be reached only by a winding, precarious horse trail, upon which food, medicines, and everything else had to travel.

In the old days the Havasupia lived—"for thousands of years," one of them said—on the grassy and wooded plateaus above the canyon. They had a range of about two and a half million acres. And then in 1882, President Chester Arthur set up a "reservation" of maybe five hundred acres for them at the bottom of the canyon. In 1969, the federal Indian Claims Commission, in violation of a Supreme Court ruling, illegally took away their "aboriginal title" to their land.

And so they were "confined" to the dry canyon forever.

In despair the Havasupia asked for some of their lands. Congressman Morris Udall and Senator Barry Goldwater sponsored a bill to return 169,000 acres that had been given away to the U.S. Park and Forest Services, and Congress eventually acceded.

The return of the People's land brought protests by environmentalists, led by the Sierra Club, who wanted to preserve the "wilderness" for "wild life" and for "recreation," not for Indians. Who knew what the Indians might do to the "wilderness"?

"All these so-called environmentalists coming up here and begging to keep this land away from us—to protect the plants and wild animals, which they just found out about last year," said a Havasupia witness who went to Washington for hearings on the land bill. "These people can't even know what they are talking about. They haven't even seen most of the lands they want to steal from our people. These people are really ignorant of nature, as most of them know only what they read in books. We live on the land. We'd like to put some of them out there with nothing and see if they figure out how to stay alive.

"We are talking of survival, while they talk about recreation. Where does the greed of these people stop? These people wanted to keep the land from us for animals they called cattle. Now they want to keep it from us for animals called mountain sheep.

"They forget that human beings live in nature, too, something we've known all along."

On the Ogallala land of the Lakota Nation there is a woman who is the granddaughter of the famous holy man Black Elk. Her name in English is Grace Black Elk. And this is what she said to me:

"One day soon, the white man will come to us, and say: Help us! We have used up the energy of Mother Earth! We have wasted the energy of Father Sun! We beg you to teach us how to use our energy wisely! So that we can survive! We are afraid! So please help us! You Indians know how! So teach us!

"And I will say: Sure! Let us see your Application for Survival. Go write your proposal and submit it to us. And we will submit it to our councils of chiefs for consideration and discussion.

"And then I will say to them: Come back in two years!

"But, they will say, this is an emergency! We have an energy crisis!

"We know, I will say. We sympathize with the plight of the white man. So we will very sympathetically file your plea away. We know this is a matter of life and death for you. So we will have to consider this very carefully. In two years we will have a meeting on your Application for Survival. Even a conference. Even a congressional hearing. This is the way we learned from you to consider matters of life and death.

"So, I will say, come back in two years.

"Now, what is this 'energy crisis' the white man has? It is *his* 'energy crisis.' The white man created it, because he does not re-spect Mother Earth; he has to consume the energy of his Mother the Earth, for his electric toothbrushes, electric hair dryers, electric light bulbs, electric lawn mowers, electric heaters, electric air conditioners, electric music!

"Why?

"Because he doesn't know how to use his hands any more. To make the things he needs. To do the things he has to, to survive. Yes, he needs the energy of the Mother Earth because he doesn't have his own energy any more. He doesn't think any more.

"Sometimes I talk in the universities. To the students. And I ask them: What do you think of the 'energy crisis'?

"And they say: The President will have to take care of it. And the scientists. So, they say, we can't do very much about it anyway. We have no power. We can grow a little garden.

"I tell them: Forget the President and think of yourself. You have power in you. That energy you have in yourself. That is a power. That energy in your family. That energy in the sun. That energy in the earth. And they look at me and they do not understand me. Some of the white students and young people maybe are beginning to understand, but most of them look at me and do not see. And most of their parents are blind.

"Mother Earth has no 'energy crisis.' Father Sun has no 'energy crisis.' The People, the Indian People, they have no 'energy crisis.'

"Who does?

"It is the white man, who has broken the Sacred Circle of Life.

The Guilt Is in Our Blood

🐾 TESTAMENT OF a South Dakota lawyer,
the son of "pioneers"

In the pale dawn of a winter morning, a man drove into the
hills. The town was still asleep. On the sides of the road the snow
was banked in high drifts, blown by the prairie winds. No one was
on the road but for the lone car that had silently followed him
each morning, at an embarrassed distance, as he drove to his
morning prayers in the Chapel in the Hills.

His silent companions were agents of the FBI.

One morning on his way to the chapel the man stopped his
car by the roadside. The second car stopped uncertainly behind
him.

He got out. And he casually walked down the road to talk
to the two men who were watching him. "Good morning," he began, with a mixture of irony and friendliness. "If you fellows have
to follow me to church every day, why don't you ever come into
the church to pray with me? Be a whole lot better than sitting in
your cold car outside the church, just waiting for me. Don't you
think?"

And saying that, he got into his car and drove to his prayers
in the little chapel in the sacred Black Hills of the Lakota.

It was a Lutheran church and he was a "good Catholic," but it
was the "most peaceful place" he knew. Sometimes he "even
prayed for those FBI men sitting in the cold outside the church."

The wooden-stave church with its stone altar and bare crosses was a replica of a stave church in Borgund, Norway. It was built in memory of Norwegian pioneers on the Dakota prairies, the Reverend Anton Dahl and his wife, Lena Dorthea Elstad, who had come as evangelists to the Lakotas' old land of Red Wing and Battle Lake, Minnesota, in the 1880s.

So it was fitting that this man prayed in their chapel. For he too was descended from hard-faced pioneers, though his family had come from Sweden. "My people settled here in South Dakota three generations ago," he said. "That makes me a grandson of the founding fathers, I suppose."

A lawyer well known in the state, he was the classmate and crony of some of its leading citizens and a bridge partner of its most famous statesman. That is, he had been, until he had become the legal defender of the Lakota elders from the reservations and the militant young Indians from the urban American Indian movement at Wounded Knee.

Suddenly he was a renegade, a heretic, an "Indian-lover." He was bemused, but bewildered, by the federal agents who followed him about. "Perhaps they think I am praying with the militants," he said. "Or perhaps the thought of a Catholic in a Lutheran church is suspicious?"

But it was no joke to him. His life, his family, his law practice had been threatened.

"And we have had those obscene phone calls in the night. We get threatening letters. There is garbage thrown on our lawn. Our kids are picked on. Our tires are slashed. You walk down the street and someone who knows you all your life looks the other way and won't say hi. In a small town in South Dakota, this just isn't done. Lord knows I haven't carried an argument to anyone. But rather than argue with you, they won't even talk to you. Everyone is hysterical about the Indians."

He begged that his name not be used, though everyone knew it. He sighed wearily. "It's not that I am ashamed of anything I have done. But I just don't wish any more pressure on my family, on my kids, on my wife.

"Sometimes I think it would be better to move out of the

state. But after living here for three generations, that's difficult to even think about," he said.

If that was so, why did he go on defending Indians in the courts? Why did he do it?

This is what he told me:

When you walk down a street in Rapid City, South Dakota, behind a Lakota man or a young Lakota girl, and you look into the eyes of whites who walk toward you, what do you see? You see fear. You see hatred. You see it in their eyes, even when they try to hide it with a smile. On the street, in the middle of town, in midday, why are they afraid? Why do whites look at Indians that way?

The whites still don't see the Indians as human beings. They see animals!

In South Dakota, where we live in the shadow of Wounded Knee, and we have all our lives, why the hell do we treat Indian people as inferiors? Why do South Dakota whites seem to take naturally to racism against the Indians?

My analysis of it is that it is a feeling of guilt that causes racism against Indians.

Folks here know some of their history. They drive past the Wounded Knee signs on the highway. They know that for every white killed by an Indian, hundreds of Indians were massacred by whites.

Now, we don't massacre Indians any more. We kill them in more civilized ways. We are more civilized in our racism.

Any white merchant in South Dakota, if he examines his conscience, can tell you about a thousand little incidents in which he has treated an Indian person as an inferior, as a second-class citizen, as less than a human being. When you call it to his attention, his first reaction is one of fear. Then of anger. He has done these terrible things over the years. Not major crimes. He has not killed anybody. He has not beaten anybody. Maybe he has had Indians thrown in jail over the years, but that's about all. And all of a sudden it's thrown up to him by the same Indian people he did these things to. That it's wrong. That it's racism. That he wouldn't do it to a non-Indian person. And he realizes, perhaps subconsciously, that it's true.

The emperor has been told he is naked. His reaction is one of anger.

In seeing what has happened at Wounded Knee, he begins to fear that the more militant Indian isn't going to take it any more. His first thought is: *If they ever start to get even, I am really in trouble.* So he becomes frightened.

For the guilt is there. The guilt has been there ever since the year 1. The guilt is in our blood.

Once in a while we will patronizingly adopt an Indian and say: Well, I have a friend who is an Indian. It is the same as: Some of my best friends are Jews—and it means as little. What it means is: when you see on the street the Indian whom you have adopted, you say hi to him.

They wouldn't go to have a cup of coffee with an Indian. Not in their home town. Because if they did anything like that, the community and the business people in town would ostracize them. They would be called "Indian-lovers," or worse. So they certainly wouldn't invite an Indian into their homes. They don't really want an Indian for a friend, because they don't really think of an Indian as a social equal, or even as a human being. It is a sop to the Christian conscience.

What hypocrites!

But they don't fool anyone. Least of all the Indians.

Every Indian knows that when he gets caught in a white man's town, in the white man's systems, in the white man's court of justice, he doesn't stand a chance. That's why they always plead guilty, don't ask for a lawyer, just go to jail.

The safest place in all the world for a white man is an Indian reservation. Because every Indian, drunk or sober, knows that if he tangles with a white man he is going to end up in one of the white man's institutions. It is a foregone conclusion that if an Indian is called into any court anywhere in the Dakotas, he will be sent away. There has been a little change in that since Wounded Knee, but not too much.

Still, every once in a while an Indian beats the system and walks out of jail. He feels proud and he says: Okay, fellows—I fought your system and won! He had better watch out. They will go after him. They will get him.

As a lawyer, I know. I have seen it happen.

The word gets around to the law-enforcement people that certain individuals, certain families of Indians, are defiant. So they say: We'll get them! Of course, the law-enforcement people know these Indians are taking advantage of their constitutional rights; but constitutional rights are apparently wrong for Indians in Dakota. So they say: We'll get them! And they do. If you win a temporary victory in court, the law-enforcement people back away for a while. But sooner or later, in one way or another, they "get" those "uppity" Indians.

South Dakotans are blind to the value and the beauty of the Indian way of life. It is willful ignorance. They don't know; they don't want to know. They are totally blind. It is going to be a long and continuous battle to even teach South Dakotans that the Indians are human beings.

There are some fine people in South Dakota. Naturally. Some of our church people have risked their pulpits and occupations to help the Indians. Some of the Jewish people have been beautiful. Some of the university people and the students have been sensitive and courageous in defense of the human dignity of the Indian people and their rights.

Once these sensitive people, and the youth and the intellectuals on the East and West coasts, begin to see the merit of the beautiful culture of the Indian people, which should not be destroyed, which should be respected, then public pressure will filter into South Dakota. And we will conform. But that process will not be one of seeing and appreciating the Indians' ways on their own merit. It will be more selfish than that.

You will begin to see thousands of young people turning on

to Indian spiritualism. You see them now, coming to Crow Dog's Paradise, on the Rosebud Reservation. You see them rejecting the really crass materialism of the white man, of their parents.

As the word of this spreads in the youth culture, you are going to see the so-called liberals on the two coasts begin to perceive the value of what the Indians have. It is really a mystic trip. Perhaps you have to believe in it or it won't work for you. I am a good Catholic, but I believe in the Indian religion. I have learned from my meetings with the spiritual leaders of the Lakota, like Black Elk, Crow Dog, and Leonard Crow Dog.

And now you want to know how I got involved with Indians. . . .

I am just a small-town lawyer. So if it hadn't been for our family background, I suppose I would be as bad as some lawyers in South Dakota. By that I mean . . . we're Democrats. My wife's family and mine. For many, many years a Democrat in South Dakota was as rare as a Republican used to be in Mississippi. So we were outcasts. Liberals. Anyone who calls me a liberal now—well, that's still a fighting word, but it used to be a pretty radical word out here.

Back in 1957, I got started in the civil rights thing. At the time I happened to be in the military. In Arkansas! I was Governor Faubus standing in that schoolhouse door. And I was properly outraged.

Still, no one had ever denied me my civil rights, nor had I ever been discriminated against. Never been arrested. Never been bitten by a police dog. Never been hit by a billy club.

Never been black. Or Indian. But I tried to help.

And then George McGovern, who is an old family friend, convinced us that the war was wrong. I remember one night discussing with my wife how Martin Luther King had said that the war was racist. I couldn't understand that. And my wife said to me, "Can you imagine us bombing northern Sweden?"

All of a sudden the meaning of the war came home to me! That massacre at My Lai was just like the massacre at Wounded

Knee! That war in Vietnam was just like the war we fought against the Sioux in South Dakota!

Yes, I felt the guilt of it.

Little by little I began to learn a little about Indian culture. The spirituality of the Indian people. The basic honesty and bravery. The fact that they would do almost anything rather than embarrass someone else. And that, to me, is a tremendous thing.

So I got involved in the Indian movement. I had defended Indians in court before. But this was different.

I feel that Indian people are never going to love you as a white man. They have a backlog of hate that they have earned. And you will never get rid of it all. But if you try to do things to help them, as I have been trying to do, perhaps they will hate you a little less.

THE INVENTION OF
AMERICA – I

ON one side of the room was a wall-to-wall, ceiling-to-floor reproduction of the Declaration of Independence.

The man with clear eyes, so sharp he had to squint, looked up at the words on the wall. "Look at all those words! Justice! Justice! Justice! Justice! We have never had any of that justice and now you people want us to celebrate!"

Now it was embarrassingly quiet in the conference room of Washington's American Revolution Bicentennial headquarters. In the shadow of blown-up patriotism cast upon visitors by the facsimile of history on the wall, no one had ever uttered such heresy. The church-hush mood of the room made anything but a worshipful murmur seem blasphemy.

The director of the nation's "two hundredth birthday" puffed silently on his pipe, as if he were cremating those words. Dolefully he eyed the Dakota man who had spoken so undiplomatically.

The man who had spoken had the wind-lined face of an ex-

Marine. He was one. On his car bumper there was a faded cry: "A FEW GOOD MEN." Robert Burnett was his name; he was the tribal chairman of the People of Spotted Horse, the Sioux of the Rosebud Reservation, and he was a legend in the Dakotas, whose pride, it was said, could be as fierce as the prairies.

Once when he was picketing the tribal headquarters in a civil rights dispute, the FBI had come to arrest him. It was said that he beat up those FBI men, then sued them for trespassing on Sioux tribal land.

"That's how the Indian has survived, by fighting for his pride. That's the American spirit," he once said.

In Washington for the usual ritual meeting with government agencies were several such tribal leaders. They'd attended the President's "prayer breakfast" at the White House. Someone thought it would be "good publicity" to invite them to the Bicentennial office and get them "involved" in the celebration, which they had been ignoring.

"Indians are already patriotic," snapped Burnett.

Something seemed to be going wrong. But what? A box of Bicentennial lapel pins was brought in and dumped onto the table. Everyone was invited to pin one on. "Hooray," whispered Doreen Bond, of the Northern Cheyenne. "Here come the beads and trinkets."

In his deep and solemn voice, the tribal chairman of the Crow, Pat Stands Over Bull, said: "Up where I come from, the white man wants to have a little celebration at the Little Bighorn. I don't know what the white man has to celebrate," he said, thinking of Custer's defeat. "But the battlefield is on our reservation and we don't want them coming out there with their carnival."

"Make them erect a statue of Sitting Bull," suggested an elderly Crow.

"Yeah," said Pat Stands Over Bull. "I just bet they'll do that." There was laughter by the Indians.

Hoping somehow to salvage the meeting, the director laid down the pipe he had been puffing and bravely appealed to the skeptical tribal people. Here is a "tremendous opportunity," he said, smiling, "to awaken the entire nation to the richness of your heritage" and to the Indians' "contribution to America."

"The entire nation is our heritage," muttered one of these tribal officials as he left. "We *are* America!"

On a summer afternoon on the prairie some years ago, Burnett and I had squatted in the shade of the old tree behind his house. It was the Fourth of July, but we were not celebrating. The sun was too hot. In the dusty heat of a prairie afternoon there are only two things to do: sit in the shade of a tree, and wonder. We did both.

In his fist my friend held a leaf of grass. "Grass is like a human being. It is strongest when it is nourished by the earth. That may be why Indians don't understand white men too well," he said. "You seem to live in the air. Like hawks. You seem to move all the time. Like hawks. You seem to have no roots, no history, no place. What is America to you? It is somewhere that you visit on holidays and on vacations, like tourists, going to visit a distant relative.

"And you don't seem to know where America is, so you go on searching for it."

In the beginning, no one knew where this land was, except those who lived here. The ancient biblical and European historians had little or no knowledge of the nature of the Americas. Even the "Islands of the Blessed," of Homer and Plato's "Lost Continent of Atlantis," were beyond the edges of knowledge, where only fools and poets ventured. They were an abyss.

The earth had three, not four, corners. So it was believed there were three directions, not four. When the Three Kings came bearing gifts to the Christ child, they came from the three corners of the world. In modern belief they are depicted as white, black, and yellow Kings, coming from Europe, Africa, and Asia. But there is no king of America, no red king who brought gifts to the infant Jesus. In the Holy Trinity, the threefold miter of the pope, and the three crosses on Calvary, the symbols of the three-cornered world are still preserved.

Saint Augustine thought the *orbis terrarum* was a three-cornered globe. And what then lay to the west? Nothing but a "watery wasteland of spirits," Augustine said, "where no snow falls, no strong wind blows, and there is never any rain," a land of nothing, in the midst of nowhere, and inhabited by no one.

And so Europeans did not travel to America, as Marco Polo had to China; they "discovered" it, they "invented" it, as the Mexican historian Edmundo O'Gorman so brilliantly observed in *The Invention of America*. The conquistadors did not "invent" America in their own images so much as in the images of their myths. The New World was the Old World of their fantasies.

As gods might, the Europeans believed they had created the New World by their "discovery" of it. If that was so, why couldn't they just as boldly "invent" the creation myths of its origins? They did.

In his ecstasy Columbus thought he had come to the "Gates of Paradise," and the People, so "gentle and loving" as to be unbelievable, must be descendants of Eve and Adam, to the east of Eden. That was the dream of many early voyagers: to discover the lost Garden of Eden, the Promised Land of biblical prophecy. And the People were in all probability, therefore, refugees from the Flood, in Genesis.

The creation myth that was by far the most popularly believed by the scholars of the day was that the native Americans were Jews. In the universities and churches of the learned men of Europe this was scientifically proved, beyond doubt. Here were the "Lost Tribes of Israel," found at long last. A Flemish monk, Louis Hennepin, summed up the proofs of Hebraic origins in his *New Discovery of a Vast Country in America*. "These savages originally sprung from the Jews," he said, because it could be seen that they lived "in a form of tents, like as did the Jews"; they anointed themselves with oil, as did the Jews; they bewailed their dead "with great lamentations," as did the Jews; they had beliefs of "the Creation" that were in "conformity" with concepts of Moses; they seemed to have God's curse "laid upon them," as did the Jews; and they were "subtle and crafty," as Jews were thought to be. So the monk thought they must be Jews.

Scholars did not all agree, of course. It was thought by some that the People of America had not come from Israel at all. They were Carthaginians, or Phoenicians, or Egyptians, or Babylonians, or Celts, or Africans, or Welsh, or Chinese, or Japanese, or even Indians—that is, from India. There are scholars who believe to this day in one, or more, of these myths of foreign origin.

These creation myths of the Europeans seemed hopelessly opposed to one another. But they had one belief in common. All of them agreed the Americans had come from somewhere, anywhere but America. That religious myth has persisted for five hundred years. So potent and ego-satisfying has it been for the descendants of the Europeans that it has been accepted by anthropologists as a creation myth of scientific fact, known as the "Bering Strait Theory."

Modern scholars seem to agree that the first Americans were not Babylonians, but probably Mongolians. They walked to America through the icy wastelands of the Siberian Arctic. They walked across the land bridge that is thought to have existed in the Bering Strait. They walked into America over the glaciers and tundra of Alaska. They walked south, from there, to what became their ancestral lands. And some walked all the way to the farthest tip of South America. They walked for centuries, some twenty-five thousand years ago, during the Ice Age, and the scholars do not know why.

An old friend, the scholarly Herbert Blatchford of the Navajo Nation, once said to me: "If the land bridge of the Bering Strait existed, it had to be a two-way street. You could walk either way. So maybe it was the American Indians who walked across it first. And we populated Asia!"

Some of the tribal histories did tell of the People coming from the north, and some told of the People coming from the south. None of the histories of the origins of America of which I have heard—and they are thousands of years old—said anything about a long walk from Siberia. The People of America seemed to believe they came from the land of their birth. That was perhaps too rational a thought for the believers in the European myths to listen to.

One summer a few years ago, the famed archaeologist L. S. B. Leakey announced that his team had found tools of native Americans in California, which he had dated as being perhaps 75,000 years old. That could not be possible, since it was 50,000 years before the first Americans were supposed to have walked across the Bering Strait! And then came word of an even more impossible discovery. "In an ancient Mexican stream bed," a scientific team of the U.S. Geological Survey found some "relatively sophisticated tools," which "were dated by several techniques." They were about 250,000 years old! Here was a dilemma indeed! "We are painfully aware," said the geologists, "that these results deepen the dilemma already recognized that so great an age for man in the New World is archaeologically unreasonable."

(And yet it was not "archaeologically unreasonable." The grand old man of Southwestern archaeology, Edgar Hewett, had voiced what he called a "common sense" archaeology many, many years ago. "I can not recall ever having heard the question, 'Who discovered Europe, Asia or Africa?' There is no reason to ask it. I know of no reason for thinking that America was ever discovered," wrote Hewett. "The human animal probably wandered back and forth over the Arctic lands without knowing or caring whether he was in Asia, Europe or America. . . . And he never stopped until he covered the habitable globe. Upon which continent he originated no one knows, nor ever will know. The quest for the 'Cradle of the Human Race' must take its place along with the other follies of science.")

The origin that had been "invented" for the People of America was not in accord with the creation myths of the Europeans. Nor were the People, for their "invention," too, had been "unreasonable."

In England, John of Holywood wrote in 1499 that these

strange "creatures" in the New World had skins that were "blue in colour" and heads that were "square." The early Spanish governor of Cuba, Velásquez, wrote of a tribe that had "dog faces and flat ears"; while De Oviedo described humans who were like monkeys, except that they were "half feathered and half furred," and they sang "like larks." Even the precise historian of Columbus's chronicles, the monk Peter Martyr, told of men in the Land of Inziganin who had tails that were three feet long. And yet they were not as wondrous as the "Headless Men, whose Eyes were in their Breasts."

No wonder the scholars, jurists, and wise men of Europe debated whether the People of America were human. In Spain it was decided for Catholics in 1537, when Pope Paul III issued his bull *Sublimis Deus,* that "the Indians are true men"; while in England the Protestants would no more than concede, with Cotton Mather of New England, that they were, at most, "half-men, half-beasts."

To the Europeans of the Renaissance these strange creatures were reincarnations of the bestiaries and demons of their medieval myths. As the historian Lewis Hanke has said, the Europeans had "set forth on their conquest [of America] expecting to encounter many kinds of mythical beings and monsters depicted in medieval literature." And so they did. For these enlightened men of the Renaissance "tended to look at the New World through medieval spectacles," and what they saw was the Old World in the New.

After all, had not Columbus sought "to unite the world and give to the strange lands the form of *our own*"? The Spanish humanist Hernan Pérez de Oliva had sensed this in 1528, when he wrote his remarkable book *History of the Invention of the Indies.* For their "dream was a European dream which had little to do with the American reality," noted the English historian J. H. Elliott: "And perhaps dreams were always more important than realities in the relationship of the Old World with the New."

If these Europeans did not find what they were seeking, they thought they had. When the seafaring brothers Niccolò and Antonio Zeno sailed toward "Groenland" in about 1390, they solemnly reported the discovery of a feudal kingdom among the Eskimos, much like that of fourteenth-century Italy. Some historians have cast dubious eyes upon the logs of their voyage, but the Zeno brothers had no doubt that they had discovered a land of "many Cities and Castles," where there were "Latine books in the King's librarie" and a great Gothic "Church of the Moneasterie" beside the glacial seas of the Arctic—a sight that would have delighted the Eskimos of "Groenland," had they seen it.

Many of these attempts by Europeans to reshape America to their own medieval images were comic. But not always.

When King James I of England heard that Powhatan, the father of Pocahontas, was "King of the Indians," he sent a royal messenger to Virginia, in 1608, to "crown" the tribal elder with a Tudor title and a scarlet robe of royalty. Upon his arrival, the king's messenger had "foul trouble" convincing the old and dignified Powhatan to kneel and receive his honor. He utterly refused.

"Neither knowing the majesty nor the meaning" of the crown, said Captain John Smith, Powhatan "endured the persuasions, examples and instructions" of the king quite politely. But he still refused to kneel.

So the king's messenger jumped the old man from behind, "leaping hard on his shoulders" until he was "a little stooped." And so he was crowned. In triumph the English gunners fired a salute, the noise of which was "barbaric" to Powhatan. The bewildered elder "remembered himself," however, and rising to his feet with dignity, he graciously thanked his attackers for whatever it was they thought they were doing. Powhatan undid his worn cloak and old moccasins. He gave these to the king's messenger in return for the gift he had been given.

And to this day, the worn cloak and old moccasins of Powhatan are on exhibit in a British museum. The triumph of empire!

These image transplants seldom took root. Most often, though native Americans rarely became Europeans, the native Europeans became imitation Americans. And the irony of history, wherein the conqueror is conquered by his conquest, repeated itself.

In name alone the colonies of New England, New Amsterdam, New France, New London, New Britain, New York, New Jersey, and New Spain partook of this New World. The medieval myths of the Renaissance men were to be wholly changed by the spirit of America: the Europeanizing of the wilderness was not a great success, nor were the People greatly impressed. In fact, the very opposite seemed to be happening: the Europeans, as the frontiersman J. Hector St. John de Crèvecoeur said, were becoming "white Indians."

Europe had sailed forth on the winds of swift change. That the winds may have blown both ways was rarely recognized. And that the stronger wind may have blown imperceptibly from America to Europe was not even explored; for the thought that the discovery of the New World delivered Europe from its medieval sloth and provincialism would have been historical heresy to the white man's sense of racial supremacy.

"The immense debt of Western culture, in general, and especially Western technic, to the more primitive people [sic] has rarely been acknowledged, or even recognized," Lewis Mumford wrote in The Condition of Man. "It is from the Amerindian culture of the New World that over half of the world's agricultural wealth is derived." More than that. The embryonic sciences of medicine, botany, astronomy, chemistry, and physics in the Renaissance were greatly advanced, if not inspired, by the new phenomena discovered and catalogued by the Europeans who came to America. In the year that Columbus reached the shores of the Indies, Copernicus was not twenty and Galileo not yet born. Their concept of the world would be forever altered by the existence of America. It was not surprising, then, that Sir Francis Bacon was to name the New World of scientific discoveries the "New Atlantis."

The discovery of the New World created an "upheaval in the mind" of Europe, said Mumford. It "hastened the end" of the "disintegrating medieval culture" by opening its medieval myths to the knowledge of the ancients. The world of European thought was small—orderly, rigid, narrow-minded—and it was over-whelmed by the flow of new visions, new ideas, new worlds. The new "values, meanings, and forms" of knowledge found in America were "sometimes worthy to be put alongside the best that Palestine, Greece and Rome could show," said Mumford. And these constituted the real "discovery."

In the New World there were "new islands, new lands, new seas, new peoples; and what is more, a new sky and new stars," wrote the ecstatic Portuguese, Pedro Nunes, in 1537. For was this not "the greatest event since the creation of the world"? cried López de Gómara in 1552. It was second only to the coming of Christ! Even that agnostic Scotsman Adam Smith, two hundred years later, in his *Wealth of Nations,* could not restrain his biblical awe of this new creation myth: "The discovery of America and that of a passage to the Indies are the two greatest and most important events recorded in the history of mankind."

Nothing in the memory of Europe since the Crusades to the Holy Lands of the East had been as invigorating and liberating to its spirit as its journeys to the Holy Lands of the West. For it was a New World of the mind, not merely of the map.

The Old World became a new world itself. In the year of the "discovery," the callow Martin Luther was about to enter the Order of Saint Augustine. But as he was later to write: "We are living in a New World, today, and things are being done differently." It was as the scholar Lipsius was to write ruefully to a friend in Spain in 1603: "The New World, conquered by you, has conquered you in turn."

Who conquered whom?

If America so deeply affected Europe, how much greater was its effect on those Europeans who had settled in America. That is still our least-known history, yet to be told, for it has been hidden by the belief in the "discovery" and "invention" so religiously preserved in our myths and books.

In the Plymouth colony in Massachusetts, the Pilgrims built a village that was hardly English. It was more like that of the

Algonquin People. Even to the stockade of trees that surrounded it, and the garden crops of corn, the village was more American than European; it had to be to survive.

And had it not been for People such as Squanto, a sachem of the Wampanoag Nation, the Europeans would probably never have survived. Squanto is portrayed in white myths as that "friend of the Pilgrims" who taught them how to cook a turkey for the first Thanksgiving; though in paintings of that momentous event he is often depicted sitting in a corner eating the dark meat. In truth, he was a learned man who had been across the seas many times, as many as fifteen years before the *Mayflower* had even landed; a scholar who had studied in England, he had traveled throughout Europe to observe the customs of the strangers.

It might have been that Squanto had been delegated by the chief sachem of the Wampanoag, Massasoit, and by the Tribal Council, to work with the warlike Pilgrims in a futile attempt to keep them peaceful. But the Europeans could not have imagined that the "Heathen and Infidels" were seeking to civilize *them.* They believed, as Governor Bradford said, that Squanto "was a spetiall instrument sent of God for *their* good."

(The seal of the Society of Massachusetts in Nova Anglia depicted a naked native, in a field of tobacco, a bow in his right hand and an arrow in his left. And from his mouth came the plea: "Come over and help us.")

These People of America taught the Europeans much more than how to grow corn and cook a turkey. In the teachings of wise men such as Massasoit were the foundations of the "American way," the philosophical and physical origins of democracy, then unknown to Europe.

One story of the acculturation of the Europeans into the "American way" shall have to do for now:

When the Reverend Roger Williams, in 1638, preached from the pulpit of the Salem church that perhaps it was not Christian to whip parishioners who had missed a Sunday sermon, he was hounded from his church. It was Chief Massasoit, the chief sachem of the Wampanoag, who offered Roger Williams, the "father of religious freedom" in America, a sanctuary on his tribal land, which later became Rhode Island. There was established the first European colony in which freedom of religion was practiced. As Sachem Massasoit said: That was not a new idea to his People.

In gratitude, Roger Williams thanked God, not Massasoit: "God was pleased to give me a patient spirit to lodge with them in their filthy, smokey holes," he said to his fellow Europeans, not to the Wampanoag.

In the imitation Plimoth Plantation built for tourists there is now but one prominent mention of Sachem Massasoit. The automatic food machines in the cafeteria bear the name Massasoit Vending Company.

Often the histories of how Europeans became Americans have been forgotten, if not ignored. The origin of what is unique in the "American way" of life has been sought by scholars in all the obscure corners of our past. It has been traced to English common law, the Magna Charta, the British parliamentary systems, the philosophy of the French revolutions, the Spanish Laws of the Indies, and the Calvinistic Reformation, as well as to the descendants of the European pioneers on the frontiers of the West. But the most obvious origin of the "American way" has been largely ignored—the native land and the native People themselves.

And why not? If Europeans could "invent" America and the Americans, why couldn't they "invent" the history of America?

In 1744, when the colonists had begun to be troubled by the oppressive taxes and restrictions of English colonialism and were starting to think of independence, the governors of the colonies met in Lancaster, Pennsylvania, to talk of what, if anything, they could do. They had no strong idea of what America might become. They were weak in the face of the mighty English empire. They were disunited. And so they listened, as before they might not have, to the words of a sachem of the Iroquois, Canasatego, whom they had invited to address them. He sensed their troubles at once, and he advised them:

"Our Wise Forefathers established Unity and Amity between

the Five Nations [of Iroquois]. This has made us formidable. This has given us great Weight and Authority with our neighboring nations. We are a powerful Confederacy; and by you observing the same Methods our Wise Forefathers have taken, *you* will acquire such Strength and Power. . . ."

Ben Franklin, an astute observer and admirer of tribal life, understood immediately the advantages of the Iroquois system of democracy. He soon applied its lessons to the dilemma of the colonies. In 1754 he admonished the delegates to the Albany Congress to heed the wisdom of the People: "It would be a strange thing if Six Nations of ignorant [*sic*] savages should be capable of forming a scheme for such a union, and to be able to execute it in such a manner as that it has subsisted ages and appears indissoluble; and yet that a like union should be impracticable for ten or a dozen English colonies."

It was "more necessary and must be more advantageous," Franklin told the assembled white colonists, for them to do as the Iroquois had done. And the would-be Americans did indeed form "such a union" as Sachem Canasatego advised.

Not merely the unity of the Iroquois Confederacy, but the way it was achieved, was a lesson that these colonists were to learn. The nature of the Six Nations' government had been established so democratically that each was separate, but equal, within the whole. For no Iroquois nation dictated to any other. It was a manner of democracy that these colonists were to rename the "system of checks and balances" between a local (state) and national (federal) authority, when they wrote it into the Constitution of the United States. And that was uniquely American.

In *Our Brother's Keeper*, Edgar Cahn has said: "The Iroquois Confederacy was a model for our federal system." It was the "Indian way."

The way of the People of America had even more practical uses for the colonists in the winning of American independence. It was symbolized by those patriots who at the Boston Tea Party dressed as Iroquois, in "Indian blankets," and painted their faces with "war paint." On that day, in Boston Harbor, they sang as they dumped the English tea into the water:

> Rally, Mohawks!
> Bring your axes!
> And tell King George
> We'll pay no more taxes
> On his foreign tea.

It was not a masquerade, as it has been depicted. The symbol of courage, of boldness, of individual daring, and of defiance in the face of impossible odds, was the Indian. The "Mohawks" at the Boston Tea Party foretold much about how the Revolution would be fought.

Not too well known were the "Indian tactics" of General Washington himself. The Virginia gentleman had wished to fight in the gentlemanly manner of the English—line on line of soldiers, face to face, in the martial pattern of the Middle Ages. That European military tactic ended with the disastrous defeat on Long Island. After that, Washington remembered what he had learned in his youth among the tribal People of Ohio, and in the ambushing of the English General Braddock in the French and Indian War. He ordered the remnant of his army in the Pennsylvania woods to "fight like Indians."

To the anger of the English, who called them "savages," the Revolutionary Army fought from behind trees and rocks, usually ambushes and surprise attacks, then slipped away into the woods. It was not at all gentlemanly, it was too American, but it brought the victory of Trenton, which some have said was the turning point of the war.

Delighted by the success of his Indian tactics, Washington petitioned the Continental Congress for permission to make "buckskins" the official uniform of the Revolutionary Army. The Congress responded with a discreet silence.

It was the spirit the land gave to the People, in the way they knew it so intimately and fought for it, that the colonists learned to respect. The military records of which tribe fought on which side in which battle paled beside this, although there were times when the tribes' heroism seemed decisive. The colonial newspapers had numerous stories of these exploits, and they read like parables.

A typical account was that of "Sachem Ninham of Wappnachi village" in New York State, who with sixty followers "joined Washington in Albany" and was sent, with Lafayette, to "check the British"; he forced them to retreat. At the Battle of Van Cortlandt, in 1778, Sachem Ninham was killed. "I am an aged tree," he said. "I will die here." The Battle of Van Cortlandt had been fought where his People's village had been before the land was stolen by the English. He died for his land, not for Washington.

"Literally did they redeem the pledge they had given at Albany, the pledge of 'Ruth,' " said Washington. He thought the people of Wappnachi had died so that his army could escape. The general did not understand why they fought.

And yet few of the Europeans who had become American would ever know the debt they owed to the People. They did not comprehend, most of them, the sources of their own strength. In the beginning of the Revolutionary War, the Declaration of Independence did not mention the People except to curse them as "merciless Indian Savages," and at its end, the Treaty of Peace of Paris did not mention them at all. The new Americans thought that they, too, had "invented" America. And so they invited not one native of America to join their imitation of the Iroquois Confederacy.

"Ever thought much about what makes the United States so distinctly different from any other country on earth? It's because of the Indians," declared an editorial that was reprinted in tribal newspapers of the 1960s, from the *Navajo Times* in the Southwest to the *Tundra Times* in Alaska. "If it had not been for the rich Indian democratic traditions, it's hard to tell what kind of government we might have today . . . the idea of several states within a state (Federalism), the belief that Chiefs are servants of the people rather than their masters, and the insistence that the community must recognize the difference between men and their dreams, and respect it, all were in practice here, before Columbus landed."

Not only that, but women's rights, to vote and to govern, were practiced by many tribes. Even the "lack of peasants" and the unpopularity of the feudal caste system were "inherited from our Indian predecessors."

"Scholars are just beginning to learn that the effect of the Indian culture on white customs far overshadows the effect of white methods on Indian practices. By absorbing a lot of Indian culture, attitude and abundant products (cigarettes, chewing gum, rubber balls, popcorn, cornflakes, flapjacks, maple syrup) the United States is completely different and unique, as a nation, and the people are different too."

In that way the people of Europe "entered into Indian history." And they became American, as the *Aborigine,* an early journal of tribal scholarship, has noted: American history is "Indian history."

That man could alienate himself from his history and his land was nothing new. It was known in the time of the Aztecs. An ancient poet-priest had written of this in Nahautl, before the coming of the Europeans:

> Do men have roots, are they real?
> No one can know completely,
> What is Your richness, what are Your flowers,
> O Inventor of Yourself!

The Governor of All the Tribes

❦ TESTAMENT OF James Canan, Area Director,
Bureau of Indian Affairs, Billings, Montana

A man of sensitivity and intellect, he was not the stereotype of a
government bureaucrat. James Canan had devoted his life to
Indian affairs; he had spent twenty-five years in government
service, "working for the tribes," he said. In the years before he became the area director of the tribes in Wyoming and Montana, he
had helped develop the strip mines of the Navajo Nation.

"Is it true as they say that the Bureau is the errand boy of the
strip-mining companies?" I said.

"That's not so!" he answered.

"Some people say that it is no coincidence that as soon as the
Cheyenne People asked that their strip-mining contracts be canceled you recommended strip mines to the Crow People. They
say you timed this to undermine the Cheyenne. They say the Bureau of Indian Affairs should be called the Bureau of Corporate
Affairs."

"Nonsense!" he asserted. And now he was indignant; he had a
right to be. "I am no one's errand boy," he said. His Irish temper,
if that's what it was, turned his cheeks angry red.

"We're concerned with the economic development of the resources of the Indian people. Look, we've been working on this
for a long time. We're the guardians of their land, by law, not by
choice. We're just doing our job."

In the modernistic Federal Building in Billings, Montana, where the soundproof, air-conditioned offices of the Bureau of Indian Affairs were nestled, the largest space seemed to belong to the planning offices, which had prepared the "Crow Ceded Area Coal Lease Mining Proposal." One of the planners had told me it was "Canan's baby."

"The principal role of the Bureau," Canan had candidly said of the coal mining, was "in working up the sale."

And that it did. The Bureau's proposal recommended the strip mining of the Crow lands because "The income of the local people, especially the Crow Indians, will give them the opportunity to increase their standard of living and self-determination." Not once, but seven times, this was repeated. And there would be better roads, a "minimal" displacement of ranchers, only a "few" white workers, and merely "slight to moderate" changes in the "rural culture," the Bureau told the People, somewhat disingenuously, since its report to Washington predicted that "social changes associated with urbanization are probable."

It was true. There would be noise and dust. Sacred sites might be "completely and permanently destroyed." The mine itself would be "visually offensive." And all wildlife, "all but perhaps the small rodents," would "probably be displaced." Still, that was "offset" by promises of money: "increased personal income," "stable employment," and "investment, tribal development and family income."

Canan was no romantic. He was no "Indian-lover." He knew more of the coal in the earth than he knew of the spirit of the earth. "Indian history here is vague and not very evident," his planning office said in their report on the Crow.

Then why had he devoted his life to Indian affairs? In all honesty, he said, he was not sure.

From his youthful dreams he remembered no interest in Indians. As a young man he was restless; he attended three colleges and graduated "with not a very clear idea of what I would do." The job he had hoped for with the Quakers "fell through, for reasons that I can't quite remember." A "temporary job" with the

Interior Department was offered him in 1949. In a sense, his life's work was "an accident." With no knowledge of Indians, through either study or personal contact, he was given "management training" and assigned to the Bureau of Indian Affairs' Washington headquarters as a "business economist" for the tribes.

By 1960 he was "expert" enough to be sent to the Navajo Nation as the Bureau's assistant area director "in charge of resources," during the time when the strip-mining and power-plant leases were being negotiated. There he helped shape one of the largest energy projects in the country. He did so well he was appointed area director of all the reservations in Montana and Wyoming, where he was to guide the development of an energy project that might be even larger. If he succeeded. But he was having trouble.

The old days were gone. No longer would a Tribal Council vote politely for whatever men like Canan proposed, whether they agreed or not. Some no longer listened to him. Some hated his guts, he said. And now the Cheyenne had canceled his coal leases, the Blackfoot were taking over their schools, the Kootenai had set up toll booths on the highway, and the Crow had "closed" the Bighorn River to white men.

So I asked him: Wasn't it time to resign? Had the Bureau outlived its time? Were the Americans going to take over America? Once he had said that he had "no regrets" for the things he had done and the life he had lived and the advice he had given the People. Was that still true?

This is what he told me:

Now, look at it this way: Why are the Indians at loggerheads with the government?

It is because the Bureau of Indian Affairs' area directors and agency superintendents have veto power over the Tribal Councils. When a tribe passes a resolution, *I* have to approve it. That, I suppose, makes *me* the governor, or the president, of all the tribes, although I am not a member of the tribes.

Colonialism? Some would say that it is. It is all part of the system of checks and balances written into the Indian Reorganization Act of 1934 by Commissioner John Collier. And that was supposed to offer our style of legislative democracy to the tribes.

Sovereignty—that is the issue!

What is sovereignty? It is not simply a matter of civil rights. It is not simply a matter of self-determination. And it has never really been defined. Until it is resolved, nothing will be resolved. It is the issue underlying all others. If you try to solve other problems first, aren't you putting the cart before the horse?

Consider my job: On the one hand I am supposed to iron out the problems of preserving the Indians' identity within the larger society. But at the same time I represent to the Indians the government of the larger society.

I have a dual role. And I am damned if I do and damned if I don't.

Some of the tribal chairmen will hardly talk to me any more. Some will not talk to me at all. It is not a complete breakdown in communication, but it's almost that.

There is a lot of what I don't like to call reverse racism. But that's what it is. All these tribal resolutions on expelling whites from the reservation, on barring white reporters from Tribal Council meetings, and prohibiting *any* scholarly studies of Indians by whites, as the Northwest Affiliated Tribes just did— what is that but reverse racism?

Things have changed.

More and more tribes say they want to run their own affairs, to run their own schools. They demand local control. They want to have a say in who teaches their children and what and how they are taught.

On the Northern Cheyenne, at the town of Busby, the people came to me and said, We'd like to run this school. I said, All right. Half the teachers stayed. Half the teachers left. They didn't want to work under the tribe. And then the Cheyenne said they wanted complete control of the Busby school. And some more of the teachers left.

Now, how can the tribe run the schools if the white teachers won't teach! I don't know when the day will come when the tribes will run the schools.

Self-determination is one thing; but self-government is something else. On some reservations, if the tribes act like "little nations," that creates problems. On the Blackfoot Reservation there are 2,500 Indians and 13,000 whites. If the Blackfoot have jurisdiction over the whites, that means the majority of the people, who happen to be white, will have no vote, no say in the government.

The Indians say: We have self-government. We can do as we please. Well, that creates a problem.

I don't know the solution.

During the Nixon administration the catchword in Washington was "self-determination." In the Bureau we were supposed to *give* each tribe the *right* to make up its own mind about assimilating or keeping its identity. But the decisions were made in Washington. The programs and the money to run them came from Washington.

Every time there is a change of administration in Washington, there is a change in policy. The Bureau has to carry it out. So it is no wonder that the tribes don't trust the Bureau.

Until the 1920s the government told us the Indians had to assimilate. They were the "vanishing race." They had to get into the "melting pot" and give up their identity. Then in 1928 there was the Merriam Report: the Indians were supposed to preserve their identity. And Commissioner John Collier developed that idea in the 1930s. Then came World War II, and the Senate committee led by Senator Burton Wheeler of Montana was hostile to Collier. Senator Wheeler called up the Bureau and told Commissioner Zimmerman to write a report on "How We Can Get Out of the Indian Business." Until his dying day Zimmerman swore it was not his idea. He was forced to write it. In the 1940s he wrote his report calling for the termination of federal responsibilities to these tribes. Then in the 1950s, under Eisenhower, we had the "termination policy": once again the Indians were told to give up their identity, and assimilate.

Then we had the "relocation program," to get them off the reservations and into the "mainstream," as the melting pot was now called. Then in the 1960s, under John Kennedy, we had Commissioners Phileo Nash and Robert Bennett, who told them: Get into the mainstream, but don't assimilate.

None of the policies ever came from the Indians. They came from Washington.

Everybody thought, when I came to the Bureau twenty-five years ago, that the tribal governments would soon die out. Yes, we had to work with them, but they were transitional. America was supposed to be a melting pot. The Indians, like everyone else, were supposed to melt. They were dying out.

I never believed it.

This country is big enough for people with different cultural identities to live within it. Peacefully and democratically. That, it seems to me, is the real problem: How do we work out the government and jurisdiction of such cultural pluralism? Now we recognize the right of tribal governments to continue. Cultural pluralism is national policy. But the problem is in what way, and to what degree, the people in different ethnic groups can *really* exercise these rights.

In Europe there are several countries that have ethnic groups living *independently* within their borders. Like the Basques in Spain. Some even have their own governmental structure inside the dominant society. Europe, in this sense, is way ahead of us.

We have to find the way.

THE INVENTION OF
AMERICA – II

ON the gentle shore of Massachusetts south of Boston, there is a shrine where thousands of white people go every year to worship a large stone. It is Plymouth Rock, upon which, according to an ancient myth, the Pilgrims landed. Neither the shrine nor the reverence of the worshipers has protected the sacred rock from cracking almost in half, as has the Liberty Bell.

When the first settlers on the *Mayflower* came ashore, they were hungry from the ordeal of the long voyage on meager rations. Reverend Theodore Parker, the noted abolitionist and friend of Emerson, once recalled a story told in his family about that day. As soon as they came ashore, the Pilgrims began to raid the fishnets and steal the corn in the fields of the Wampanoag People. It was a theft that weighed as a debt on their Puritan consciences. And they later repaid it in English shillings, the reverend said.

There is no shrine that commemorates that first dinner of

stolen fish and corn. Nor is there any shrine to the Wampanoag People, whose fish and corn it was. Any more than there are shrines to the American wise men and philosophers who implanted the ideas of tribal democracy and individual freedom in the medieval minds of the Europeans. There are statutes and picture postcards and patronizing references to "the contributions of the Indians" to America, as if it was the People of America who were taught to be "Americans" by the Europeans. There can be no such shrines, because it is the Europeans, not the Americans, who to this day are revered and worshiped.

After all, a shrine to a stolen fish would be an odd memorial to the founding of a nation.

In time the spirit of America was to be expurgated from American history. That happened on the frontier. When the westward movement of the Easterners began, even those, like Thomas Jefferson, who had known the sources of our uniqueness and therefore wished the earth be taken from the People by "honest and peaceable means," never "without their consent" lest the American spirit be corrupted, then cried for its death. "We shall be obliged to drive them [the People] with the beasts of the forest into the stony [Rocky] mountains," Jefferson had written of the frontier in 1812.

On the "Sea of Grass" of the West was a "new" New World to be "discovered." It was to be re-"invented." Here was that "Promised Land," a Western writer boasted, for here "the fabled lands lay, the Elysian fields, Atlantis, El Dorado." The West was a second "Garden of Eden"; even more, wrote other Western writers, it was the "Garden of the World" and the "bane of true Godliness." Its conquest was "God's battle," said William Thayer, in *Marvels of the New West:* "It seems as if God had concentrated His wisdom and power upon this part of our country, to make it His crowning work of modern civilization." Nothing less than heaven, it was "Providence illustrated."

And it was more than that: it was the fabled and long-lost "road to India," as Thomas Jefferson described Lewis and Clark's search for the Pacific Ocean to the Congress. Walt Whitman was

to name it the "Passage to India." So it was, said Senator William
Benton, that "the road to empire" in the West at last would realize the unfulfilled dream of Columbus; the "riches of India"
awaited, and the American "Indians" had better not stand in the
path of the modern conquistadors.

The men of the Renaissance had conquered America with
such seeming ease because the People did not exist for them, and
they "invented" them in the images of their own "creation myths."
So, too, the men on the frontier conquered the West by proclaiming the People did not exist; but on the frontier of the West the
feudal fears and medieval creation myths would be too mystical
and metaphysical. So they were Americanized. The fantastic
creatures of the bestiaries were simply "beasts."

In the "wild West," said General Custer, the People were
"wild animals," merely "beasts of the forest." And that, said
Commissioner of Indian Affairs Francis Walker in 1872, justified
their annihilation. "With wild men, as with beasts," said the government's "guardian" of the Indian People, "there is no question
of national dignity." For "beasts" had no culture; they could
not be a nation nor could they own land. "It is nonsense to talk
about our having driven most of these Indians out of their lands,"
President Theodore Roosevelt was to say. "They did not own
the land at all, in the white sense." And years later the President's
son, Colonel Theodore Roosevelt, Jr., was to refine the "beast"
theory to a succinct sentence. "Warring against colored nations
was more dangerous and more exciting than big game shooting,"
he said, "but still more or less in the same category."

After all, his father had said: "This great continent could not
have been kept as nothing but a game preserve for squalid savages."

That the "beast" theory was popular on the frontiers was not
surprising. One Kentucky backwoodsman of the early 1800s
voiced it when he allowed as how hunting for "game" such as
"bar" (bear) and "painter" (panther) was great fun, but "thar
ain't no game like Ingins." It was an enthusiasm that Daniel
Boone and Colonel Frémont would have shared.

That the "beast" theory is popular among some government historians nowadays *is* surprising. Not that they would go hunting human "game." And yet in *Prospector, Cowboy and Sodbuster,* published by the Interior Department in 1967, the concept of the People being little more than troublesome "game" is much the same. The white settlers not only tamed "the wild land," the departmental historians wrote. "They brought civilization." In executing that feat they "forced the nomadic Indians onto reservations, drove the game into the hills"; the "hostile" Indians and "wild" game had to be subjected to "pacification," one way or another.

If the People were beasts, then they had neither a culture nor a history worth considering. Nor was it conceivable that the pioneers would learn anything of value from them. They literally did not exist.

On the Conestoga wagons and stagecoaches to the West, the creation myth of the Renaissance was reborn. But it was uglier and cruder. The refugees from the Irish famines and German revolutions of the 1840s who crowded the pioneer trails were not explorers or adventurers; they were hungry and desperate people.

The poor peasants and store clerks who wished to go West were ill equipped for the rigors of pioneer life on the frontier. They had to harden themselves. One way of doing so was through fear and hatred, that "thrill of horror" of the "savage" that was insightfully described in *Our Wild Indians* by Colonel Richard Dodge; it toughened their senses and made them feel bold, even when, as the colonel noted, there was nothing to fear.

And the pioneers feared the land itself. In a fond reminiscence of frontier life in a volume of *Prose and Poetry of the Livestock Industry* published by the National Live Stock Association as late as 1905, the frontier "wailed out the warning to rash mankind; 'abandon ye hope, ye who enter here.'" It was an "almost unknown region [of] every conceivable horrid aspect, and dreadful conditions . . . this howling, hopeless, worthless cactus-bearing waste . . . inhabited by savages of extreme fierceness and cruelty and haunted by prowling beasts of unexampled ferocity."

The Europeans who settled in the West were terrorized by it for generations after. They had sacrificed all the comforts they valued. They had left their ancestral homes. They had little idea where they were going. They were not Americans. In the "new land" of the frontier the early settlers were Swedish and Norwegian farmers, Dutch burghers, English landowners, French fur trappers, escaped African slaves, Mexican vaqueros, Spanish priests, Russian aristocrats, Chilean miners, Chinese railroad workers, Australian sailors. And many of the largest ranches and cattle companies in the West were owned by Europeans—French marquises, English lords, and czarist barons. Not even the American army of the frontier was wholly American. The famed Seventh Cavalry of General Custer had a rather large contingent of professional soldiers and adventurers from Ireland, Germany, and Italy. One was Captain Myles Keogh, an Irishman, whose only previous military experience before he faced Crazy Horse on the Little Bighorn had been his service in the papal guard at the Vatican.

That was the paradox. In fighting the Americans, the Europeans became Americans. And it was the "beasts" who Americanized them—by "Indianizing" them.

None of the white settlers knew the lay of the land. None of them knew its meanings. These were things they had to learn from the People, who had lived there for thousands of years.

In the beginning the People had welcomed them into their villages. They fed them. They gave them their own beds. They led them to their richest pastures. They guided them through the mountains and showed them where to ford the rivers. Early wanderers, such as Lewis and Clark, almost all had "Indian guides," but it was the People along the way who taught them how to survive in an alien land that was a wilderness to them. They nursed them when they became ill. They loved them when they were lonely. They accepted them into their families and tribes when they were lost.

As the Arapahos were to sing in sadness in their Ghost Dance years later:

> My children, my children,
> When I met the whites,
> I gave them my fruits.

Even the pioneer trails were not made by the pioneers. They were mostly the old trade routes of the People, hundreds and thousands of years old. So, too, in the lands of Gran Chichimeca in the Southwest, "the Iberians in their explorations moved along the same old *puchteca* [Aztec merchant] trails," wrote Charles Di-Peso, director of the Amerind Foundation. The conquistadors, like the pioneers, walked in the footsteps of the native Americans; they blazed few trails of their own.

These "aboriginal thoroughfares," as H. H. Bancroft called them, spanned the continent, east to west and north to south. And the historian likened them to the Roman roads in England, which became the basis for our automobile highways. On the frontiers the white settlers were guided not only by these native roads and native peoples, but by native ways that they adapted to their own if they were to survive their journeys.

On the earlier frontier of the eastern Blue Ridge and the Appalachians, the frontiersmen and women had become as "Indian" as they dared to be, according to Crèvecoeur in *Letters from an American Farmer*, 1782. "We metamorphose ourselves" and "adopt those savage customs," he said. "Behold me under the wigwam; I am so well acquainted with the principal manners of these people, that I entertain not the least apprehension from them. I rely more securely on their strong hospitality, than on the witnessed compacts of many Europeans. . . . Men are like plants" and they bear the nature of the "soil in which they grow. . . .

"Still the danger of [my] Indian education alarms me!" Crèvecoeur wrote. The pioneer might learn the "Indian ways" too well and unlearn his European culture. He was a stranger "on a foreign land." And so he prayed: "I beseech thee, O Father of nature, that our ancient virtues and our industry may not be totally lost . . . on this new land."

Those who had stayed behind in the Eastern cities, imitating

European manners, both idolized and ridiculed these frontiers-men as "playful Savages" and "rational barbarians," who were "no better than the Indians" they fought. And the irony of it was that those who thought they were the most "Indian" in dress, in mannerism, in talk, in the way they lived, were the proudest self-proclaimed "Indian fighters": Daniel Boone, Christopher ("Kit") Carson, Davy Crockett. And yet these folk heroes of the whites were often portrayed as "half Indian." The farther west they went, the more "Indian" they became. In the "wilderness" the mountain men "lived exactly upon the Indian system," noted George Catlin during his prairie journeys of the 1830s. And they were, like the traders and trappers, wholly native American "in dress and manners." They learned much more than they taught, for the civilization of the cities was ill fitted to the civilization "in the country," Catlin said.

On the prairies of the West the rancher and the cowboy owed more of their heritage to the People than they knew. Their ancestor and teacher was the Mexican vaquero, an inheritance reluctantly recognized by the Anglos just recently, though it was written in every word of the cowboy world—his land: *Tejas, Las Californias, Nuevo Mexico, Nevada, Colorados;* and his home: *el ranchero, el corral;* and his tools: *la reata, el lazo;* his animals: *broncos, burros;* his ancestors, *los Indios;* and himself, *el vaquero* —the buckaroo.

An old-time vaquero of California, Arnold Rojas, remembered that when a cowboy "was especially skilled" it was said of him, "*Se crio entre los Indios, pues*" ("Well, he grew up among the Indians"). He said of himself, "*Me crie entre los Indios*" ("I was raised among the Indians"). "A man took pride in calling himself *Indio*," Rojas wrote. In those days, "The old Spanish and Mexican [land] grants used Indian *vaqueros* almost exclusively, until the Gold Rush."

More than the cowboy's skills or senses, his spirits were *Indio.* A lone rider, he was a wanderer who loved the land like a brother. A man of few words, he held his thoughts close to his chest; he did not talk, he acted. Once the *Indio vaquero* was like that,

Rojas said, and the cowboy, Anglo and Mexican, learned that from him. "He was pithy and often spoke in metaphor." He was daring, but "sparing in speech and serene under all circumstances." Maybe the Lone Ranger and his faithful Indian, Tonto, ought to have changed places.

In a moment of forgotten truth in one of his first movies, *The Big Trail*, a young John Wayne is a wagonmaster leading an early group of Hollywooden pioneers into the wilderness. Someone asks him how he knows so much about the West.

"Everything I know," he says, "I have learned from the Indians."

All the land was the land of the People. The nature of the land gave to them their nature, as they gave their nature to the land. That was the history of the American West, retold as myths that were truth. It may be that the Europeans' intense feelings of guilt, which came with the taking of the land in the way it was taken, and the intense angers of the People at losing their lands, combined to distort this knowledge of what the land meant and corrupted the history of America.

"To destroy tribal people is the same thing as going out and destroying all the books in all the libraries, all those records and documents of history," said Gerry Wilkinson, of the National Indian Youth Council. "It is a gut kind of thing, the gut fear that white men have of the earth, of their birth, of their ancestors."

In the memory of white men, the history of the West became that of the wars against the People, and of "Indian uprisings." These battles have been written and rewritten in thousands of volumes and hundreds of cinema and television tales. And yet these were a history of conquest and death, not of the People of the West. In the end the history of America was to be confined to historical reservations of human artifacts, guarded by the white historians.

The People would soon become nonexistent once more. So much so that when they defeated the Seventh Cavalry of General Custer on the Little Bighorn, credit for their triumph would be given to Napoleon Bonaparte. The *Yankton Dakotaian* and other

Western newspapers widely and seriously reported that Sitting Bull had "studied the campaign of Napoleon" in his tipi. In a contemporary history of the battle. W. Fletcher Johnson wrote: "Sitting Bull has read French history carefully and he is especially enamored of the career of Napoleon, and endeavors to model his campaigns after those of the 'Man of Destiny.'"

Nothing the People did was of their doing, whether it was victory or defeat. As did most histories of the "Indian Wars," the account of the battle focused on Custer's defeat, not on the Lakota and Cheyenne victory.

By the beginning of the twentieth century, the People had all but vanished, historically and numerically, from the eyes of the whites. "We became invisible when we were no longer a threat," Vine Deloria, Jr., has said.

In his misanthropic love of the American West, Frederick Jackson Turner, the "father of frontier history," was to say that the People had little or no influence on that history. The frontier, by itself, had "Americanized" the Europeans, and the native democracy that developed had arisen from the "free land." "It came stark and strong and full of life from the American forest," like a frog from under a mushroom. The People were reduced to mere scenery that got in the way. "American history has been to a large degree the history of the colonization of the Great West," wrote Turner, by the white "settlers."

The People had no history but for their fight against the "colonization." As the Europeans had "invented" America in their own image, so the descendants of the Europeans "invented" American history in their own image. "There is little of significance to present day readers of American history earlier than the discovery by Columbus," stated a *Guide to the Study of American History* written in 1896 by two renowned scholars of the day, Edward Channing and Albert Bushnell Hall, in association with Frederick Jackson Turner himself. Since the "Indian [had] little history in the modern sense," they said, the very "term 'American history'" began with "the dominance of Anglo-Saxon ideas and institutions."

Once again the creation myths of medieval Europe were up-dated. It was no longer that belief in the supernatural monsters of the Renaissance, but a rational belief in the supernatural Western men, who created history out of themselves in an im-maculate conception; a belief that has dominated the re-creation of American history to this day.

Nowhere was the creation story more innocently transcribed than in the *Manual for Citizenship* published by the Daughters of the American Revolution for many years. It began like this: American history was dated "from the discovery made by Colum-bus." Before that time, "No one lived in [the] country but savage Indians and wild beasts." They had "no cities or villages or houses." And so the "real settlers" had to come from Europe, for neither "savage Indians" nor the "wild beasts" could qualify as "real settlers." It was these Europeans, "mostly" from England, who "brought their laws and free institutions with them." And they "made" America.

Fortunately, these histories were not very historic. The Peo-ple were no more invisible than they had ever been, and the histories of the People did not disappear when they were for-gotten.

They were exported. And the myths and methods that had sub-dued the native People of America were to be employed to sub-due the native People of the colonial world. Not merely the myths, but the men who had conquered the West, were sent overseas in the war against Spain in 1898, as they had been in the war against Mexico in 1838, to combat ever-darker-skinned men and women.

In the conquest of Cuba, Puerto Rico, and the Philippines, the U.S. Army was led by General Nelson A. Miles, who had earned his rank as chief of staff by seeing to the surrender of Chief Joseph of the Nez Percé and Geronimo of the Apache; he was the veteran of many "Indian Wars." (The commander of the U.S. Army in the war against Mexico, General Winfield Scott, had earned *his* rank as the executor of the infamous "Trail of Tears." As the "Trail of Tears" was the prelude to the invasion of Mexico, so the trail of Chief Joseph led to Havana.)

The soldiers were "mostly" old "Indian fighters," said Colonel Theodore Roosevelt. His own Rough Riders were men who he said "had taken part in the killing of the great buffalo-herds and had fought Indians when the tribes were still on the warpath." More than half were cowboys and cattle ranchers; eight were "Sheriffs and Marshalls," three were "Stagecoach drivers," and five listed their trade simply as "Indian fighters." Almost all had been recruited in New Mexico, Arizona, and Oklahoma. Some of them were Indians.

Once the People of America had been defeated, these mythmakers merely continued the war elsewhere. It was, as has been said, a "Tropical Indian War."

In the wild charges and ambushes of the Rough Riders there was more than an echo of the Seventh Cavalry. One correspondent nostalgically noted "how much Custer would have enjoyed" the Battle of Santiago. Many of the attitudes and tactics of the troops were extensions of their deeply rooted anti-Indian feelings. When the Spanish empire fell and the U.S. army of occupation established military rule in Puerto Rico, an officer in the port of Fajardo reported in disgust that these islanders were "like the Indians"—shiftless and lazy and happy.

No wonder the New York *Herald Tribune* wrote of that war as being fought with "warring distracted tribes, civilized, semi-civilized, and barbarous." In an editorial that might have been the rewrite of one left over from the "Indian Wars," the paper's editor, Whitelaw Reid, explained: "It is not imperialism when duty keeps us" among such tribes "to help them, as far as their capabilities will permit, toward self-government on the basis of [our] civil rights." The Interior Department had been, and still is, saying that about the American tribes.

After all, it was to be expected that men to whom the conquest of "savages" was the manifest destiny of civilization would feel morally justified in fighting them anywhere. They perceived the darker-skinned tribes of the world as they perceived the red-skinned tribes of America.

That had happened once before and it would happen often again. In time the echoes of the "Indian Wars" had been quieted, and the People had "uninvented" themselves. But the belief in the ancient creation myths of the Europeans continued to haunt the nation and distort its self-knowledge. And seemingly doom it to forever "reinvent" itself, and everyone else, in its image.

When the soldiers of the U.S. Army were sent among the tribes of Vietnam, a newspaper in Pueblo, Colorado, heard eerie echoes of the massacre of Sand Creek, which was not far away, in the government policy of "Vietnamization." In the defoliation of the "enemy rice paddies" it saw the slaughter of the buffalo. In the Green Berets' outposts in the Mekong Delta (one was supposedly named Fort Dodge) it saw the frontier forts of the West. In the herding of the Vietnamese peasants into "protective villages" it saw a similarity to the Indian reservations. And in the napalm bombing of the innocents it heard the shrieks of the dying at Sand Creek.

One Navajo Marine in Vietnam voiced this feeling when he wrote home: "Sometimes I feel I am fighting myself."

And yet there are people who seem to learn nothing from their myths. In a curious interview with the Italian journalist Oriana Fallaci, Secretary of State Henry Kissinger once offered an explanation of his success in negotiating the peace treaty that "ended" the war in Vietnam; his charismatic self-image was that of the lone gunslinger who rides into town to bring peace and justice singlehandedly.

It was "a Wild West tale," said Kissinger.

The Myths of the Machos

𝕍 TESTAMENT OF Arlyn Rounds, Woodard's Indian Store, Gallup, New Mexico

In these mountains there was an "unwritten law" of the West.

The man who came home to find his wife in bed with her lover might legally kill her, or her lover, or both. This was not thought of as murder; it was simply a defense of a man's honor, or, the sanctity of his marriage bed, his right of macho. But the woman who found her husband in bed with his lover had no equal right. Nor honor.

One rural spring in the early 1970s, at calving time, an equal rights bill of sorts was proposed in the state legislature to offer a deceived wife the same rights as her husband. By an overwhelming vote of two to one, the outraged male legislators shouted, No! Indignant at this and similar invasions by women of the men's traditional province of morality and politics, one of the legislative body's powerful members, Senator Aubrey Dunn, an apple farmer whose committee held the purse strings of the state government, voiced the offended pride of the machos by proclaiming that the women—"little old biddies in tennis shoes" —had gone "too far."

This was "man's country." In the mystique of the Western frontier, the Pioneer Mother was revered in statues of tarnished bronze in front of every courthouse but rarely inside. The myth of the machos was still alive in the West. It rode on the highways in old movies, as it once had in dime novels, and boasted of its prowess in cowtown cafés, strutting about on Friday night in local cantinas and bars; it appeared as well in the men's rooms of the state legislature, like verbose ghosts of Zane Grey fantasies.

It was the land of Billy the Kid and Kit Carson. Here a man was a man and a woman lived in the shadow of the movie Western, in which the cowboy slept with his guns on his hips. He sooner would do without a woman than his pistol.

Maybe the frontier was gone, but in the minds of these machos it still lived on.

On that highway of myth known as Route 66 there was a town in the desert of New Mexico that had done its damnedest to preserve the spirit of the old frontier. It was here that John Ford had filmed many of his Western epics.

That town was Gallup.

It wasn't the "toughest town in the West," but it was "tough enough," a city father boasted, sitting in his air-conditioned office, talking as tough as John Wayne, or Walter Mitty. "There are no fancy frills. There is no pretense in this town. It's a no-holds-barred kind of town. Rough. But honest. Where a man has to prove he is a man. It's not an easy town for a woman." That was why, said the city father, there were more bars in town per citizen than probably anywhere else in the country. Not, as some said, "to exploit those Indians," but because these bars were part of the "town's character." There were thirty bars, or more, for no more than fifteen thousand people. One year, more than one hundred babies were abandoned by their mothers in these bars.

Of all the towns of the West, it seemed an unlikely one for a daughter of the aristocracy of Detroit's auto industry, educated in New York City, a devotee of the Fifth Avenue shops and the boulevards of Europe, to seek as a refuge and to settle in.

Ms. Arlyn Rounds didn't seem to think so.

She had lived alone with her children on a ranch whose library was full of books. She had taught school on Indian reservations. She had managed a business of her own in Gallup. She did not believe, she said, in what she called "the myths of the machos."

She smiled as sadly as a tolerant and indulgent mother at the thought of the town's shopkeepers, with their boyish faces and pot bellies, who imagined themselves reincarnations of the Western heroes they watched on television—"conquering women and Indians" in their dreams.

But wasn't she uneasy in this world of male fantasy?

No, she said. "As a woman you have to preserve a sense of humor and a sense of humanity and a sense of independence and dignity about yourself, and about men."

And how did she do that?

This is what she told me about herself:

Sad. Yes, it is sad.

The macho thing is really sad and somehow funny. And yet it's dangerous, too. Mostly for the machos themselves. Because it's not a true picture of what they are and what they can do. Some of the shopkeepers in town want to be John Wayne. They have revolvers in their cash registers. And they have shotguns in their broom closets beside their aprons.

Most of them are gentle, generous, intelligent men. They are not Wild West types. They probably couldn't hit the side of a mountain.

But they are frightened.

Of whom? They are frightened of Indians whom they have known all their lives. They are frightened that the Indians may burn down their stores. They are frightened that the Indian "militants" will take over the town one night.

In Gallup, we, the whites, are the minority. Where else in the country is there any city where the whites are outnumbered so greatly? I don't know of any place.

So there is a fear here, which increases the macho.

The death of that young Navajo Larry Casuse, whom they called a "militant" because he accused the town of exploiting Indians—his death was a whole Keystone Kops thing. He kidnaps the mayor. Where to? To a sporting goods store two blocks away. So they have a shoot-out. And he is killed somehow. It

should never have happened. Or did people *want* it to happen!
This is the frightening thought I have had. Was this a tragedy
that the men in City Hall *wanted* to happen? Why couldn't it
have been stopped at City Hall? I wasn't there, but I wonder.

Are we, I wonder, sometimes caught up in the fates?

For nights after he died I did not sleep. I had visions of a
blood bath in town.

Some of these men, these respected men in town, when I
talked to them, weren't rational. There was no rationality. There
was fear and hysteria. And I think some of them would have
wanted to see "Gunsmoke" enacted on the street.

It's as though they had been caught up in their macho image
of themselves. Both the white and the Indian men.

And yet, on the whole, the relationships between the Indian
and white men seem to have worked out peacefully. I don't think
the Indian wants to take over Gallup. He has got enough trouble
running his own businesses at home. He just wants to be his own
boss, to run his own businesses, at home.

Really, the violent ways are not the Indian ways. But I do
think we are going to see a generation of "militants."

These kids are mostly at the college level. Where there is an
enlightenment of the mind. Where they are inspired. If the college is doing its job, it has to be a place for the "revolution
of ideas." The entire atmosphere of a college is that. It has always been so. It will always be. It *should* be.

And yet if there is so much violence, so much macho, so
much hatred, why do I stay here? What is a woman like me
doing in a town like this? Why did I come here?

I love Gallup. I really do.

When I came here things were not yet bad in the East. But
I could visualize how bad they would become in the cities. And
I had children. I wished to give them human values they could
not get in the Eastern cities. I wished them to be independent
and to be their own person. Not only that, but to feel, to identify, with other people, as I did.

When I came here I was a teacher. I wanted to teach Indian

children. That wasn't fulfilling enough for me, however, because a teacher on an Indian reservation has to be a fighter against the government system of education, the BIA, and in those days you never could win.

As a woman, I still feel there are things in my life I must do that I have not done. That doesn't have anything to do with the things I must do for myself, but has to do with the things I feel I must do for other people, probably to satisfy myself. That way, as a woman, I am fulfilling the reason that I was born.

That sounds too moralistic! It's a miracle I did not become a missionary when I came West.

Once, I went back to the East. That was after I got my divorce and I sold my business here in town and went back to Grosse Point, Michigan.

At the time of life when most women of my age are settling down and becoming secure, I went excursioning off. I wanted to lay to rest any desire I might have had to live that "good life" I had left back in Grosse Point.

But it was no good.

I went to work for General Motors. Where else would I go to find a job but to the people I knew, whom I had grown up with, in the auto industry? And I lived in a very nice all-white upper-middle-class neighborhood.

And yet you could smell, you could taste, the fear. The city was an armed camp. In the West I never locked my doors. My God Almighty! In that city I began to roll up the windows of my car, and I locked all the doors of the house at night. In a few months I found myself acting in fear, just like the rest of the people do back East.

I would say: I will not live like this!

My mother would say: You will be killed!

And I would say: If it is ordained that I be killed, I would rather die than live in a self-imposed prison!

And we packed bags and baggage and came back to the West.

In those cities of the East people live in a terror that covers them like a skin. So they come out West for two weeks to try to shed it. But they cannot. Here they are terrified of Indians.

They have never been in Indian country. They have been reading God knows what about Indians. And they want to know if they are safe! When the tourists ask me if it is "safe" to visit an Indian reservation, I have difficulty giving them an intelligent answer. God! I get so violent internally.

What are they afraid of? Is the fear of everything Indian so ingrained? Or are they frightened by the West, by the freedom and independence of the West that they feel?

Sometimes I think that the freedom in the air here really does frighten the people from the cities.

My grandfather taught me to be independent, to be myself, to be free. He always used to say to me: You were born in the wrong century. You should have been born a hundred years ago. You are really a mistake of nature.

My grandfather was that way, himself. My grandfather was a technological man. He had a pride in things man created with his own hands. And his great fear was that we were getting away from making things ourselves, with our hands, by allowing the technological advances—which he admired as an engineer—to take over. He was fearful of what these technological advances were doing to the human being's ability to be a human being.

That was something that I learned from my grandfather: the value of human dignity. . . . Now we don't too often think of the innate dignity, the beauty, of the human being.

And maybe this is what the Indian is saying: These things you build, your cities, your schools, your prisons, are taking away the dignity of human beings.

People come here looking for Indians. And yet when they see them, they don't really see them.

Why do they come?

I think people identify with the Indians because we're all really unhappy.

We are unhappy with our way of life. Life has changed, but this was nothing we had a say in. No one asked us. So we had to accept these changes passively. And we don't like it, we don't like what it has done to us. It has destroyed our values. It has accelerated the way we live, without giving our life any direction.

So we feel lost. Because we are.

My grandfather, I remember, talked in the thirties of "the good old days." Well, in my generation I don't think many of us can look back to, or talk of, the good old days; not many of us have known many good old days to look back to. When were they?

So far, this has been a wild century.

And so, when the Indians began saying: Hey, I am going back to my old culture! Hey, I don't want your civilization! It's phony! It's hollow! It's empty!—well, maybe this is why so many people are identifying with the Indians.

They have a culture that is hundreds, thousands, of years old. And that is still alive in many, many places. And they can go back to it.

We can't go back to our own past. We have destroyed it. We can't go anywhere. We have noplace to go.

THE LOVERS OF INDIANS — I

Man is to woman as the little moon
is to the large sun.
Bernard Second, Mescalero Apache

In the grand old hotel of a prairie town known for its mythic fear of the "dirty Indians" on a nearby reservation, two courageous white men were having supper with me. The men had stood up to public ridicule by defending the rights of the town's original settlers. And for that they were branded "Indian-lovers," a name of contempt, for few white people in that town dared express "love" of an Indian in public.

One man was simply a small-town lawyer. One was a nationally known civil rights lawyer who had come West to fight for "Indian causes."

As the evening, and the whiskey, wore on, I asked the civil rights lawyer why he had become involved with Indians on the lonely prairies, so far away from his life. What made him stay here? The lawyer began to recite the rhetorical litany of the injustices that had befallen the People. It was time, he said, that their human rights and their treaty rights were recognized, and he personally was going to fight for that day. He had dedicated himself to winning justice for them.

It was an ennobling and impressive speech. No less so because I had heard him give it once before, on a television documentary.

And so had the happily drunken small-town lawyer. He leaned across the dinner table, spilling a glass of water, and whispered loudly, "Thash not why he stays here. I will tell you why he stays here."

Why?

"Pussy," the small-town lawyer said. "Indian pussy."

In saying that he began an ecstatic tale of the "three days and three nights" he had spent in a room upstairs in the grand old hotel with a young Indian girl. "That girl sure was crazy," he said. "We never got out of bed."

The men grinned at one another in the dreamlike memory of a shared fantasy.

> Licence my roving hands, and let them go,
> Before, behind, between, above, below.
> O my America! my new-found-land . . .

And so John Donne, Canon of Saint Paul's Cathedral in London, immortalized the erotic fantasy of European men that America was a woman of their deepest dreams. His early-seventeenth-century ode of love to America was fittingly titled, "To His Mistress Going to Bed."

In the beginning, America was a native woman. . . .

The "Virgin Land" was often portrayed by the male artists of Renaissance Europe as a beautifully nude and strong-bodied goddess, Venus adorned with a feathered headdress, who reigned with the royalty of Elizabeth of England or Queen Isabella of Spain—but for her voluptuous nakedness. And she was exotically depicted astride the land or the sea, riding an armadillo or a crocodile, awaiting if not welcoming the white men of Europe with the promise of a new Garden of Eden. She was the origin of romantic fantasies that have persisted until this day.

From the time the first Renaissance seafarers came to these

shores, they not only compared the New World to a woman, but symbolized their conquest of the land as they might a conquest of love. And the figure of the native woman became the symbol of America.

In a new Garden of Eden there had to be a new Eve, or paradise would have been a sterile place. And in seeking Eve they found her by recreating her to fit their image of her. "It is your own thought that became Aphrodite," Euripides wrote of man's image of the Grecian goddess of love and birth. "Aphrodite is the name of all human folly."

So it was to be in America. The image of the native Eve was created of and by man, as the biblical Eve was created from the rib of Adam. Her character and the character of the land were to be given the shape of the desires of the European men who had created them; an unobtainable dream, all the more potent because of that.

In 1497 the explorer Amerigo Vespucci, for whom America was named, "discovered" that dream. On the coast of Brazil he thought he had come upon the daughters of Eve, the perfect women: "They are very well proportioned, so that one does not see on their bodies an ill formed limb or feature. And although they walk about utterly naked, they are fleshy women, and that part of their sex that if one has not seen it one would think invisible they cover with their thighes except for that part which is modestly speaking, the mound of love. In short, they are no more ashamed than we are of showing our nose and mouth." Not only that, but they rarely were "wrinkled" and they looked "as though they had never given birth"; a "Virgin Land" of eternal virgins.

More wonderful even than these lovely women was the way they made love. "They showed themselves very desirous of copulating with us Christians," wrote Vespucci; for they were women "full of lust." And for their "extreme of hospitality" he self-righteously and unconvincingly lamented, in print, to his Catholic readers that these "loving" women were "worse than heathens."

The chronicles of Dutch, French, Spanish, and English seafarers were as romantic, and as dreamlike. One of many was A

New Voyage to Carolina, by John Lawson, printed in London in 1709, containing an Anglo-Saxon version of Vespucci's Garden of Eden. The women, "when young, and at Maturity, are as fine shaped Creatures as any in the Universe," Lawson rhapsodized. "Nor are they Strangers or not Proficients in the soft Passion. They are of a very hale Constitution; their breaths are as Sweet as the Air they breathe in, and the Woman seems to be of tender Composition, as if they were designed rather for Bed than Bondage." And most pleasing to the Englishmen, "They never love beyond Retrieving."

Sadly for him, John Lawson's appreciation of the native women was not appreciated by native men. When he returned to the Carolinas a few years later, he was "seized by jealous Indians, and put to death."

In the macho fantasies of the men of Europe there was one aspect of the conquest of America that the "prudishness of later centuries tended to obscure," wrote one historian: "the carnal bond." The Old World was in upheaval; it was casting off those feudal inhibitions that once veiled women in the mystery of religious superstition and bound them by the codes of Roman patriarchy, where love was chivalrous rape and sex was a sin against God. It was an era of sensual rediscovery, of Boccaccio's *Decameron*, of the lusty adventures of Rabelais, of Ariosto's love lyrics, of the full-bodied Venuses of Titian and the women of Rembrandt, of Michelangelo's sensuous religiosity, of the passionate plays of Shakespeare and Don Quixote's unrequited quest for romantic love. In savoring the freedoms of America, the men of Europe may well have been seeking a bodily freedom they had idealized but, like Don Quixote, never realized.

Men of the Renaissance thought of women with medieval imagery. A woman was made in the image of the Virgin, to be held pure and immaculate. She was a "blessed vessel of God." Yet she was as well a handmaiden of the "Serpent in the Garden," the temptress of God's damnation: for she possessed, as she was possessed by, the awesome power of creation embodied in the mystery of her sex, which made her susceptible to witchcraft and sorcery. In the thrall of these fears men sought to conquer women, or to be freed of them.

The fear of women as witches who denuded men of their stately powers was codified by two Dominican monks in the *Malleus Maleficarium*, published in Germany in 1486. In this manual for men who wished to rid themselves of the "Satanic" sex of women it was written, based on the writings of such Church fathers as St. Jerome and St. Augustine, that there were "wanton women" who "obtained cohabitation" with "Incubi." Though witches might be either male or female, they were more often women, wrote the monks; for women were "more carnal than a man" and were "of inordinate affections and passions." So women were "feebler in mind and body than men." The monks wrote: "To conclude: All witchcraft comes from carnal lust, which is in women insatiable" ("Why Superstition Is Chiefly Found in Women").

And it was this fear of women that led to their prohibition from ships in the Age of Exploration. If a woman was found aboard ship, she was often thrown overboard. On their ships men created their own world. Ships were the domain of men. And "women were as much excluded from the conquest [of America] as they were from the voyages of exploration and discovery," as Charles Ferguson wrote in *The Male Attitude*. In the mind of the conquerors it was they, and they alone, who would create the New World: "There was no concept of conception, no gestation, no fetus, no growth in the uterus, no birth." Man seemed intent on implanting his images upon this land. He explored it. He discovered it. He conquered it. And there may be inherent in the conquest of peoples by armies of men an enthronement of male dominance and male myths.

And so these men were in no mood to understand the reason for the social freedom and political power of tribal women. They mistook the independence of these women as "licentiousness," which affirmed their own sense of male superiority. And when they experienced the natural equality of native women, they did not comprehend it at all. Nor could they conceive of a matriarchy that was not as authoritarian as a patriarchy, but then most non-tribal people still do not understand that rule by women is innately different from rule by men.

The strength of the women of the Iroquois and Algonquin peoples was particularly confusing. For these Indians, "God exists in heaven, but not alone," said the Dutch colonist Adriaen Van der Dronk in 1655, in his *Description of New Netherlands.* "He has there with him a goddess, a female person, the most beautiful ever known." On earth, as in heaven, the Iroquois women reigned beside their men and sometimes above them. They chose the leaders and decided the affairs of state. It was unheard of in Holland.

More incredibly, the women were "very free and do as they please." And when "they become old they will frequently boast of their connections with many of their chiefs and great men." In the eyes of Van der Dronk and his fellow patriarchs, this had to be because of "prostitution."

And if these women had the audacity to behave as if they were "heathen goddesses," the moralistic patriarchs of the Dutch Reformed Church would teach them Christian humility, more befitting to women. They would convert them through sexual conquest. "Our Dutchmen run after them very much," complained the settler Johannas Megapolensis in 1644.

On the shore of the Virginia colony the English gentlemen were more openly romantic. Several went into the hills "to the Indians" in the first year of the settlement. By 1611 forty or fifty men had "married" native women. And by 1613, the Spanish traveler Diego de Molina noted that not just the men had "gone over to the Indians," but the Englishwomen, too, were "intermingling" with the native men. So strong were their passions that when a Virginia pastor preached a sermon chastising this love of the heathen, he was stoned from the pulpit by the men of the parish.

If they did not comprehend the spiritual relationship of native women to the land, they seemed to sense its strength. And they were captivated by it, personifying America as their mistress. The countryside was a "Paradice," wrote Robert Beverley, a colonial leader; it was "so delightful and desirable" one's "Eyes are ravished with the Beauties of naked Nature"; even the flowers made love in the meadows. One day as he walked in a pasture, he wrote, a "Flower of Flesh Color" had caught his eye. "The Form of it resembled the *Pudenda* of a Man and Woman lovingly joined together."

A man who imagined flowers making love could easily be seduced by the "Virgin Purity" of his fantasy. The "Indian damsels," too, had an "excess of Life and Fire," Beverley said, "which makes them frolicsom, but without any real imputation of their innocence." His fellow colonists were too vulgar to appreciate this. He admonished: "However this is enough for the *English*, who are not nice in distinguishing betwixt guilt and harmless freedom to think them Incontinent." These women were "not to be resisted."

The colonial government met this threat of romance by enacting what may have been the first racial laws in the land. Not only was the marriage of white men and native women outlawed, but children born of their loving were denied the rights of inheritance and property. By 1705 these children were to be legally defined as "mulatto," but the racial laws of the South were originally instituted by Europeans against Americans, not Africans.

And if love had become illegal, it had become immoral as well. Beverley disagreed. No "good Christian," he wrote, "should have refused a wholesome, straight bedfellow when he might have had to fair a portion with her as the merit of *saving her soul*." Love of native women "for Christ" might be a way of "converting these poor infidels and reclaiming them from barbarity." Not by a Bible, but by a phallus. . . . "Even their copper colored complexion would admit to blanching." Besides, "Intermarriage had been indeed the Method proposed very often by the Indians in the beginning, urging it frequently as the Rule. And I can't but think it would have been happy for that Country, had they [the English] embraced this proposal"—the "intermingling of blood" that Thomas Jefferson was to dream of as national policy.

That was the moral dilemma John Rolfe had faced in publicly declaring his desire to wed Pocahontas. His love for her was not of "unbridled carnal affection," he said, but was "for the honor of our country, for the glory of God, for my own salvation [from sin] and for the converting to the true knowledge of God and Jesus Christ an unbelieving creature, Pocahontas." And so the marriage was sealed and doomed. Pocahontas died soon after.

In his belief—if he believed it—that his beloved "unbelieving creature" was less than human because she was a Native American and a woman, Rolfe may be forgiven for not even knowing his wife's name. It was not Pocahontas, as he called her. Her name, in her own language, was Motoaka.

In the Massachusetts Bay Colony of the Pilgrim fathers Rolfe's dilemma became a neurosis which was to sicken the loves of men and women for centuries thereafter. The Puritans lived in a patriarchal theocracy that sanctified male dominance by an authoritarian religion. One can imagine the incomprehension of these settlers when they found that north of Plymouth the tribes were ruled by a woman, the "Squaw Sachem" of Massachusetts, Nanepashemet's widow. She was so powerful that she was one of the sachems who signed the Treaty of 1648. And she was so loving that she offered the site of Cambridge to her guests in honor of her affection for one of them, Captain Edward Gibbons.

Many of these Algonquin tribes were led by women. And the puritanical patriarchs no doubt thought themselves bedeviled by them. There was Wetamoo, the "Squaw Sachem" of the Wampanoags, Awashonks of the Sogkonates, Cochenoe of the Shinnecocks, and several more.

One of the Puritans who did recognize the power of native women was Thomas Morton of Merry-mount. In 1625, the "Lord of Misrule," as the colony's governor designated him, had established his own free settlement, "inviting Indian women for [his] consorts, dancing and frisking together like so many fairies, or furies, rather; and worse practices. As if they had anew revived and celebrated the feasts of the Roman goddess Flora." It was a "School of Atheism, as it were," fumed the governor. And one of those who attended these festivals was the "Squaw Sachem" of Massachusetts.

The "New English Canaan," Morton had christened his colony. And he did lovingly celebrate America, as he said, "Like a faire virgin, longing to be sped,/And to meete her lover in a Nuptiall bed." In this spirit he composed hymns and songs to the land, as to a lover:

> Then drink and be merry, merry, merry boys,
> Let all your delight in Hymen's joys;
> Lo! to Hymen, now the day is come,
> About the merry Maypole take a room.

And so Thomas Morton was "deported" to England. If the Puritans had been able to "embrace the Indian warmly," as had Morton, was the wistful comment of historian Wilcomb Washburn of the Smithsonian Institution, "it is not impossible to imagine a quite different United States." But it was not to be. All that remains of the memory of Merry-mount is a road sign on Route 3, outside of Quincy, Massachusetts.

The Idyll of the Daughters of Eve was about to be abruptly ended. In righteous anger, the Puritans imposed their severe strictures on the freedom of women. And any humanity between native women and white men was mercilessly punished. As early as 1623 one colonist had been accused of "keeping Indian women," while Edward Ashley was chastised for "comiting uncleanes with Indian women." Now the punishment would be death. When one colonist publicly announced his wish to marry a native woman, he was beheaded, his body "drawn and quartered, his legs and arms torn out, and his severed head placed on a stake in the town common.

So fearful of the women were these Puritans that they sought to exorcise them. "They believed in the priesthood of true male believers—and male control of society," wrote Charles Ferguson. They had "contempt for women as persons and Woman as [an] idea." And they thought, wisely, that strong women, native or white, were a threat to their patriarchal rulers. They were right.

One strong and independent woman did indeed arrive in Boston, in 1634. She was Mrs. Anne Hutchinson. After Sunday sermons, when men alone were allowed to discuss the affairs of the colony in church, she gathered the women in her home to hold their own meeting. These women had few rights. None had been allowed to sign the Mayflower Compact. And they had rebelled against the autocracy of the men in their first year in America. In that winter, when of eighteen wives but five survived, they had protested: "For men's wives to be commanded to do service for other men—they deemed a kind of slavery." Anne Hutchinson quickly found an audience for her doctrines of religious democracy and of salvation by love. You cannot sin, she said, if you possess the grace of God "in your heart." That, cried the patriarchs, was "the worst of all heresies."

To the Puritans, love of God was less of a sacrament than fear of God. It was to instill this fear that the council of men, in 1637, decided to slaughter the entire Pequod Nation. "By this means the Lord struck a trembling terror into all the Indians." But the congregation of Anne Hutchinson refused to join the slaughter. For this she was accused of heresy in rejecting the commandment to honor her father, that is, "the fathers of the Commonwealth." A Reverend Hugh Peters raged: She should have been born a husband, not a wife; her sin was her sex. And so she was banished from God's "chosen Land" and went to heathen Westchester, in New York, where she and her family were ironically killed in an "Indian raid."

The fear of women grew to hysteria. A few generations before the Salem "witch trials," the women who had attended the meetings of Anne Hutchinson were accused of "lying with the Devill."

John Josselyn wrote of one of these women, in 1638, as if she were a feudal grotesque, for, it was said, she gave birth to an infant "without a head, but having horns like a beast, and ear scales on rough skin like a fish called thornback, legs and claws like a hawk," a child "in other respects as a woman-child," a "female Devill." Josselyn was describing not a native woman, but a Puritan woman of Boston, whose sin was that she had talked of the equal love of God.

Eve, as a dream and as a human, was to be driven out of the Garden once more. Not to the East of Eden, but to the West.

The figure of America was no longer clothed in innocence in the imagination of the men of Europe. She reappeared fully armed and warlike. And more and more she was portrayed as a woman warrior. In the 1500s, a frightened Dutch engraver had forecast this image by showing America as a muscular naked woman warrior, her pubic hair flowing upward like wings of flame as she strode over the corpses of her victims, a spear in one hand and the severed head of a white man in the other. The caption read: "Cruel America has devoured many men."

In the eighteenth century it became more and more popular to depict America as an armed native woman. She was usually shown guarding the land, like a nude Statue of Liberty, welcoming the Europeans not with a torch but with a huge and ominous spear—a curious confusion of sexual symbols. The motif was to reach the height of its power in an awesome mural of a female warrior queen that Tiepolo painted on the ceiling of a German castle. His majestic Eve, wearing a great headdress and with a medicine pouch between her breasts, rode upon a Mississippi crocodile large as a dinosaur, as she blessed a panorama of all the world's races. She was a Roman goddess. On a silk pillow at her feet lay the heads of three white men.

It was understandable, then, that when the American Revolution began, one London publication depicted the founding fathers as a native woman, naked but for her G-string of feathers and her weapons. She cried out, "Liberty for ever!" as she swung her fists at the symbol of England, a regal lady who was beating America on her bare breasts and intoning: "I'll force you to Obedience, you Rebellious Slut!"

My People Are Dying of Guns

🐾 TESTAMENT OF Grace Black Elk, Ogallala Nation, Pine Ridge, South Dakota

In the quiet of an evening there was a social dance. The drums beat softly. Some medicine people had spoken from time to time. One of them had sung an old song. And then he sat down again and the dances went on, in a small circle in the middle of the room, until someone else spoke.

She stood by her chair, a stout, strong woman. And she began to weep.

"My people are dying!" she had said, her words weak. But when she began to cry, her words became stronger, "My people are dying! My people are dying!"

It stunned the people in the room to hear her cry out as she did. The quiet of the evening had been good to feel. And the medicine people had spoken philosophically of the "good feeling" of "being Indian" and at peace with the earth. She stood in the middle of the room now. And she cried, "There is nothing good in being a good dead Indian! My people are dying!"

Her eyes were unforgiving, black with anger. And the tears did not soften them. Her body shook when she cried, but she did not stop.

She was not a young woman. And she was not ashamed to weep in public.

She was Grace Black Elk. She had come from the Ogallala Nation and she had been one of the defenders of Wounded Knee

II. She had seen so many of her Lakota people die in her life that she could not halt her weeping.

At Wounded Knee II, she had said: "I know they'd like to shoot us. But we don't care. We want to think for ourselves. We've got a mind. The Great Spirit gave us a mind. And we can't live by somebody else's thinking."

One of the young Lakota women said of the women there: "We have the warriors, out in those bunkers. We have the women. And the women here are just like thousands of years ago. Some of the women are packing around guns and stuff. That's their thing. But the men are here with their families.

"And it's cool," she said.

They said that Grace was one of "the stronger ones." She did not need a gun to be a warrior.

In the room the silence surrounded her when her tears came. Many of the people could not look at her. They glanced at the floor.

Some of the things she said were hard to hear, because they were so painful. But some were full of laughter.

Some of the things she said were easier to remember. I did not write them down when she spoke. Nor did I go to the dance with a tape recorder. And so these are things I remembered later that evening, when I came home.

This is what I think she said:

In Denver, where I live, who is my neighbor? No one knows who lives next door. . . . That's no way to live.

The thing that was most wonderful at Wounded Knee was that we were one family. Our people came there from everywhere, all the tribes. The Lakota people were our own people, who we knew, but the other people became our people, too.

Everyone was one!

We had whites there. We had Chicanos there. We had the yellow. We had blacks there. It didn't matter who you were, what your color was, if you were a man or woman. Everyone there was a sister and brother.

Money was no good to us in Wounded Knee. It was no use for someone to have money. What good was our money? What could money buy in Wounded Knee?

Nothing! That was what money was. Nothing!

So we learned the ways to live without money. And we learned what money was really worth for living. I had $250 when I came to Wounded Knee. Suppose I had $250 in Denver? I would spend it right away. And what could I buy for that? Happiness? Dignity? Peace of mind? A good spirit? Sisters and brothers? In Wounded Knee I had all of these things and more things. Things I could not buy in Denver with my money.

So we learned that you can have money and be poor.

In the night, sometimes, these marshals and these FBIs would begin to shoot at us, for no reason. In our sleep. Everyone would go for cover. Then in the morning we would see someone lying there and we would shout: Are you hurt? Are you alive? No one asked who it was. All that mattered was were they alive. The important thing was *life!*

All these marshals and these FBIs were interested in was death. In killing us.

Once I liked these FBIs. I was on their side.

In Denver, on television, the FBIs were always the good guys. They came to help anyone in trouble. They risked their lives, you know, to help the poor people. So I said I was with the FBIs, I was always on their side.

But in Wounded Knee, when the FBIs started shooting at us for being on our own land, then I changed my mind.

After one day these FBIs came to see me. There was this knock on my door. I opened it. There were these two FBIs, very big men, and at first they startled me.

We are FBIs, they said.

Good, I said. I am FBI, too.

So they opened up their wallets and showed me all their shiny badges.

I looked at them and I said: I want one of those badges, too.

Because I am FBI, too. Because I am protecting my country, too.

They looked at one another in a confused way. They didn't know what to say.

So I said: When you go to see the Great Spirit, will you take your badges? To get into heaven? I think, maybe, if you do show your badges when they open the gates of heaven, maybe you won't get in.

They said: Mrs. Black Elk, we want to talk to you about Wounded Knee.

So I said: That's what I am talking about!

And I shut the door.

I could hear them standing there, by the door, laughing.

When I was younger I was a Catholic. That's the way I was baptized. Prayed to the saints. Went to the mission school. And believed in the Catholic religion.

Some of my Lakota people were baptized several times. One man told me he was baptized two hundred, maybe more, times. He was a Baptist, Methodist, Episcopalian, Catholic. Everything. But I was brought up as Catholic.

One day I asked a priest to tell me: What about our People who lived before you came? They weren't baptized. They lived for thousands of years like that. They lived good lives as they could, though maybe some part of them, like their hands, or a foot, or their tongue, did something wrong. Since they were not baptized, when they went to heaven did they have to leave behind their hands, or foot, or tongue, that did something that was wrong?

He didn't know what to say.

God is not like that. If God created everything, then He created every part of us equally. Everything that the Great Spirit created has to be holy. The earth has to be holy. The grass has to be holy. The human being, every human being, has to be holy, too.

Life is holy. That is my religion and that is what we should pray to. My religion is that everything the Great Spirit has given us on this earth is holy. Who needs statues?

So I am not Catholic any more. It is not religious enough for me.

I am a poor, uneducated woman. I am just a poor Lakota woman.

Who am I?

But I know this: My people are dying!

My people are dying on the roads. My people are dying in the hospitals. My people are dying in the prisons. Why are they dying? Because of the crimes they have done, because of the alcohol these so-called Christians sell our men, our boys, our women. And my people are told they are guilty of this and they are punished for this. But no one says these so-called Christians are guilty for selling the alcohol. And *they* are not punished. *They* are not dying.

My people are dying of the tyranny of the white man in the Bureau of Indian Affairs. Who has taken their land. Who has left them in hunger. They are dying of hunger on my reservation.

My people are dying of guns! When the white man came here we had no guns. He brought the guns to us. He taught us to kill with guns. He teaches our young men in the army to kill with his guns. And yet the white man says: Let there be Peace on Earth. Every Christmas he says that, Let there be Peace on Earth, while he goes everywhere on earth. And he kills people.

On Sunday the white man goes to church and he prays. And on Monday he goes to work and he makes bullets with the same hands he prayed with on Sunday.

If the white man wants Peace on Earth, let him stop making his bullets. Let him stop making shotguns. Let him stop making M-1 carbines and worse guns. Then, maybe, we may have peace.

In the old days, a "good" Indian did not say anything about these things. He would be silent. He was a "good" Indian because he did not go where he wasn't wanted and he did not say anything the white man did not want to hear.

I will not be silent! I will not be silent!

My people are dying! My Lakota people are dying! My Ogallala people are dying! And I will not be silent any more!

So I tell the white man he is wrong. He is going in the wrong direction. He will be dying, too. He will be dying, too, if he does not become human.

At Wounded Knee we risked our lives for our people. For our Lakota people. For all human people. For our sisters and brothers of every people. That's a good way to live. And to die.

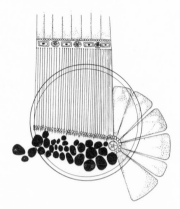

THE LOVERS OF INDIANS — II

ONE by one the men who had dispossessed Eve set out to seek a new Garden of Eden. They went West. But this time they searched for a paradise of men. After the fall of Eve there were many men who took the Virgin Land as their lover. On the frontier they would be their own masters. So they thought.

"The superb masculinity of the West," said one of them, was created for men:

> O to return to Paradise!
> O bashful and feminine!
> O to draw you to me, to
>   plant on you the lips
>   of a determin'd man . . .

Not words of love for a woman. It was a love song for the earth. "Away with old romance," thundered old Walt Whitman. In the West the new romance was "to plough, hoe, dig" the new land. The seeds of his manhood would "plant companionship thick as trees, along all the rivers of America." He wished to "teach robust American love" to the soil. He needed no woman, any more.

The man and the land; it was an unequal romance. And in some ways it was perfect; a man plowed the earth and dug in it, laid railroad beds upon it, prospected and claimed it, and was buried in it, until he was part of it. In all this the earth lay willingly beneath his plows and hammers, yielding to his desires, as a man's lover, or mother. The civilization of the white man was "masculine," said the historian of the early frontier of the West Francis Parkman. "The Germanic race and especially the Anglo Saxon branch of it, is particularly masculine."

In the Gardens of Eden in the West there was no need for Eve. She had been succeeded by the perfect woman—the earth. "Ma femme," Walt Whitman said. The wilderness was "the realm of men and their erections," said Henry Thoreau, the "earthly paradise of American imagination, a Garden of Eden" for Adam.

"Here is *man* in the Garden of Eden; here is Genesis and the Exodus," affirmed Ralph Waldo Emerson. "America is such a garden of plenty," there was no need of Eve. "When our population, swarming West, had reached the boundary of arable land, as if to stimulate our energy, on the face of the sterile waste, beyond, the land was suddenly in parts found covered with gold and silver, floored with coal. It was thought a fable . . ." And it was; in this fantasy of the fertility given man by Mother Earth, there was no mention of a woman.

And these frontiersmen, with their "excess of virility," suckled like newborn infants, wrote Emerson, upon "milk from the teats of Nature." The earth was less a lover than an all-embracing mother. Even the fiercest of these men in the wilderness, as Charles Wilkins Webber had said in his homage to Daniel Boone, plunged into the "virgin forest," in the popular metaphor of the time: "deeper and deeper, with yet more restless strength, into the cool profounds of the all-nourishing bosom of his primeval mother." It was man's desire to return to the innocence of his childhood, Walt Whitman said—"To Thy immortal breasts, Mother of All."

"Man's unceasing search for the lost self in the womb of the race," the author of *The Frontier Mind*, Arthur Moore, named it, "the universal longing for rebirth and recovery of primal strength." As though in the West men could begin again, and forget the memory of their past immorality, by being reborn. It was a desire of many men, the frontier fantasy. So much so that the historian of the late frontier, Frederick Jackson Turner, wrote of the West as a mother, the eternal mother, where "European men and ideas were lodged in the bosom [of America]," giving birth to the "perennial rebirth" of man. "She opened new provinces and dowered new democracies in her most distant domains with her material treasures," just for men. And she bestowed her motherly cornucopia upon these men, for their pleasure. She was pliant and passive, as a womblike dream.

It was a dream. The land was not the mother or servant of men. Nor was the earth as soft and compliant as a submissive mistress; nor was it the mother to anyone who walked upon it. Rather, it was cruel and ungiving. The land of the West was desert and its bosom was the rocky mountains. As always, the reality was more poignant and human than the fantasies. That was to become its tragedy, for the unrequited dreams of white men on the frontier were never to be satisfied.

And yet there were women in the West, whose strength the white men seduced and abused, but did not recognize. These were the native women, the first "pioneer mothers" of the frontier settlements, without whom it is doubtful if the white men could have survived. On the early frontiers there were few explorers and surveyors, fur trappers and mountain men, without a Sacajawea (the guide of the Lewis and Clark expeditions), who was the teacher and guide, lover and mother, to their "lost self" in those strange lands.

In the West the government census of 1870 counted about 172,000 women. But native women didn't count and weren't counted. In Montana there seemed to be "eight men to one woman," that is, "eight white men to one white woman"; in Wyoming there were six to one; in California in 1860 there had been twenty-three to one; and in Colorado it was thirty-four to one. And yet the uncounted native women may have outnumbered both.

One of the myths of men in the West has arisen from this "scarcity of women." Some male historians have thought women "had scarcity value, and were treated with exaggerated respect —that is, the 'good' women" (*America Moves West*, by Robert Athearn and Robert Riegel), but native women were neither scarce nor respected. And the men's thoughts about women, not their fantasies, may have come, in the beginning, from their images of native women, who were often the only women they knew: the "daughters of Eve" and the "whores of Satan" were replaced by the "lewd Squaw" and the "Indian maiden."

On the shores of the earlier colonies, the strength and independence of the native women had been a source of romantic myth for the white men. In the West these women were the enemy. The People of the prairies had learned the lesson of the defeat of the tribes in the East. And they fought the white man from the beginning; in turn, the conquering men now collected women like scalps. The "sensualism of the savage" was no longer a promise of paradise, said John Frémont, one of the conquerors; it was a "fiendish" snare for "civilized men." In the past, the conquerors of the land lost their "dignity in loose amours," wrote the Reverend Theodore Parker. No longer should the white man "mix his blood in stable wedlock with another race." On the frontier the pioneer had to maintain an "antipathy" to marrying native women he slept with, and "distinction of race" had to be "observed." If not, the native women might conquer the Christian by "loose amours"; the "sexual swinishness of the savages," as the Victorian Karl Marx was to call it, was threatening to "civilized men."

Conquest of native land and native women went hand in hand. The "dusky maidens" were the color of the earth. And they were to be treated in the same way as the earth.

On the frontiers in the 1700s, the French fur trappers set forth the manner when they "made free with [native] men and married their women"; but they did so as callously as in "Sodom of olden times." These Frenchmen were freer of self-righteousness than the English, but they nonetheless held native women in contempt. "Savages know neither love nor delicacy," said Pierre-Antoine Tabeau, who accompanied the Loisel expedition on the upper Missouri in 1803. In the West, a man "truly takes romance by the tail," he said, for the native women did "the most obscene things." So the French were not obligated to be moral, or loving.

It was a sanctimonious pose. For the French fur trappers "were mostly, if not entirely, connected by marriage with the Indians," observed one John Townsend in his *Narrative of a Journey Across the Rocky Mountains* in 1830. So "dark" and so "wild" were these fur trappers that, though "calling themselves white men," they were known as "French Indians," or "Squaw men."

So it was everywhere in the West. There was "an almost total want of chastity" wherever the white men went, wrote David Thompson in his *Narrative of His Exploration in Western America, 1784–1812*. Because, he said, "The white men who have hitherto visited these [native] Villages have not been examples of chastity; and of course religion is out of the question." One frontier writer put it this way: "To many of [the] young men their brief season on the frontier was a 'Mardi Gras' with no Lent to follow." And one traveler to the gold rush diggings at Sutter's Mill in the Sierra Nevada simply noted, "All these men live with Indian or California women."

In their memoirs these pioneering white men often went to great pains to insist upon their "antipathy." To "marry an Indian squaw and live with her tribe" was not an act of love, but an act of business, an old-time trapper, Caleb Greenwood, wrote in *I Married a Crow*. The White man "gained a home, with all its comforts" and "was allowed to pursue his occupation without fear of molestation," by this pretense of marriage. Anyway, "A trapper led a lonely, solitary life." The disclaimer was a necessity of Western history. The white men who lived among the tribes "were classed as 'Indian men' and bitterly hated by the other faction known as White Men," recalled a rancher in West Texas, W. K. Baylor. "Go with the Indians and you are an Indian," he said half a century later, remembering the white men who had "favored" the Comanches. They were "savage as any hyena and merciless as any tiger"; they were traitors.

These feelings of hatred led to the degradation of the men and women, native and white. In the mining camps and frontier forts of the pioneer West there were few wives of white men, except among the officers. And the women who gathered or were brought there were often whores or women who were treated as whores.

One of the military dispatches from the mythic Fort Laramie, in 1846, typically described these "numerous squaws, gaily bedizened," and the men's "mongrel offspring ramb[ling] in every direction through the fort." A few years later, in 1855, Second Lieutenant Sylvester Mowry wrote from Fort Yuma, in Arizona: "the principal occupation of the officers was drinking ale" and "roging" the native women. "Yuma is a hell of a place. We are surrounded by squaws all day long. Entirely naked [but for] a little fringe of bark." A "tender moment" with fifteen or twenty of the "dusky maidens" could be bought for a pound of beads; cost, $2.50. And though he had developed a "moral aversion to squaws," the lieutenant wrote, he had "several virgins in training."

"Indian women have not the slightest idea of virtue," said one straight-faced report to the Interior Department from Fort Sumner in 1866.

This was not merely the conceits of vulgar racism. It was "scientific" fact, widely believed by white men. One of the internationally renowned sociologists of the nineteenth century, Dr. Cesare Lombroso, had proved it with an array of statistics in his study *The Female Offender:* "In female animals, aboriginal women, and in the women of our time, the cerebral cortex is less active than in the male." And since women were more "primitive," they were closer to the "lower animals" and more "promiscuous." "The primitive woman . . . was always a prostitute and such she remained until semi-civilized epochs." She was a "born prostitute."

"Red Indian women [are] difficult to recognize for women," said Lombroso, but: "We have only to remember that virility was one of the special features of the savage woman" to understand that the "prostitute has a greater atavistic resemblance to her primitive ancestress, the woman of pleasure." These "Red Indian women" were "strangers to the coldness of normal women," he said. "They love with all the intensity of Héloise."

"In normal women love is weak," the good doctor explained.

The matings of male fantasy with the female reality was to create schizophrenic offspring. More than once.

In attempting to justify to themselves the inhumane and sadistic nature of their behavior, these men of the West seemed to become irrational, enraged at the sorrows of their victims and given to a worship of he-man machismo that thrived on self-inflicted pain.

Never had white men so voraciously seduced and raped this land. And never had they murdered women with less of a qualm. The "Sabine rape" of the West, Emerson named it, of which "Roman heroes" might be born. In the aftermath of the massacre at Wounded Knee, one smiling army officer was pictured posing with a Lakota infant on his knee, while the child's mother lay dead in the extermination ditch.

Sand Creek was the pinnacle of this peculiar sort of insanity.

In a strange ritual after their massacre of hundreds of Cheyenne men, women, and children in 1864, the Colorado Volunteers, under the command of the Methodist minister Colonel John Chivington, performed a sexual sacrifice that was to be repeated by soldiers elsewhere in the West. No one at the time, or since, has commented on the meaning and purpose of those blood ceremonies; though many have wept at their horror.

One soldier severed the sexual organs of a Cheyenne woman

and stuck the flesh in his headband. One soldier skewered a girl's sexual organs upon a stick and held them up in triumph. One soldier neatly sliced off the sexual organs of a woman with his hunting knife and stretched the skin across his saddle horn. One soldier found "a child of about three, perfectly naked" and at point-blank range shot it to death. One soldier opened the womb of a pregnant woman with his saber, and her unborn infant fell out beside her. There were women who had hidden in arroyos and sand holes, in clusters of five to thirty, who were methodically slaughtered by sword and gunshot, one by one. On the frontier those fallen in battle were often scalped and mutilated; but why this ritual of desexing women who were dead and castrating young girls? Not warriors, but women.

And so the fantasies of Eve in the Garden of Eden ended. But they did not die completely.

The official rifle-practice target used by the U.S. Army in the West had been affectionately named "The Kneeling Squaw." One hundred years later, in the National Guard armory of Bradford, Vermont, during the spring of 1973, Dr. George Margolis of the Dartmouth College Medical School found a "bullet ridden target" in the shape of a "hippie girl." The Sunday soldiers had filled the target's breasts with bullets. Few had shot at her head.

The romance of rape had left its hidden heritage. In the he-man of the macho traditions of the West, these myths about native women were transferred to white women. Schoolmarms and camp whores replaced the virginal "Indian maiden" and "lewd Squar." On the frontier, either a woman was placed on a pedestal or her place was in the gutter, a dual unreality that white women inherited from their men's mythology about native women.

In the no-man's land between these myths, any woman entered at considerable risk. "Wyoming wants women, and wants them bad," wrote the frontier editor of the Laramie, Wyoming, *Boomerang*; but: "There are very few households here as yet that are able to keep their own private poet." So only a woman who could sew a buttonhole and did not look like a "cross-eyed hog" need come West. In the Montana Territory, the early-day historian Thomas Dimsdale typified this male attitude when he intoned: "A woman is queen in her own home; but we neither want her as a blacksmith, plough woman, a soldier, a lawyer, a doctor nor any such professions . . . from strong minded she males, generally—'GOOD LORD, DELIVER US.' "

Of course, the women of the West, native and white, were all these things and more. In the mountains and the prairies there were more women who did "men's work" than in the cities of the East. There had to be. If they did not, the white men could never have survived either the elements or their own rhetoric.

Though the West had only 5 percent of the nation's population, it had 15 percent of the female "literary and scientific persons," 10 percent of the women doctors and journalists, and 14 percent of the women lawyers. In the lands west of the Mississippi there were 452 physicians and surgeons who were women.

So enduring are the he-man myths of the West that few, if any, women doctors, lawyers, journalists, or "literary and scientific persons" have ever appeared in the thousands of Western movies, novels, and television serials. The women in these fables are still the schoolmarm and town-whore version of the "Indian maiden" and "lewd Squar."

Even these women, created by the myths of men, were becoming unnecessary to the fable. The Garden of Eve, where women created a Paradise for men, was replaced by a Garden of Adam, where Paradise existed because there were no women at all.

In the myth of the Western man Cowboy Country had become wholly Man's Country. The mythic "Marlboro Man" of cigarette fame symbolized the changing scenery of masculinity: "Marlboro Country is and will remain an entirely male land," it was explained. And Vice-President John Benson of the Leo Burnett advertising agency put it bluntly: "We've discussed the idea of a woman in the ads. But the minute you put a gal in the ads, you domesticate the guy. You take away his mystique."

For had not America become a fatherland rather than a

motherland? As Russell Baker of *The New York Times* commented: ". . . surely the American flag is the ultimate male sex symbol. Men flaunt it, punch noses for it, strut with it, fight for it, kill for it, die for it. . . . Philosophically speaking the masculinity of the American flag is entirely appropriate.

"And women?" Baker went on. "Male pleasures and woman's sorrow, it sounds like the old definition of sex."

The romance of the West was the seduction of America. And as the women were conquered, so the land was conquered, fondly and forcefully, gently and brutally, with love and hatred: it was the romance of rape.

One afternoon last winter, I was talking to one of the most prosperous white Indian traders in the country. In this modern office, surrounded by relics of the past, he was a hardheaded businessman until he began to talk of native women. Suddenly his voice was soft.

"Sex," he said. "If Freud had ever gotten into the relationship between the Indians and whites, he would have laid it off to the sexual thing. There may be a lot in that. Like in the South, almost every guy with a plantation was screwing the good-looking black daughters of his slaves.

"Everyone who is spouting off about being part Cherokee or Mohawk or whatever—it is their great-great-grandmother who always was an 'Indian princess.' Never was their great-great-grandfather an Indian *man*.

"There has been so much animosity between whites and Indians in North and South Dakota, Montana, Idaho, and Wyoming that it's just unbelievable. Not being a Southerner, I don't know for sure, but I think it is the same kind of feeling Southerners have for blacks. It is both love and hate.

"Listen! The Indian women are not as shy and coy and standoffish as they appear. Not when it comes to sex!

"I have had so many opportunities, though I have not done it, of trading shells and stuff right here in the store, for a 'piece.'

Sure! I could screw four different women in a day. And they would either be Indian women or white hippies pretending to be Indian. I come on strong to them, kidding them about sex."

No sooner had the white trader said this than the telephone on his office desk rang. It was his white, suburban wife asking when he was coming home for supper. "I was just thinking of calling you," he said, a sly smile quickly disappearing from his face.

"Yes, dear," he said into the telephone. "Yes, dear, I am coming home right away."

It Would Be Real Interesting If It
Turned Out That All Indians Are "Fake"

✌ TESTAMENT OF Bob Ward, Indian trader

The sign said: "THE ORIGINAL TRADING POST. ESTABLISHED IN 1603.
TRADER: BOB WARD."

On a summer desert day, the dimly lit shop was as musty as
an old ghost-town general store. The atmosphere was hushed, distant, mysterious, dreamlike, romantic, surrealistic, archaic, and
historic. It was all that the city people with the anticipatory eyes
and expectant cameras had come to seek in the West.

"We sell history," said the trader, "to people who have none.
These people are dissatisfied with their own culture. Maybe
they're dissatisfied with the United States as it is. And they want
something different, something better."

The shop was cluttered with the past. Its showcases were
crowded with ancient revolvers and modern Indian jewelry; its
walls covered with old photographs and relics of the old "Indian
way"; its ceiling hung with cradleboards and animal horns; its
floor worn by the feet of generations of Pueblo people who had
come to sell their heritage to the traders and of the tourists who
had come to purchase it.

"It will not work," the trader said. "After thirteen years in
this business I found out that no one gets close to Indians. Not
even other Indians. These people aren't going to get into Indian
culture, no matter what they buy."

Then why was he an Indian trader?

Bob Ward had the ways of an old trader. He was a hardheaded romantic, who cherished his eccentricity; a loner in the tradition of the Yankee peddler. There was that odd boyish mixture of naïveté and shrewdness I recognized as a characteristic of all those scroungy, mean, honest, sly, and blasphemously straight-talking men I had once known in the trading posts along the wandering two-lane road from nowhere to nowhere that was fondly remembered as "Bloody 66."

In those gone old days there were no Hong Kong trinkets, no Italian moccasins. And like so many younger white men in the "Indian business," Ward would probably have traded his Lincoln Continental Mark IV to have traveled into the desert before the media "ruined Indian art." But he had come down the road too late.

And why, then, was he an Indian trader? He had not answered my question.

"Oh, I am looking for a lot of things and running from a lot of things," he said. "When I first came to Arizona, it was after a disaster in marriage and a disaster in business. And it was just a matter of getting away. For a long time I had been collecting Indian stuff. When I was growing up in Fresno, California, we had a lot of Indians. From the time I was two years old I had lots of exposure to Indians. So it was a natural thing to go into the Indian business.

"The funny thing is that I had very short hair. I was very clean. And the old-timers then had long hair, were rough characters. And they treated *me* like a hippie. Now I am considered one of the top traders in the business, and I am just as prejudiced against these long-haired young people, the hippies and the 'new Indians.'

"Yah! I started out as the biggest 'Indian do-gooder' in the whole world. I thought the Indians' country had been taken away. And all that. But they're systematically buying it back," the trader said, "with welfare payments."

His father was a sharecropper "in cotton and grapes," he said.

So as a boy he "chopped cotton." And he had fought for his survival the hard way; he had no use for pretensions. Even his own. One of his furies with the modern world, and he had many, was with the media "Indian fad." Though this had made him wealthy.

And why did this anger him so? I told him he sounded like an old prospector cursing because he stubbed his toes on gold.

This is what he told me:

As a kid growing up, one of the funny things I remember is that picture over my head. He looks like a Mexican don. He is my great-grandfather. And as the family history goes, he is supposedly Cherokee. He was on the Trail of Tears, from what I was able to find out from older relatives. His father was in one of the groups that split off and went to Texas.

Till I was in my twenties I didn't even know I was part Indian. I didn't even know this photograph existed. This is why: it was behind an old-time photograph of my great-grandmother, who was Irish. And one day I was cleaning the frame and I took the photograph out. And behind it, here was this man who looked like a Mexican.

So I asked my mother who he was. Well, she said, he's one of your ancestors. My dad had told her not to tell anyone that was her grandfather. His complexion was too dark, his hair was too dark, his eyes were too dark to be one of the family. Look at me: I'm blond-haired and blue-eyed!

But I am part Indian. Not that it makes much difference.

Now it has become fashionable. And I wonder: if the Chinese fad gets as big as the Indian fad, how are people going to say they are part Chinese?

The media began looking at the Indian fad about seven years ago. Dealers and collectors in New York went directly from the African fad to the Indian fad. And the funny thing is that African "trade beads" are now passed off as Indian "trade beads." Now those New Yorkers—they seem to start more fads than anyone else—are converting the Indian fad to the Chinese fad. How? I don't know.

So many people in this business go into it strictly for the profit. And there are tremendous profits to be made. There are dealers who have Navajo silversmiths and painters, Hopi kachina carvers, who work for them in their stores. And it becomes the work of a mechanic and a draftsman. The Indian is the mechanic, while the white trader is the draftsman, who says: Okay! This is what I want you to do next! Well, that Indian could be the best silversmith in the world, but he isn't creating anything. He is like a carpenter working on a building designed by a white architect, and making money for some white contractor.

No one knows how many millions of years it has taken to create the Indian art we now have. In the last fifty years it has gone backward in creativeness. Why? The Indians have let the white man manipulate their talents for economic profits; it's just a matter of economics. If only the Indians would use their own talent and their own creativeness.

A good trader? Someone who respects not just the Indian people, but has respect for the physical nature of the things he is dealing with.

Sure, I drive a new Continental Mark IV and have a new house and a new motor home and a new Jeep and all that stuff. But I have got it by being sympathetic to Indian art. There's a big difference.

The funny thing is that there is so little animosity among Indians toward the dealers who are the biggest cheats. I could never figure that out. Maybe it is a sort of reverse sense of humor.

And that's the way the Indians deal with me. They'll do their damnedest to cheat you, but it's done open-eyed. And you know it and they know it. If you push back only as hard as they push, it's all right, it's part of their sense of humor. They appreciate that. That's just the way their mind works. You can't change it and you can't improve on it and you just let it go and accept it.

Now, I don't know what Columbus found. But I'd guess that

the Indian we know today is still the same, pretty much, as he was five hundred years ago. At least, in the way that he thinks. Because he is still pretty easy to take advantage of.

Of course, he's adapted. He would be extinct by now if he hadn't. But he still thinks the same way.

The minds of the Indians operate so that they can be Indian when they want to, or white when it's profitable, or Chicano when it's necessary. They can do whatever does them the most good.

They're crazy smart!

Are they "real" Indians? Yes, I think so. But it would be real interesting if it turned out that all Indians are "fake," if some of these "new Indians" woke up one morning and said: My God! I am an Indian! I better start acting like old Cochise or Geronimo! And then, all of a sudden, they started becoming Indian.

A lot of these "Indian riots" are just an opportunity for them to let the public see them do their thing. These guys like the limelight. It's the same thing that makes an Indian war dancer such a spectacle to see.

Maybe there were five thousand National Guardsmen out there, with tanks and guns, to blow them away. But they still are going to make their name known. So the world knows that they are there. And if you have a few Charles Manson types, well, they can lead them right into oblivion.

If you give an Indian a microphone, you are going to get a whole lot of stories that have no bearing on anything except the microphone. This is why so much crap, so many lies, are put in print by the media.

Up to ten years ago the reservation Indians, like those Hopis and Navajos who lived way back, were unavailable to anyone. Even to each other. All of a sudden they are constantly exposed to outside elements: to Indians from the university coming to visit, to whites coming to visit, to book writers coming to visit.

Now I'm afraid they are getting pretty "Americanized." One of the biggest things that has happened to them is they got four wheels with four hundred horses attached to them. And that will make their life very bad. That mobility!

It is the same as far as the white Westerner is concerned. There is very little of the old West left, because of that damned mobility that has shrunk the world.

Fifty years ago it was almost impossible to get across the mud in the streets. Nowadays you can go anywhere. That one thing, the availability of travel, is just changing the Westerner into a whole different kind of person. And the damned media let us know what's going on in New York, in Boston, in Saigon.

And for the last four or five years, the people from the other parts of the country, and the world, have been coming to the Southwest. They rubbed off some of their bad points on us, and mixed them with some of our bad points. So it's not such a neat place to live any more.

That's why I am seriously thinking about Alaska. I've got this strong urge to go to Alaska. You keep reading that it's the last frontier. And it is sort of like the Southwest was when I first moved here, a sort of Wild West place where you have to take care of yourself. And where there are open spaces.

If I move to Alaska, I will have to go into the Eskimo business.

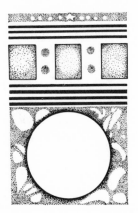

THE MYTHS AND RITUALS
OF THE WHITE INDIANS – I

Our Indian People are plain People. Beads and
Feathers were the creation of the White Man, who
brought the idea to America. It was the White Man's
way of keeping the Indianness.
  Bonita Wa Wa Calachaw (Keep from the Water)
  Spirit Woman and Artist (1888–1972)

In solemn ritual beneath the Grecian drapes embroidered with
gold thread, designed by my father, the tribal officials had
gathered in the East Room of the White House at the invitation
of the President. Dwight Eisenhower was in a good mood; he
loved Indians. And he welcomed his guests with fine words and
bad jokes, as Presidents have done ever since the defeat of the
tribes. It was an ancient white ritual.

One of the elders thoughtfully had brought a peace pipe. He
took it from his attaché case and blessed the President.

Since the tribal officials had become accustomed to the political rituals of the whites, they came prepared. They were re-

splendent in headdresses of eagle and turkey feathers, with beaded necklaces dangling on the breasts of their gray business suits. In politeness they hid their humor and discomfort, but wearing the costumes of two civilizations at once did get tiresome.

That evening, three of the elders were resting in weariness, in the offices of the National Congress of American Indians, waiting for their planes. In those days the offices were in an aging brownstone near Embassy Row. And the elders in their business suits, their "Indian" costumes in their luggage, looked like senior civil servants.

A photographer of a leading news service came in. He had been sent to photograph "those Indians," he said as he sat down to wait opposite the tribal officials. He didn't recognize them without their feathers.

An hour passed. "Where are the Indians?" the photographer finally asked.

"Here," one of the elders said, smiling.

The newspaperman was not amused. "I can't photograph you in business suits!" he blurted. "Don't you have some feathers? War bonnets? You know, something 'Indian.'"

So the elders opened up their luggage and donned the war bonnets they had worn to entertain the President. In the morning newspapers across the country a photograph appeared of the three old men in feathered headdresses—seen from the shoulders up. Their business suits had vanished.

In the eye of his camera the photographer had seen neither men nor Indians. He had looked into his own imagination, as if his lens were a mirror of what whites believed Indians should look like. Faced with real human beings, the photographer turned them into a white fantasy. And in doing so he turned Red Indians into White Indians, who were clothed in the white myths that whites wished to see.

It was a strange paradox. At that time, in the 1950s, the government had decreed that the time had come for the Vanishing Race to at long last officially vanish. They had been pro-grammed to become white.

That was the time, during the Eisenhower years, when the Congress of the United States decided the tribes must be "ter-minated." And in 1953 the government had enacted the "Ter-mination Act," once and for all to end its own treaty promises and legal responsibilities. Eleven tribes were officially declared to be nonexistent, and the Interior Department had adopted rules to divide and lease tribal lands—to whites. Soon the People would have nothing left but feathered headdresses.

That was the time, in the 1950s, when the "Unfinished Indian Wars" had begun again, wrote the former Commissioner of Indian Affairs, John Collier. Some of the whites, he said, were "con-vinced that the Red Indian having lost a continent, it is time now to square accounts with him altogether, by taking away the last of his tribal property, and ultimately, his tribal identity." Once that was done, the Red Indian would be replaced by White Indians; it was the act of "final termination," Collier said.

Some of the People might be reluctant to terminate them-selves, the government reasoned. And so it began a program to entice, cajole, and force them into the ghettos of the cities—which were then euphemistically known as the "Mainstream of the American Way of Life." It seemed clear to everyone then that rural life was backward, and that the cities were the fulfillment of the "American dream." So why deprive the tribal People of the cornucopia of wealth that was pouring forth in the shopping centers? The government program, called "Relocation," was so successful that by the seventies one-half of the tribal People lived in the cities.

Of course, by then the urban whites had begun their nostalgic migration back to the rural countryside. The Circle of Life would once more turn in the great mystery, but that was something whites could not foresee.

But why, then, preserve the fetish of the feathered Indians while seeking to de-Indianize them? It seemed mere perversity, or was it simple greed? Maybe it was both, but maybe it was neither.

That was the time, in the 1950s, when few whites thought, or knew, much about Native Americans. Fewer cared. "The tempers of American Indians have reached a boiling point," commented *The New York Times*. And then it mused, with a mixture of incomprehension and disbelief: "Who are the American Indians? Why should they boil, and why should the rest of us care?"

That was the time when a publisher of *Ramparts* magazine wrote to me: "Indeed, it's true. No editor really wants anything about 'real Indians.'" Even the editors of a crusading journal of liberalism, who had published a Lo-Pity-the-Poor-Indian article, told me when I suggested they publish one from an Indian point of view: "One Indian thing every two years is about as far as we can go." And a prominent university scholar laughingly voiced the disdain then common: "I thought all Indians were in museums."

That was the time when I was writing a book prophesying a tribal renaissance. One editor with whom I discussed the idea declared: "No one is interested in Indians. They don't sell." When that book was published, I was asked to appear on NBC-TV's *Today Show*. But a producer refused to permit any Indian to appear with me. "You are the expert," he said. "Hell, what do you need an Indian for?" As the editor of a national Sunday supplement with fifteen million readers told me: "No! We do not want any interviews with Indians. An Indian would be biased in favor of Indians."

That was the time when a mournful elegy to the vanishing of the Vanishing Race, sorrowful with compassion, was published in the *Harvard Law Record*, entitled "American Indians: People Without a Future." It was written by a young student named Ralph Nader. One hundred years before, a similar elegy had been offered to the Vanishing Race by a young student at West Point: "We behold him [the American Indian] now on the verge of extinction . . . soon he will be talked of as a noble race who once existed but have passed away." That one was written by George Armstrong Custer.

In this dreamlike world of myths and superstitions the whites believed in, there emerged the White Indian. Though he had been born of the Noble Savage invented by the early European settlers, he did not really reach maturity until he became the Vanishing Race of modern times.

Soon after the nineteenth century's "Indian Wars" had ended in the military defeat of the tribes, the vanquished warriors were hired as stage performers in "Buffalo Bill's Wild West Show" and similar circuses. Once the War Department's plans for the "annihilation" of the "Savages" were shelved, it became fashionable to perform "Custer's Last Stand," using the very warriors who had fought in that battle, but often they were dressed in theatrical clothing to make them seem "more real." The death of the West became an entertainment. And the Noble Savages became White Indians. So popular was this spectacle that it toured Europe, where it was seen by Queen Victoria and blessed by Pope Leo XIII.

Always, in years past, the whites had sought to preserve the image of the People they sought to doom. By refusing to see them as they were, by ignoring them and by their inability to listen to and to comprehend them, these whites of necessity recreated them as white myths. Neither knowledge nor ignorance in any way affected them. For once the Vanishing Race was created, the White Indians achieved a kind of immortality. They were to become a white totem, a touchstone, a sacrilegious deity that symbolized the lost innocence of the land.

One peculiar thing about the Vanishing Race was that it was forever vanishing yet never vanished. Had it done so, it would relinquish its power. So it had to go on vanishing perpetually, as if offering itself in sacrifice as a surrogate symbol of rebirth, a vicarious faith in America, a reaffirmation of the continuity of history for those who no longer had faith in their own history. No matter how often the Vanishing Race was wiped out in films or fantasies, it always reappeared. It had to.

And that may be one reason why the mythic members of the Vanishing Race have been so popular. They are survivors.

In each generation there has been a revival of interest in the White Indians. The "Indian fad" has been reborn every twenty years, said Frederick Dockstader, director of the Museum of the American Indian in New York. But, he said tartly, it has always been a "white fad," in which Indians have been "manipulated" by whites for whites.

On a cold winter day, December 1, 1967, the latest revival of the Vanishing Race was proclaimed by *Life* magazine—which itself vanished soon after. "The Return of the Red Man" was heralded on the cover by the reemergence of the "Spirits of the Warriors" in psychedelic war paint. The warrior who was depicted seemed to be a Mohawk, but it was difficult to tell; he had blue eyes, green and red hair, a yellow and purple nose, and pink ears. In spite of his colorful disguise he was, however, just a modern version of the White Indian.

The reincarnation of the Vanishing Race this time took the form of "rock bands" and communes of Ph.D. dropouts, said *Life*. It was a "hippie discovery," for the "Indian way" of life had become a "Happy Hippie Hunting Ground," where the white long-hairs of the counterculture masqueraded in the "ways of braves and squaws." In San Francisco's Haight-Ashbury the young " 'white Indian' may sport a feather and a headband" that were "believed to provide 'good vibrations' during an LSD trip," *Life* editors informed Middle America, conjuring up fearful images of its sons and daughters who had become howling red "savages" and "barbarians" by forsaking their suburban parents' civilized homes to "go native."

Still worse, the hippies' "Indian ways had infected the non-hippie world," *Life* said, as if describing a social disease. The fashion model "Twiggy" had been seen in a new "red Indian dress"; the Paris designer St. Laurent was fashioning "fringed belts" for evening wear; the exclusive Norell had created a cocktail gown decorated with the Cherokee alphabet. Lord knew "where it would end." . . .

These White Indians were appearing in the most unexpected places dressed like cultural transvestites. In *Teen* magazine a white girl posed in buckskins: the "POW WOW LOOK" was created. The old-fashioned Christmas catalogue of Sears, Roebuck offered sheets, pillowcases, draperies, and towels adorned with such designs as San Juan Pueblo pottery, Coushatta basketweaves, Kiowa Horse Parades, Blackfoot Arrowheads, Cheyenne Horsemen. There were best-selling books, hit movies, and even a Pulitzer Prize for an Indian writer, Scott Momaday. On a morning television show it was announced that "sand painting had become fashionable" for housewives. "You don't have to be a medicine man to become a sand painter," said the host. In a sunbathers' magazine the nudist "King and Queen" were crowned with a beaded headband and a war bonnet, their only clothes. And in the Vatican, Pope Paul was photographed wearing a feathered headdress of his own.

Said *Time*: "Indians are becoming fashionable." And as Calvin Trillin wryly noted in *The New Yorker*: "It is almost possible to hear the drums in the East Sixties" of Manhattan. While in the *Berkeley Barb*, an oracle of the underground press of the New Left, a White Indian had risen in the centerfold, adorned with a Christ-like halo. His naked squaw lounged erotically and obediently at his feet, like a little dog. That bit of radical-chic macho had appeared, it is true, before the rise of women's liberation. At that time though, the "hip tribesmen" seemed to think the male fantasy was quite "spiritual."

And while these "hippies have sort of adopted the Indian as the symbol of their way of life," wrote the *Berkeley Barb*, their suburban parents had begun to invest in the Indians' culture. "POPULARITY OF INDIAN OBJECTS SOARING," reported *The New York Times*. On Madison Avenue, at the Sotheby Parke Bernet gallery, the "first major sale of American Indian art, including Navajo rugs," was announced by Harmer Johnson, the gallery's director of "Primitive Art." "We expected the sale would fetch $40,000 to $50,000, but instead it fetched $170,000." On Fifth Avenue, a silver-and-turquoise necklace and bracelet that may have sold for no more than a few hundred dollars in a desert trading post was now advertised for $18,000. In the *Capitalist Reporter* the news was treated as a religious revelation: "INDIAN ART: TRIPLE YOUR MONEY," they proclaimed, "IN TWO YEARS." Even old pots were "investments that rank with good contemporary paintings" and "gold and real estate." And "the end isn't even in sight," said Harmer Johnson.

More than simple stone, the "spirit of our heritage" was being offered the buyers of Indian jewelry. It did not matter that many of these "ancient relics" and "sacred jewels" were not Indian-made, but had in fact been manufactured on assembly lines, often by hippie entrepreneurs who had gone West to seek the spiritual way of the Indians and, not finding it, stayed on to cash in on the White Indian fad.

Even the spirit will be packaged and marketed in a commercial society. One store advertised "the priceless spirit" in the jewels, at "Bargain Discount Prices." Another offered a "Genuine Indian Pendant" of sacred turquoise to be worn in the navel for "truly sensual" belly dancing. The White Indians may have bought the spirit in the stones, but in doing so they were no nearer to whatever they were seeking.

"They have stolen everything else. So now the whites want to steal our culture," said Clyde Warrior long ago. And so it was, as John Major Hurdy was to say in *American Indian Religions*: "The American Indians have religion (maybe we should steal that from them, too)." But it was not that simple.

"Someday the jewels on their necks will be so heavy they will choke themselves on our spiritualism," said Alonso Ortiz, a young scholar from San Juan Pueblo and an anthropologist from Princeton University. "They want to buy spirituality through materialism. Because they live in a society of materialism. And that's all they know."

If the whites had known little of the Indians before, they knew little more now. But the fad had grown from fantasy to a fascination that did not seem to rise and fall in the usual pattern of public interest. There was something profoundly disturbing and uneasy in the strange mixture of nostalgia and persistence with which these White Indians pursued a culture they did not and could not comprehend, and had for so long sought to destroy.

"Spread of Indian culture continues to grow—among non-Indians," declared Tyrone Steward, the publisher of *American Indian Crafts and Culture* and *Indian America*, both white magazines. "The beads, bells and feathers become symbols of the surface image and attract the masses," but "dedicated purists [have] come to believe in the Indian way and become entirely engrossed in a pattern of living Indian," he said, even "to putting their newborn [babies] in cradleboards.

"One of the ironic things is that many non-Indians become more 'Indian' than the Indians," Steward continued. "A dear friend of mine said something like this: 'I know I can never be an Indian, but sometimes I forget I'm a white man.'"

And yet the deeper the interest in Indians became and the wider the acclaim for Indian culture, the less it seemed to have to do with the real People. The masquerade of these White Indians was not so much a farce as it was false.

In the conquest of any culture something is gained and something is lost. The conqueror easily gathers up the material spoils —it is always the spirit, the soul, the essence of a way of life that is most difficult to conquer. When the Romans conquered the Grecian gods and goddesses and carried them away into their own religion, they clothed them in the robes of Olympus but not in its philosophy, they recreated their forms but not their meaning, they imitated their bodies but lost their spirits. For all her beauty, the Venus of Rome would never become the Aphrodite of Greece, risen from the sea.

So it was with the rituals of the White Indians. Once they had created the Vanishing Race by their deeds. Now they wished to recreate its culture as they desired it to be by their myths. Like the Romans who hoped to adopt the glory of Greece through conquest and clothing, they could not.

In the City of New York there is a store where White Indians may buy "red skin" cosmetics.

The face and body makeup comes in a rainbow of shades on an Indian Brown Base. Once the White Indian's skin is ethnically browned, the unexposed body may be clothed, via a Do-It-Yourself Kit, with a plastic Ghost Dance Shirt, a Chief's Bonnet of Imitation Eagle Feathers, a Silk Mohawk Wig or a Synthetic Nez Percé Wig, an Indian Princess Dress with Imitation Elk's Teeth, and an aluminum peace pipe that doubles as a fake tomahawk.

Someone has "to preserve the fascinating heritage of the red brothers," says the proprietor of the store.

History Has Passed Us By

❦ TESTAMENT OF Ike Merry, Director,
All-Indian Inter-Tribal Ceremonial

The old Yankee peddler didn't just sell "things." He peddled ideas.

And with his profits he earned the cloak of history, a disguise he wore as defiantly as a pair of old pants. He was the philosopher of traditions that no longer existed. When the fabric of history had worn so thin it was preserved as an antique in the museums for tourists, the Yankee peddler left the country roads of New England. He went West.

In the West the Yankee had no history. He was an immigrant, a newcomer, an alien. So he began the search for a history that offered a new beginning and an old tradition. He "discovered" the Indian once more.

Mountain men and squaw men, traders, cowboys, and ranch hands, journeymen tinkers and medicine show doctors, hobos and circuit preachers, thieves and newspapermen, all had this in common: They were pilgrims to a Garden of Eden, a perfect Nirvana, that was forever beyond the very next hill. They were strangers in paradise.

Old Ike was a modern refugee in this pilgrimage. In his case, "old" was a word of affection, not of description, as it usually is among a people without a history.

Edward ("Ike") Merry was a twentieth-century pilgrim. In a time of technological men it would be neurotic to admit to romanticism. So he did not. In a voice remarkably like that of

Humphrey Bogart, he told me he had journeyed to the West "because of my sinus condition." It was the truth, but it was not. He was a hard-mouthed Yankee, from New Hampshire, and his self-deprecation was mostly an exaggeration.

Back East he had worked for the iconoclastic publisher of New Hampshire's *Manchester Union*, old William Loeb. "He's not a New Englander!" scoffed Ike. "He's an Oyster Bay aristocrat. He emigrated up from Wall Street into New Hampshire in search of the 'real America.' He's an outsider!" Infuriated by the "outsider" who ran a newspaper as a projection of his own ego, the native son went West, where he himself was the outsider.

In the old days a newspaperman traveled as light as a bindle stiff. The cigarette dangling from yellowed teeth, a misshapen fedora, and a battered typewriter were all the equipment he needed for his trade. And except for his cynical view of life, his religious disbelief in belief, all of a small-town newspaperman's worldly belongings would "fit in his hat," as they said. He would go from town to town, like a medicine show barker. That was how Ike remembered it.

"There was one newspaper in a town. So if you couldn't get along with the editor, who usually was the publisher, well, you would move on to the next town.

"And that's how I ended up here!"

In a "crummy little town" in the desert, he discovered his Garden of Eden. He was as surprised as he was awed. He had found a belief.

And what had he found?

"Ceremonial! It captured me! It was bigger than me! It was a pure idea!"

For a generation Ike was the director of the All-Indian Inter-Tribal Ceremonial, billed as the world's largest extravaganza of American Indian dance and horsemanship since Buffalo Bill's Wild West shows. In its heyday the Ceremonial attracted 100,000 visitors yearly, from all over the world. In time Ike got to be known as "Mr. Ceremonial."

It became a religious devotion to him. The newspaperman

from New Hampshire was the "savior" of the disappearing culture of the Indians; he ran the Ceremonial like a crusade.

"Sure, I preached. I cajoled. I devoted my life to preserving the Indians' cultures. There are very few pure ideas left in this world. There isn't much beauty left either. And in its way, the Ceremonial was that pure idea of beauty."

One young Navajo scoffed: "The Ceremonial was a projection of his white ego."

In the town there were protest marches held to halt the Ceremonial. The commercial "EXPLOITATION OF INDIANS" was pointed out by one picket sign. Another read: "GIVE US BACK OUR CULTURE." There was no peace in his Garden of Eden. There was gunfire in the streets. In fear, one year, the merchants canceled the Ceremonial.

Ike resigned.

"No!" he thundered in his Bogart whisper. "I did not resign! I quit! When a man resigns he sends a letter that says how much he enjoyed his work, but he has had a better offer. When you quit you stand up on your chair and piss all over your desk!

"After twenty years you find out you have been nothing but the town idiot! 'Jesus Christ! All he talks about is the Ceremonial!'

"Maybe I'm a damned gadfly!"

He had become that lone wanderer once more. He had nowhere to go. "Now I am sixty-two. I am here. Where am I going to go?"

This is what he told me:

All of us had primitive beginnings.

Now, what sets an Indian apart from the rest of us is that we left our primitive beginnings a thousand years ago. He didn't. Now, I don't think that's a virtue. To claim that I am superior to you because I am as primitive as my ancestors, the way the Indian militants do, that seems a peculiar virtue to me.

They are human beings. They laugh and cry just like everyone else. Sure. But the Indian is just the ragtag end of a culture that reached its peak a thousand years ago. He is just a little man trying to hang on to an identity that was of great significance long ago. It doesn't tear him down if you see him in that light. He would understand himself a lot better if he saw himself that way.

And the Ceremonial was an attempt to create that understanding. The average American still sees the Indians in terms of John Smith—I mean Pocahontas.

Nowadays there are few "real" Indians left.

The Ceremonial was more meaningful fifty years ago, in 1921, when it began. In the first programs there was a real interest in real Indians: *Meet the American Indian before he is no longer the American Indian! See him now before he changes! Here are Indians you don't know anything about! This is your opportunity to know him before he is gone!*

Whoever wrote the first programs was a man of considerable insight. He understood the purpose of the thing.

Our approach to the Indian was: *This is you! This is your culture! You never look at your culture! You just accept it!* So we helped the Indian to be Indian.

At the time, the Ceremonial was a big thing. The town had no paved roads, in or out, until 1934. It had one little railroad line, one hotel. So the Ceremonial was like Chautauqua, the big tent.

One fellow told me, "For weeks before the Ceremonial we used to dress up like Indians, run around, have foot races." It was a big social event. The old-timers really loved the Indian, to play at being Indian, to see the Indian dances. So there was a good feeling on both sides. Everything was settled with a handshake.

When I first came here, the officials of the old Santa Fe Railroad had been with the line maybe thirty years. They had real affection for the Indian, for the Southwest. They collected Indian things. That generation is retired now. Or dead. They have been replaced by a group of younger, more industrially oriented officials, to whom the Southwest is just a job.

Same thing with the old Fred Harvey hotel people. The old-

timers would buy things of the Indians, but they wouldn't sell
them. They would fall in love with them. They would put them
in the vault. But the new generation of Fred Harvey people
feel: Hell, we're not a museum! I guess they just sold it all. The
old-timers would turn over in their graves if they saw the things
they sold. Yes, there has been a change.

Once the town became a spot on a ribbon of concrete running
across the country, everything changed. The Ceremonial was a
flame a few of us kept alive. But it died.

Now the sole business of the Ceremonial is business. Is it
commercial? Everything is commercial. The Ceremonial is dead.

Everything changed. The Indians who had come for years to
dance, they were getting old. We paid them five dollars a day.
But they didn't dance for that five dollars a day. They danced to
say: I'm proud to be Indian, to dance my best. Well, that
changed. Now the Indians would come in and say: Why not give
us twenty-five dollars a day? Hell, what's twenty-five dollars a
day? they'd say. It is nothing! For all the costume changes, the
long trip, it's nothing!

Look, it's the spirit of the thing that's dead; it's the good
feeling that's dead. It's not a pure idea any more.

These militant Indians who say the Ceremonial is an insult
to their culture, their religion, have lived in Los Angeles or
Chicago all their lives. They are trying to recapture something
that has died. They never knew it. They don't know what it was.
They are not real Indians. They are mostly half-breeds.

After dealing with the Indians as I did for so many years,
dealing with these militants wasn't easy. These militants give
you no quarter at all. And they would make outrageous demands. I mean demands they knew could not be met.

On the day the Ceremonial opened they would come in and
say: We're going to occupy your office! And they would occupy
it.

I would sit there trying to work, while exchanging sarcastic
pleasantries. So the police chief comes in and he says: You want
them out? And I say: Yes. And he says: Get out! And they scat

like the wind. Someone then comes in and says: Well, we ought to talk to them. So we bring three or four into the office, and there's talk. That's exactly what they wanted. They say: We want a permit for a parade to protest the Ceremonial. Someone says: Maybe we can give you a permit if you promise to do this or do that. We don't want any trouble. So they've breached the wall. It was like Hitler marching into the Ruhr. If we had fired one shot, they would've turned back. But we didn't.

My position was: Fellows, there is a line. This is where *I* draw the line.

One Saturday night I was going to supper when Casuse, the militant leader, met me. And he said: Here's our final demands. Take them.

Now, we had been meeting with the police, and the police had said: Our intelligence indicates this is the next stop for AIM. That was at the time of Wounded Knee. The police had infiltrated the militants; they had a couple of people in the militant group. They were talking about burning down the exhibit hall. You know, we had bomb scares and we had Molotov cocktails thrown at the downtown office of the Ceremonial.

So I said: Who are you?

He said: Casuse.

So I said: I don't have any authority to take your demands.

He said: Here is this piece of paper.

So I said: Don't give it to me.

And I started walking up to the cafeteria. He and this other guy followed me. They were back about ten feet. They were talking loud, so I would hear: The Goddamned white man! Who does he think he is! But I just walked to the cafeteria. Casuse followed me through the doors. Now this is the same guy who was going to kill the mayor! He just walked on through.

So I said: Okay, Casuse! That's as far as you go!

He kind of edges on.

So I took hold of him. I said: No further!

And he said: You filthy white man! Get your hands off me! These are our final demands to you!

So I said: I'll give you *my* final demands. Get out! And stay out! And take that Goddamned piece of paper and throw it in the rubbish with the rest of the rubbish.

He turned around and he walked down the hill.

In my mind a young Indian like Casuse needed someone to say: Look, that's as far as you go; you are getting unreasonable! If someone had done it, that would have established his position in society! And he would still be alive today.

No one ever said to him: There is a limit to the power, to the influence, you can exercise. And you should know the limit you have to live with. So that's it!

Pity the "poor Indians"? Those parlor-car liberals are always ready to shed everyone else's blood to defend the Indians. It's an easy way for them to excuse their inherited wealth, which their ancestors stole from the Indians long ago—by blaming the horny-handed individuals out here who have to deal with Indians today.

Now, some people are trying to rewrite history to say what we did to the Indian was morally wrong. As if every country hasn't done the same thing: the Romans, the Greeks, the Assyrians, the Huns, and everyone else. You can't rewrite civilization and make a morality play of it.

The people who survived, they proved they had the right to survive. If you look at history in a cold, dispassionate way, it is the truth.

To me the greatest promise of America is that this is a nation where your nationality is immaterial. The odd thing about America is that it is the only country in the world that doesn't have a common bond, like a common religion, a common ethnic background, a common history, or common family roots. None of these things hold people together. People are held together by being individual.

Any movement that is now on by blacks, Chicanos, Indians, and all the others to Balkanize our country is going to destroy the whole concept and the whole foundation of America.

So those writers who are creating and sustaining the fallacy of minorities [Ike glared at me], and the politicians who do so, are doing a disservice to the country.

I am an Irishman. I feel like standing up and saying: Look! There's more of you Goddamned Chicanos and blacks and Indians than there is Irish in this country. We are a minority in a country of minorities!

So this Southwest thing about being Anglo is the craziest Goddamned thing that I ever heard of in my life.

What is an Anglo!

There is an apocryphal story of the time this civil rights thing was at its height and Congress was sending investigating commissions all over and they sent one to some village in northern New Mexico. So they called a meeting in their county courthouse and all the people came. The chairman of the commission, he explained to the people that they were there to investigate the problems of minorities.

A sort of leading village spokesman got up. Well, I don't know, we don't have any trouble here, he said. Half of us are Mexicans. Half of us are Indians. We only got one Anglo here. And he's a nigger.

In this country when I was young it was never a disgrace to be poor. Poor, but honest! It was a disgrace to be shiftless, but not to be poor. Now it's a case of the poor making being poor a battle cry. I'm poor! I'm a minority! You owe me something. And the poor, those who are perpetually poor, who will always be poor, look to the government, to Big Brother, to 1984. A guy aspires to be politically poor so he can qualify for the benefits the politically poor get.

They demand it!

Now, that is the Goddamned thing. The blacks and Chicanos and Indians have gone from requests to demands. It was a shift in emphasis, which has upset the guidelines we had before. They don't know their position in society.

So I say the Ceremonial has had its day. History has passsed us by.

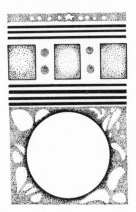

THE MYTHS AND RITUALS
OF THE WHITE INDIANS — II

IT was generally known that the man who started World War II had by his bedside the thirty, or more, of Karl May's collected works [the romantic German writer of Indian tales who had never been to America] and that these books about Indians, trappers and hunters, which strike any normal boy of fifteen as at least ridiculous were his [Hitler's] favorite reading matter," wrote Erich Maria Remarque. "Those were the Führer's favorite books."

On the sands of the rainbowed deserts in the valleys of the godlike mountains of northern Arizona there live a People whom a coal mine executive whose company was strip-mining their sacred lands admiringly called "the last of the Noble Savages." Why? They were just about "the only real Indians left," he said. It was meant to be a compliment, for "all his life he had searched for the Noble Savages"—the "real Indians."

In a romantic effort to capture the image of the Noble Savages before they all vanished, the social scientists, writers, film makers, lovers of Indians and anthropologists went among them, like missionaries in reverse, with their tape recorders, movie cameras, video systems and sound equipment to pay homage to their "dying culture." So many came that it was said, "A modern Indian family consists of a man, a woman, their children, a dog and an oral historian." It was "our last chance to preserve the culture of primitive man in America," said a spokesman of the American Anthropological Association.

One man who came seeking the Noble Savage (like most seekers he found what he sought, for he looked for little else) was a photographer filming the NBC-TV spectacular *The Navajo Way*. In his script he romantically enthused: "The only real Navajo is a sheepherder." Navajos who worked on jobs in the cities were merely "imitation white men," he told the tens of millions who watched his loving tribute to the "ancient ways of the People."

Years before, most of the People had "entered the wage economy," one Navajo official commented. That meant most of the People were no longer real Indians to their white admirer, for they had betrayed his image of the Noble Savage. . . .

Then there was the producer from a major Hollywood studio that decided to make "a Red Power movie" about a contemporary Noble Savage, but wasn't quite sure whether "Red Power" was Noble or Savage.

One morning a young man came to our home in New Mexico with a proposed budget of $800,000 for this "Red Power" epic in his briefcase. The night before, he had phoned, saying that he was ready to "fly out of L.A." at once. He "dug Indians." I invited him, not expecting he'd come. There he stood in a newly fashionable unkempt beard (this was several years ago) and with an uneasy, newly acquired hip vocabulary. Man, he said, if I would lay a "Red Power" treatment on him, he would lay $800,000 on it. I served him coffee. But he did not subside. There was just one problem, he said. What exactly was Red Power?

"It isn't like Black Power, is it?" He frowned. The studio was not much for that.

So I reassured him: "Red Power isn't Black."

There was just one more problem, he said. In this movie, which would be devoted to preserving, restoring, strengthening and revering "Indian nobility," the studio wanted their current box-office star to play the Noble Savage. The star, need it be said, was white. . . .

And then there were the directors who created their own Noble Savage in modern images. He was named "Little Big Man" and "The Man Called Horse" and "Billy Jack."

These reincarnations of the Noble Savage were so imaginative that all the latter-day warriors were white actors—not merely underneath their painted skins but within their theatrical minds. By combining the cowboy bravado of Clint Eastwood and Bruce Lee's karate expertise (these movies made karate a "big scene" on the Navajo Reservation), they created a fashionable fantasy world of contemporary Noble Savagery. A sort of tribal Godfather III. They simply turned the old Western movies upside down, so that the "Noble" white men became Indians, and the "Savage" Indians were now white men. And these Noble Savages were reborn as murderous liberals. . . .

And then there was the internationally known actor who had wished to be, or play at being, a Noble Savage throughout his fabulous career. Late one night a friend phoned me in desperation. For three days and nights a group of Indians had been in session with the actor in his New York suite. They had been trying to think of a film story for him. And they had run out of ideas, though evidently not alcohol. Would I please come right up to help? He was a lover of Indians, and they wanted to help him. I didn't go. That was fifteen years ago. Although he's often tried, the actor still has not become the Noble Savage he has always wished to be. . . .

And then there was the "classic" film that showed how a Noble Savage was all but destroyed by being educated at a university. It told of a young man who left his tribe to seek an education. On his graduation he returned to his Reservation to help his People. But he was shunned by his tribe because he was "too white." Saddened, the young man "took to drink" and, "after a long chase," was killed by his own tribesmen. The moral was clear: education may destroy the Noble Savage, whose "child-like mind," as the founder of American psychology, Stanley Hall, once wrote, may become neurotic if overstrained. Enraged by what they said was a "false image" of their People, leaders of two Chippewa tribes went to Washington to protest personally to the President. They requested "regulation of moving pictures in which they [the tribal People] are shown."

The "classic" film was *Robby and the Redskin*, made by Selig's Western Film Company. The star was Hobart Bosworth, a white man. The President the Chippewas went to Washington to see was William Howard Taft. And the year was 1911. . . .

And then there was the novelist who, like many writers before him, journeyed into Indian country in vain search of the Noble Savage, the "world of neolithic man [where] Indians do not become white men." But no matter how he searched, nowhere could he find the "real Indians" of his dreams.

So in disgust he talked to those educators, university students, health technicians and engineers among the tribes whom he met in his brief journeys of reportage. They were not "real" Indians, he proclaimed; if they "could be Indian," then anyone could be Indian. For the "Indian is a man aware of his dying. He gasps, his nerves convulse [and] he calls himself an activist," but he "is lost in the irreversible time of modern man"; he is no longer "pure." One young man who was interviewed by the writer commented: "He was a Jew. Maybe he was searching for his own lost culture. And he thought we were Jews."

The Death of the Great Spirit: An Elegy for the American Indian is what Earl Shorris named his obituary. Once again the Noble Savage was mourned by the white mythmakers who created him.

For centuries the death of the Noble Savages had been reported. In the 1600s Father Bartolomé de las Casas began a requiem that was to be sung of the "doomed Indians" ever after. The mourners have included Cristóbal Colón (Columbus) and

Reverend Cotton Mather, Daniel Boone and George Catlin, George Armstrong Custer and the anthropologist Franz Boas.

And yet the Noble Savages did not die in the myths of the whites, any more than the Vanishing Race could ever vanish. Myths that never existed in reality always seem to have the longest lives. So in our time the myth of the Noble Savage has been revived with greater fantasy than ever.

The "Epic of the Battle of Wounded Knee" II, as seen in the newspapers and on television, was the quintessence of this self-deception. It brought together all the myths and mythmakers. And the performance of the media in acting out these myths of the Noble Savage was fascinating to see. For it was a true portrayal, not of Lakota People on the Pine Ridge Reservation, but of the White Noble Savages in New York City and in Washington, D.C.

It seemed as "real" as the evening news. The People were playing themselves, and speaking for themselves. Yet their images were seen, as they were heard, through the white eyes of the cameramen and newsmen.

The Lakota protest was first seen as "A TINY CAMP OF INDIANS WITH FEW WEAPONS" (on March 5, 1973, in *The New York Times*), but it soon became "A SUSPENSEFUL SHOW OF RED POWER" (on March 19 in *Time* magazine). Not merely the images of the media, but the policies of the government, were the victims of the old White Indian myths, as the inflammatory headlines increased:

UPRISING ON PINE RIDGE

FBI BATTLES INDIANS

FEDERAL FORCE RINGS WOUNDED KNEE

ARMED INDIANS OCCUPY CHURCH

. . . BURN TRADING POST

. . . HOLD WHITE HOSTAGES

WAR DANCES OF AIM WARRIORS

It sounded like an echo of the penny dreadfuls and the scholarly volumes on the "merciless Savages" of the nineteenth century, those books that delighted in "blood-lusting" accounts of murder and bestiality, such as Reverend Henry Davenport Northrup's tale of terror, published in 1891:

INDIAN HORRORS

OR

MASSACRES BY THE RED MEN

WITH

STARTLING DESCRIPTIONS OF FAN-
TASTIC DANCES; MYSTERIOUS
MEDICINE MEN; DESPERATE BRAVES;
SCALPING OF HELPLESS SETTLERS;
BURNING THEIR HOMES, ETC. ETC.
THRILLING SCENES
AMONG
THE INDIANS

When there was nothing more dramatic to be seen than the beauty of the wind on the prairies, the White Indians posed the People as dramatically as Buffalo Bill ever did. They were creative.

Grace Black Elk simply said: "They lied."

She had been at Wounded Knee. In many of the battles then, and before, she was a Lakota leader, and she spoke bitterly. "Our young men sometimes had no bullets in their guns. Some of them were too hotheaded. Some of them would say, I'm going to get me a white-eyes today. And so we had to calm them, cool them down. And so we had no bullets in our guns until we were shot at. Then we loaded.

"They did not say these things on television. Ever!

"One day, in the television news, they said the medicine men had put war paint on the foreheads of our young men. I don't remember which said that, CBS or NBC. They lied. It was ashes from a sacred ceremony, that blessed these young men and protected them from being killed. And so when I saw the television people, I asked them: Why did you say that? You know it was ashes!

"They apologized.

"So I told them: If you admit you were mistaken, say so. If you don't, then the next time I see a priest put holy ashes on the forehead of someone for Ash Wednesday I am going to say on television the whites are putting on war paint."

After the stage lights were dimmed, the camera lenses had been covered, and the newsmen had put away their pads, a curious thing happened. The mythmakers of the media began accusing the Lakota of using them. It was all "bad theatre," with "outmoded makeup—war paint—and melodramatic lines aimed at the TV cameras," said *Time*. It was "a media coup d'état," said *The Nation*, "a group theatre" performance. It was a "staged" spectacular by "media Indians," said *TV Guide*; the wily Lakota had manipulated the innocents from New York and Hollywood.

On the prairie, life for the Lakota was poor and hard. In no ways did they resemble the Noble Savage of the media; those images were not of their creation. It was what the white eyes of the cameras had seen, and what the white eyes of the television viewers had wished to see. If the accusations of the media were true, why had they so lavishly indulged in the "bad theatre"? Why had they been manipulated so willingly? And if the would-be White Indians of the media had fantasized these struggles of the Lakota for survival and revival, perhaps they glorified Wounded Knee II not because of the needs of the Lakota, but because they themselves wished to be the would-be Noble Savages.

"So many of these people try to romanticize the Indian by making him too savage or too noble," said Delbert McBride, curator of the Capitol Museum in the State of Washington. "The image they project is the image of themselves. It is not how they wish to see the 'Indian,' but how they wish to see themselves."

"Then our People have to make the white myths into realities, by becoming living myths," said a Pawnee-Oto woman in New York City, Mrs. Mifanway Shonatona Hines, who had been a consultant to the news and television media for almost a generation as the director of the American Indian Information Center. She laughed with some anger. "It is so difficult for these media people to see beyond the one thing that they have in their mind. Themselves! And so they turn [our People] into white myths."

The quest for the Noble Savage is as old as the vision of the first European who came to America in search of an imaginary Garden of Eden, which existed only in his dreams. So it is somewhat like the quest of Don Quixote for his perfect love, Dulcinea, whose perfection lay in the fact that she did not exist. Once a desire was satisfied it was lessened, but if it could never be reached, then it went on forever. In this sense the quest for the Noble Savage would be eternal.

For in the mythology of the descendants of the European settlers there was nothing nobler than the "real Indian." If, that is, he did not exist.

In the beginning, in the eyes of the Europeans there had been no Noble Savages. The Peoples of America were no more than "beasts" and less than humans. As Governor William Bradford of the Massachusetts Bay Colony said, they were "savage and brutish men, which range up and down little otherwise than wild beasts," so the land could be said to be "unpeopled."

On the beleaguered deck of the *Mayflower*, after an ordeal of sixty-six days at sea, the Pilgrims had not rejoiced on seeing the shore of America. They had trembled in fear. For "what could they see but a hideous and desolate wilderness, full of wilde beasts and wilde men," wrote the ship chronicler, Nathaniel Morton. The country had "a wilde and savage hew," with "uncivile and Devilish" woods that were nothing less than "Satanic." So the Puritan poet Michael Wigglesworth was to describe one spring day in New England in 1662:

> A waste and howling wilderness,
> Where none inhabited
> But hellish fiends and brutish men
> That Devils worshipped.

Still, it was the "Earth's only Paradise," Michael Drayton had written in "To the Virginian Voyage" of 1605. And the People were innocent as the "Children of Paradise" in the Garden of Eden before The Fall. They had a "savage goodness," as Roy Harvey Pearce was to write in his history of Puritanism, *Savagism and Civilization.* So the Europeans were of "two minds" toward the Americans.

"The Puritan's understanding of the Indian," Pearce said, "marked his understanding of himself. . . . Whatever he saw outside, he had somehow already seen inside [himself]." So the conflict between savagery and nobility that the European saw in the Noble Savage might have been merely a projection of his own conflicts between God and the Devil, good and evil, Heaven and Hell, and European laws and American license. For it was not a philosophical conflict, inherent in the native Americans.

And yet it was in America only that the Noble Savage was both God and the Devil to white Europeans. He had brothers in Africa and Asia, where he walked the world in the shadow of the European colonizers, his creators. Nowhere, however, was he accorded the importance and stature he had on this continent.

That may well have been because nowhere else did the European seek to become a native of the land. In Africa and Asia he learned the ways of the people in order to conquer them, but he rarely became African or Asian. But in America he wished to become American. He remade himself in his image of the People he conquered, the image of the Noble Savage.

Scholars of the rationalist era ennobled their ideas of the Noble Savage with their own version of scientific empiricism. On the one hand, said the seventeenth-century master of German science, William Leibniz, these "barbarians surpass us, especially in bodily vigor, even so far as the soul is concerned." That may be because, Leibniz explained, "animals are purely empirical" and so their "practical morality is better than ours." But, on the other hand, "One would have to be as brutish as the American savages to approve of their customs, which are crueler than those of wild animals." Yet it was this very savagery that made them noble, he said.

In view of later Germanic beliefs about the Noble Savage, this somewhat schizophrenic view has rather ominous overtones. The fascination with the Noble Savage, the so-called "beast within," and the search for "pure" Indians (Aryans) that Europeans were to import from their American cousins were to cause as much misery upon that continent as on ours.

Still, the quest goes on. It is so persistent that something more than a romantic image seems to be sought; for if it were no more than that, the nightmare of the "Indian Wars" would have ended these whites' dreams of the Noble Savage and "pure" Indian (Aryan).

The German philosopher of *The Decline of the West,* Oswald Spengler, thought it was a revolt against "this loathing of the senses, of reason; this fear of beauty and happiness" that was necessary in a technological society. "Every 'real' man, even in the cities of Late periods of Culture, feels within himself, from time to time, the sleeping fires of the primitive soul," he wrote in *Man and Technics.* When a civilization declined, it was inevitable, Spengler said, that people should begin to seek their roots.

But the "search for the primitive" was more troublesome to Sigmund Freud. He thought of it as a "retrogression." Still, he too had begun to doubt the artificiality of modern living. "People who know nothing about nature are of course neurotic," Freud said, "for they are not adapted to reality. They are too naïve, like children." A strange comment for a wholly urban intellectual.

However, it was Carl Jung who was to create a philosophy out of the "search for the primitive." "If for a moment we pull away from European rationalism," Jung wrote, we shall discover a lost world of "magic coercion" and "viable serenity." He had found such a world in the "clear mountain air" of the Pueblos of New Mexico, in the tribal "Circle of Life" where he became one with "the mythic side of man," the Noble Savage reborn as the healer of the white man's psyche.

In all of this the Noble Savage loomed "larger than life," as the editors of *American Heritage* sagely and commercially had observed in their "Vanishing Primitive Man"; for "much more than most of us, they have retained an identity. Their world is so unlike ours, in its elemental values and ideals, from the magic and mystery of its rituals, to the stark simplicity of its communal life, that what are really very old frontiers seem strikingly new."

These Noble Savages may have become the "vision in a broken mirror" in which whites wish to see themselves, as the native anthropologist Bernard Fontana once suggested. It may be that the whites have become the Noble Savages.

If that was so, then it explained the "savage anthropologists," as Fontana spoofed them, who "change more slowly than the traditions of the Indians themselves." They sought to preserve the "pure" culture of the People, not for history, but for themselves. For if it was not "pure," it was "dying." So Clyde Kluckhohn, the eminent dean of anthropology at Harvard University, in his melancholy desire to keep the contemporary Indians from becoming too contemporary, protested: "They gain from us only the external, the 'objective' parts of our civilization, without its total fabric. Hence, in effect, they have for a time at least *no culture at all.*"

Some men have seen this as the enlightened White Man's Burden. The myth of the Noble Savage had been rejected by the People. And so it fell to its white creators to defend their own myth, to preserve what they thought was the "dying culture" of the People, and to become, if they could, the Noble Savages. But they could not. The failure of the myth was perhaps told best in D. H. Lawrence's *Studies in Classic American Literature*, when he lamented:

> There are these people, these "savages." One does not despise them. One does not feel superior. But there is a gulf. There is a gulf in time and being. I cannot commingle my being with theirs. . . .
> And they will call you brother, choose you as a brother. But why cannot one truly be [a] brother?
> There is an invisible hand grasps my heart and prevents it opening

too much to these strangers. They are beautiful, they are like children, they are generous; but they are more than this. They are far off, and in their eyes is an easy darkness of the soft uncreated past. In a way, they are uncreated. Far be it from me to assume any "white" superiority. But they are savages. . . . And your own soul will tell you that however false and foul our forms and systems are now, still, through the centuries since Egypt, we have been living and struggling forwards, along some road that is no road, and yet is a great life development. We have struggled on, and on we must still go. We may have to smash things. Then let us smash. . . .

So these many "reformers" and "idealists" who glorify the savages in America . . . They are death-birds, life-haters. Renegades . . .

We can't go back. . . .

And yet the processionals of those who came seeking the Noble Savage did not halt. They have grown more insistent and hopeless. They shall not cease. They shall increase.

In the travail of technology the wail of the poet Hart Crane has become the cry of the White Indians:

> *Medicine man, relent, restore—*
> *Lie to us—dance us back the tribal morn!*

The Final Termination

❦ TESTAMENT OF James Abourezk,
U.S. Senator, South Dakota

On the carpet in his den we leaned on our elbows and talked and drank beer and talked and took off our shoes and talked. After his hectic day in the Senate chambers, the genial, easygoing, outspoken, and ebullient son of a Lebanese "Indian trader" to the Rosebud Sioux, who had been elected—"by mistake," he said— as the senator from South Dakota, had to relax somehow.

"It is not easy to feel human in Washington," said Jim Abourezk.

That evening we had eaten an old-fashioned family supper. It was a home-cooked meal of frozen blintzes, Jewish-style, with sour cream, and Lebanese-style breaded pork chops, which were prepared in savory ecumenical fashion by Mrs. Abourezk. And the wines and the dessert turned this simple meal into a feast. "I like to eat," the senator had said. "And they say, 'Good food makes good friends.'

"So won't you eat another blintz," he said, laughing.

In the warmth and informality of the Abourezk house in the suburbs of Washington, D.C., we seemed to be beyond the pale of the political hysteria that had immobilized the Capitol in the last days of Richard Nixon's reign. It was as if the fears— *Lord, there but for Thy grace and that of the congressional investigators, go I*—that gripped the officials of the government had no visible effect upon the senator from the prairies of South Dakota.

At dinner, no one mentioned Richard Nixon. The food set before us was more interesting. We talked of familial things.

Once, after a Senate hearing, Jim Abourezk and I had gone up to his hotel room. He ordered a six-pack of beer, he took off his shoes, and he telephoned his wife before he did anything else. In decades of post-hearing hotel-room sessions with senators and political VIPs, that was the first time I had seen a man do these simple things. Especially the last—to telephone his wife before telephoning his office.

"It all depends," said Jim Abourezk, "what is *most* important to you."

To express his feelings about this, he liked to say, "I was born on an Indian reservation. That gave me a different way of looking at politics. You know, the Indian people believe that people are more important than politics. Or politicians. So do I."

Politics was like an "unnatural act," he said.

Wasn't he going to make a career of politics?

"Oh, absolutely not!" He was not just one more "political maverick." He was a "political mistake," he said. In his youth he had tried his hand at managing his father's "Indian trader" business, but his heart wasn't in it. So he went back to college and became a lawyer. In those days, western South Dakota had been a conservative Republican territory for generations, where a liberal Democrat had no more chance than a "Sioux militant." When he ran for Congress, everyone said he didn't have a chance. He didn't. He won anyway. When he ran for the Senate, everyone said he didn't have a chance. He didn't. He won again.

That was how he was to become chairman of the Senate subcommittee on Indian Affairs. "By mistake," he said.

"No one wanted to be the chairman," Abourezk said. "So I volunteered. They were delighted to have someone else take it. It was political suicide."

Soon after he became chairman of the Indian Affairs subcommittee he realized why no one wanted the job. The powerful

Interior Committee would not fund the work of its own sub-committee.

"God! The fact that they wouldn't give the committee a staff is just fantastic," said the novice senator. "If you don't have a staff to do the work, what's the point of having the committee? Frankly, what's the point of having hearings if you can't move legislation?

"You know, I had to use my own money to hire my own staff. The Interior Committee just wouldn't give us any money to do our work."

And why was this? I asked.

"To allow the energy companies to have their way on Indian lands, until it's too late to do anything about it," he said. It was a "deliberate stall. . . . There is no question about it in my mind. It's absolutely true."

In no time he had antagonized nearly all of the powerful interests that wished to exploit the Indian and the West. His subcommittee held hearings on its own, at which Indian people voiced their grievances on treaty violations, theft of land, lack of water, and racial discrimination. And to the displeasure of many white South Dakotans, he traveled to the village of Kyle, on the Pine Ridge Reservation, to hear the cry of the defenders of Wounded Knee II.

"Now let me tell you the truth," said a sympathetic senatorial friend. "It's fine to sympathize with the Indians. We all do. But Jim goes too far. He acts like he is an Indian. And if he keeps it up, he won't be reelected."

Why did he do it? This is what he told me:

My father was so independent he just couldn't get along with anyone. So he moved out on the frontier, back in 1895. And his character eventually changed, was changed by the frontier. He became easygoing, but a very solid man.

If you speak of one characteristic those early settlers had in common, that would be it. They were very solid. They went through tremendous hardships, because of the weather conditions and the lack of material comfort. So there was a great desire for stability and security on those prairies.

When you live in a city like Washington, D.C., as I have, you begin to really appreciate that kind of character.

God! I used to think it would be great to live in this city. It's not. It's not what you could call living. It's no good. If there is such a thing as character in Washington, D.C., it is intangible. Why? This is a phony city. And the difference is great between the people on the prairies and the people in this city.

Land has a great deal to do with people's character. I think the stability of the people on those prairies, their reliability, and their honesty, has a great deal to do with the land; the fact that they make their living directly from the land and relate directly to the land, whether they are Indian or white.

In the cities on the East Coast, living is so totally unrelated to the land that the people don't understand how a human being can relate to the land. The land is a meaningless concept to them.

They have no land!

They have no roots!

Now the development of our land is in the hands of people who don't really know what the land is. The development of the West is out of the hands of the West.

Now the energy companies in oil, gas, coal, and shale production are working their will on the American people. They are hot to exploit everything they find. They just see the West as a profit-and-loss sheet. Nothing more, nothing less! If the Indians get in their way, if the environmentalists get in their way, that's just too bad. No matter what ploy they use, they will do something to get them out of their way—whether it's the creation of an "oil shortage," or simply beating them down with lawsuits, or whether it's the millions of dollars they spend for advertising.

You have seen the advertisement that shows two little Arabs, and underneath it says: "America has more coal than the Arabs have oil. Let's dig it!" Well, after two or three years, that kind of advertising will have a powerful effect. If we have another winter of shortages, it will be even more powerful.

The energy companies have the blessing of many in Congress. And they have the acquiescence and cooperation of the Interior Department and the administration in the White House.

In this there may be the "final termination" of the Indian way of life.

Many of the obstacles to the progress of the Indian people have to do with their rights to their land and water. Who is to have these rights is purely a matter of political power. It happens that the dominant society has that political power. And it will not give it, or any portion of it, back to the Indians. Why? Because there is coal on Indian land, and the coal requires a lot of water before it can be turned into usable energy.

And so it's not a matter of Indian rights. It's a matter of white needs. The rest is all hypocrisy.

That's why I say the urbanization of the West, and of the Indians, may be the "final termination"—of both!

On the Sioux reservations you begin to see it happening in a small way. The way the government, the Bureau of Indian Affairs, is building urban housing on the prairies, without considering the desires of the Sioux. They build the houses in cluster units. They take the Indian people off their lands and force them into these housing clusters; it's the only halfway decent housing there is. And the urban housing becomes a microcosm of urban problems: the vandalism, the juvenile delinquency, the broken homes, the trouble between neighbors, the crowded conditions, the ugliness, the nervousness of urban life.

All that in the midst of the wide-open prairies, where people once had air to breathe and beauty everywhere.

But you see, these government planners are urban planners. They go into the countryside and they plan on an urban basis. They don't understand the West.

These urban planners have grown so callous to human feelings that they just move people about like so many numbers. In the cities the people are simply cabbages to them. But when you do that in the West, you destroy the way of life.

That's happening in these new coal towns and on the Indian reservations everywhere throughout the West.

That's not like people building a city and giving it their character. And giving it their face. No! It will be a faceless city.

What will the character of the West be like when this happens? It just won't be there any more. The people will become just another bunch of people, shuffling back and forth to work, the way they do in Washington, D.C. When people begin to move into these cities in the West and Southwest in great numbers, I am afraid the character of the people will change. The people are caught in this social upheaval. And it's not just the Indians and the young.

There seems to be a great resistance among the people of the West to these changes. Here in Washington they call that provincialism. But I don't think that's what it is. It is a gnawing fear that: *By God! We will be ruined if we allow what has happened in these cities in the East to happen to us!*

I'm not sure that people have figured out how to resist the onslaught. But they want to. These outside corporations, and outsiders in the government, come into the Western states with tremendous political power, tremendous economic wealth, to do whatever they want to do. And they do. It's a hell of a thing.

Self-determination? It's time that the Indians, and the West, really had self-determination and were no longer treated like children, no longer had to listen to the whims of the government. But I am not sure that any President would really change that.

No administration, Democratic or Republican, has ever been willing to let the Indian people make policy. The rhetoric of President Nixon on self-determination was great, but it was all rhetoric. Somebody may have talked him into signing a statement, and that was about all it was.

And this is one reason the people are so disillusioned with

the government. So dissatisfied. It seems that no matter what you say, what you complain about, nothing is ever done. No one listens to you. No one cares.

I overestimated the power that a congressman, or a senator, has. While you can effect a minor change, you really can't effect *any* major change.

Do I want to make a career of politics? Oh, absolutely not! After this term is up, well, who knows? I may go back home and practice law. If you remember, Adlai Stevenson once said, "You know, I'm going to go back to Libertyville, and sit under a tree and watch the people dance."

But the poor fellow had a heart attack before he had a chance to sit under that tree!

THE VANISHING WHITE MAN

On the lonely and quiet two-lane ranch road that wandered so peacefully between the foothills along the Rosebud Creek, maybe ten miles from the Northern Cheyenne Reservation, there was a monument to the death of a myth. It was a weathered plaque on a small pile of rocks that proclaimed that here by this road-side the Seventh Cavalry of General Custer had "rested" on two nights before dying on the Little Bighorn.

Even today some think the road leads to doom.

Along the Rosebud Creek the ranches of the old homesteads on what had been Indian land nestled under great grandfatherly trees. The fields were green with summer wheatgrass and alfalfa and a kind of peace.

The country was beautiful. It was Big Sky Country, wide and silent as the Montana prairie always had been. Some of the stones in these valleys were sixty-five million years old, and older.

In the sagebrush foothills there were quail and coyotes. The ponderosa pines hid the shy mule deer and the sly bobcats. On the wilder open roads of Wyoming, the herds of pronghorn were bolder; there they pranced across the highways, halting the passing autos; but here they were camouflaged by the still-ness of the hills, and wise fears.

One hundred years ago, a pioneer Montana cowboy in the lands of the Northern Cheyenne, a man by the name of Edgar Beecher Bronson, wrote of this country as "a veritable aboriginal paradise." In his *Reminiscences of a Ranchman*, he described the "plains alive with buffalo and antelope, the mountains full of deer, elk, mountain sheep and bear, the streams swarming with fish, and everywhere a thick carpet of juicy buffalo grass that kept their [the Indians'] ponies fat as seals."

Then the ranchers came onto the Indian lands. And the cattle displaced the buffalo. And the strip miners came onto the ranch-ers' lands. And the bulldozers displaced the cattle.

"And now the grass is gone," one rancher said. "It's being made into electricity."

On the Rosebud Creek a new range war had begun, within sight of the Custer monument; but this time the white ranchers would play the Indians' role. It seemed quiet. There was no shooting. And yet there was stirring in the winds. The antelope sniffed it and smelled the bulldozers coming.

In the company town of Colstrip, a few miles upwind, the strip mining had begun. There was talk of as many as seven energy-generating plants to be built in the sleepy town—popu-lation 266. One official of a local electric company told the news-papers it might become the largest power project "in the world," taking ten million kilowatts of useful energy from the earth; it would waste much more, though he did not say that. If these huge plants were built, they might poison the sky with more ashes and acids, chemicals and pollutants, than Los Angeles, New York, London, and Moscow together.

Some said a city of twenty-five thousand would be built. And some said it would be more, or less. It did not matter, for the rural way of life was doomed no matter how many, or few, mobile homes and cheeseburger stands crowded the pasture of the antelope and steer.

The romance of a boom town was a nightmare, declared a report of the Federation of Rocky Mountain States. In a typical "Resource City," modeled on towns such as Colstrip, it was found that crime increased by 400 percent; psychiatric breakdowns went up tenfold; suicides zoomed, as did divorces, more than one marriage in every two falling apart in the social chaos caused by a lack of housing, in which motel rooms rented on eight-hour shifts; schools often did not exist and could not be built by poor rural townships; and lack of simple necessities, such as sewers, turned once clear mountain streams into toxic cesspools. Living conditions were so bad the job turnover was 150 percent; there were few sources of entertainment other than bars and whores, and alcoholism became so commonplace that the local jails "were often used by wives as protection from beatings by their drunken husbands."

Of course, "Clean air and wide open spaces were gone," the report said; and the "Effects on wildlife have been nearly disastrous."

On the road into the town of Colstrip there was a modest sign: "HELP KEEP OUR TOWN CLEAN." In the blue sky beyond the sign, the huge smokestack of one of the power plants billowed grayish smoke. The grass surrounding the plant, what little there was, would soon be dying.

"The grass will die. And when it does, so will my ranch," one rancher said.

"Ranchers will vanish," said another, "like the Indians. We are the new 'vanishing race.'" He smiled bitterly.

One of the ranchers, his face hardened by the winds, his skin painted by the sun, a tall man of some dignity named Wallace McRae, was one of the new White Indians.

"My grandfathers were early settlers," he said, "coming to Montana before the turn of the century, shortly after the Battle of the Little Bighorn, where Custer met his demise while attempting to rid the West of the Red Menace." In those days, "Custer was an implement of the policy of the United States government, which dictated that the Indian, his buffalo, and his way of life were an impediment to progress. The Indian, being an obstacle to economic development, had to be eliminated or overcome."

He, Wallace McRae, now stood where the Indians had. He was an impediment to progress.

"I have become, for all practical purposes, an Indian," he said. "Like the Indian, I am standing in the way of progress because I live and work above part of the world's largest known reserves of fossil fuel.

"But I resist," he said.

Four generations of the McRae family had farmed the stones and watered them with their sweat when there was no rain. The bones of his ancestors were like stones in this land. He thought of this land as an Indian might, with respect and humility. And so it was being taken from him, as it was taken from the Indian.

Love of the land is not a clear legal title, they said.

Now they said the land he stood on was not his. He "owned the top of the soil, and that was all. The earth underneath his own feet, so rich with coal, was "owned" by the government. On most of the old homestead land, the governed "owned" the mineral rights.

If you sink into the mud, I guess you could be arrested for trespassing, they said.

Most of our public, or federal, lands were in the Western states. Some 725 million acres, more than one-third of the entire nation, it was a vast region as large as Western Europe. These lands were run by government decree. In some of the states, like Wyoming, 71 percent of the land was controlled by a single small agency of the Interior Department, the Bureau of Land Management. None of the land barons of the old West ever dreamed of possessing the land and power these minor bureaucrats controlled.

On the ranchers' land, the government could lease the coal from under their feet, their porches, their bedrooms, if they wished. And they did.

Wallace McRae had seen it happen to his neighbors:

One rancher's grasslands were selected as the site for a

gigantic 1200-megawatt electric plant. "He did not know his ranch was involved until he read about it in an item in the newspaper."

The ranch of a neighbor's family was sited for strip mining, but neither the coal company nor the government bothered to show the rancher their environmental-impact statements. So he had no idea of what would happen to his ranch or his family.

Many pastures were drilled for coal samples without asking the farmers, "under the assumption that they could not prevent the drilling." And "no prospecting permits were issued by the government."

When the academic experts of the Westinghouse Corporation did a study of the impact of strip mines and power plants on ranch life along the Rosebud, they surveyed everyone and everything in sight. But they "did not include a single rancher," said McRae.

In the Powder River Valley, just across the Wyoming line, the ranchers' feelings of frustration were voiced with Mark Twain–like irony by Roger McKenzie, a ranching spokesman: "At times it seems that we are being consumed by industry, while we are studying how, when, where, and even if we should be consumed."

After talking to maybe three hundred ranchers and ranch hands on the prairies of Montana and Wyoming, the Northern Great Plains Resource Program, in Billings, summed up what they had to say: The "majority of ranchers" in the Rosebud and Powder River regions "would really like to see the coal people go away forever. They are traditionalists. They and their hired hands think the whole business is wrong. They are committed to maintaining the land and its integrity."

It was strange, they thought, because "In the past, ranchers tended to identify strongly with big business." Why had they become "disenchanted"?

"Some ranchers," the report went on, say the coal and energy companies are "unfair, untrustworthy and inconsiderate . . . deceitful and interested solely in making money." They "send surveyors without first asking for appropriate permission." In this way they start a "scare rumor" to frighten ranchers into selling their land. And then they "get a big head start in construction work" on someone's land, "before getting formal permission" from the rancher or the government. Finally, "they argue that the heavy commitment they have made should be approved."

The ranchers are dumfounded by the immorality of the energy companies. And they feel "greatly handicapped," for, "valuing credibility, trust and honesty," they have "difficulty in dealing with corporate tactics." They "make the mistake of treating corporations—as people."

These old-fashioned ranchers feel powerless. "Ranchers are keenly aware of the tremendous power—both financial and political—held by the industrialists, who are in a position to stifle a productive ranching operation virtually overnight." And knowing this, "Very few persons believe that coal development and ranching can go on side by side."

In despair, some of the older ranchers sold out and hoped for the best. On the Quarter Circle V Ranch, in Birney, Montana, the aging owner, Burton Brewster, talked wonderingly of one-quarter of a million dollars he was offered in coal royalty for the thirty-six acres it took "to run one cow." Brewster was wistfully hopeful: "The quarter of a million dollars this one cow would generate would go a long ways. . . . With the money I am sure my grandchildren can make a better ranch."

Up in Roundup, Montana, Boyd Charter, another old-time rancher, replied angrily to Brewster: "Can you actually look your neighbors in the eye? I am as old as you are. I have engaged in the business of running cattle my entire lifetime. As I see it, it would be an utter impossibility to run cattle side by side with strip mines and power plants. Are you willing to put a plaque up on your ranch saying you sanctioned the strip mining of the place? I'd be goddamned if I'd want such a plaque up on my ranch.

"God help us," he said.

The feeling of coming doom soon became a front-page headline in the Denver *Post*: "WESTERN STATES VIEW DISMAL FUTURE." It eulogized the passing of the spirit of the old West. "Longtime residents, fearing an end to a beloved life-style, say, '*Now we know how the Indian must have felt.*'"

Across the Western prairies and mountains, up in Montana and down in Texas, the sorrows were the same. The ranchers even used the same words to curse those politicians who were sacrificing "rural life for urban death," as one old-timer said.

On his ranch in Albany, Texas, Bob Green cursed the damming of a prairie river to supply water for an industrial city fifty miles away. "The river bottom was our winter pasture and the horses stayed fat," the old cattleman said. "Now we have to feed them all winter and they don't do as well. It sounds like *Bury My Heart at Wounded Knee*. Poor old Indians; they probably felt the same way when we ran them off."

He mused, "I don't think you'll have a critter driving around in a pickup, loving this land, much longer." Ranching was becoming too "industrialized." It was a dying way of life. And the rancher was a dying breed, as the Indian had been.

If these ranchers had the feeling that they were being treated "like Indians," it may have been because they were. Ranching seemed a kind of dreamy nostalgia to many corporate and government energy experts. Those old homesteads on the prairies, like rural life itself, were secondary to the manifest destiny of urban energy demands. Some of the ranchers had begun to call themselves "White Wards of Washington." They accused the Bureau of Land Management, the BLM, of being the "White BIA."

It may have confused these white ranchers that the government mistook them for the red Indians whom they had belittled, insulted, and laughed at for most of their lives. And yet it should not have. The second-class citizenship of ranchers was a result of government policy during the energy crisis as recommended by the official report of the Joint Congressional Commission on

Public Land Review in 1970. Entitled *One Third of the Nation's Land*, this policy report on Western land use stated, in categorical italics:

"*Mineral exploration and development should have preference over some, or all other, uses on much of our public lands.*"

The energy of the grasses was to be secondary to the energy of the coal deposits. In days past, "Grazing has always been part of the western scene, and livestock ranching has had a major role in public land use," these urbanized commissioners acknowledged; but that idyllic memory of America's past was unprofitable nostalgia. The old West had to be displaced by the new West, for which "development of a productive mineral deposit is the highest economic use of the land." Thus the "primary use" of the Western prairies and forests was no longer ranching, but mining.

So then, let what *Fortune* magazine called the "New Age of Coal" begin. There was a "Persian Gulf of coal" beneath these ranchers' pastures; it would be worth billions of dollars when converted into electricity for the cities.

The sea of coal would flood the prairies. It was a tidal wave, which would sweep away ecological laws that for generations had protected the fragile land. The "restrictions upon leasing of public land coal deposits" should be "removed," or "modified," at once, the impatient commissioners said; for the "public interest requires that individuals be encouraged—not merely permitted—to look for minerals on public lands." And so, "we urge dispatch," they said.

Not merely the ranchers, but the environment itself—the grasslands and pastures, mountains and forests—were secondary to the "primary use" of the land for mining and power development, the commissioners said: "We believe that the environment must be given consideration, but regulations must not be arbitrarily applied if the national importance of the mineral is properly weighed." Land is to be "restored or rehabilitated after a determination of feasibility based on careful balancing of economic costs." That is, the costs in cash, not in grass. And

THE VANISHING WHITE MAN

besides, *"Rehabilitation does not necessarily mean restoration."* So much for the rhetoric of reclamation.

"The land might simply have to be written off," said *Fortune.* Then what of the ranchers; were they to be "written off" as well?

In setting down this statement of policy, the commissioners were merely saying what everybody had been doing for years. After all, the Joint Congressional Commission had been convened in 1964, years before the "energy crisis" became a popular concept; its policy reflected the opinions of some of the most influential and decisive men in Washington, such leaders as Senators Henry Jackson and Clinton Anderson, Congressmen Morris Udall and Wayne Aspinall, and one lone representative of industry, whom *The New York Times* referred to as "Laurance Rockefeller, conservationist."

These men had simply suggested that our national priority and business practice become government policy. For their straightforward, forthright efforts they were immediately attacked by both ranchers and environmentalists. "A Blueprint for Corporate Takeover of 724.4 Million Acres of Land Which Now Belongs to the People of the United States" was how Angus McDonald, research director of the National Farmers Union, characterized the commissioners' work. It was "a bankruptcy sale of the nation's western lands and resources." It was "the biggest land grab proposal in history." It was the death knell for homesteaders; from now on you had to be a "giant corporation" to "do a little homesteading."

Logically, the Joint Congressional Commission had recommended that the Homestead Act be repealed. The era of the small farm and ranch had gone the way of the horse and buggy.

These ranch homesteads and family farms had become "an agrarian myth," as the National Water Commission said. Every year there were fewer and fewer old-fashioned farmers. In the summer of 1973, the Department of Agriculture estimated, barely 5 percent of the people lived on farms. There were less than three million farms left in the whole country. And two-thirds of these (64 percent) were not even subsistence farms, being so small and so poor that they sold less than $2,500 worth of produce yearly, from which the farmer earned but a few hundred dollars.

Scoffing at the poor farmers, the Secretary of Agriculture said with paternalistic disdain: "They are pretty much the salt of the earth, [but they] contribute little to feeding the urban population." They could not feed themselves.

As the farmers vanished, so did the farmland. The interstate highways, suburban developers, power plants, and strip mines had begun "gobbling up" the cropland at the rate of 750,000 acres each year. By the year 2000, it was estimated, sixty million acres of choice farmland would "disappear," and so would about three hundred million acres of grazing land.

The "severe shrinkage" of our rural lands, towns, and people was becoming a national disaster, warned Leon Keyserling, the former chairman of the President's Council of Economic Advisers, in 1965. Rural life was being sacrificed to urban needs and that was economically unsound and inhuman. "It is not enough to save half the people of a ship by casting the other half into the sea," Keyserling said.

Something had to be done. Nothing was. In compassionate rhetoric, Lyndon Baines Johnson, himself a rancher, twice had urged Congress "to restore the balance between rural and urban life." The romance of the down-on-the-farm imagery had been an obligatory theme of Presidents before and after Johnson, but his appeals were more personal *angst* than national mythology; he proposed no programs of significance. And nothing was done, then or since.

In a factual declaration of what was, and still is, national policy, Undersecretary of Agriculture, Charles S. Murphy, one of President Johnson's close advisers on farm problems, set things straight with unusual bluntness. "I think it is a mistake to go too far in trying to keep people on the farm when it doesn't make sense economically," he said. We should "just recognize the fact we are going to have fewer people making a living farming. . . .

"We do not have any moral obligations to patches of land," said the undersecretary.

That was that. Here was an honest, no-nonsense statement of priorities. In our society, where most of the people and the power resided in the cities, the memory of rural life was quaint and enchanting, but it did not have the "national importance" in reality that it seemed to have in advertisements for deodorants and cereals, *Paper Moons* and John Wayne movies. The Marlboro Man had become a myth of the media.

And yet the less important ranching was, the more romantically it was portrayed. The less the countryside remained, the more city people dreamed of leaving for the countryside. Like the vanishing red man, the vanishing white man became more and more popular as a romantic ideal the less he existed in real life.

And it always had been so. The cowboy became a folk hero, as once Frank Dobie remarked, when he became a "cowboy without cows," no longer having even the "smell of cows." Before that time, he was thought of as dumb, unwashed, uncivilized, ill-mannered, and illiterate to boot. For there was little romance in cows. Not until the open range was fenced in and the cattle drives had ended and the cowboy was becoming a memory of the past did he evolve into the hero of Buffalo Bill's Wild West Show, soon to be enshrined within the "Cowboy Hall of Fame."

So it was with the modern rancher. He became a folk hero on television after his way of life on the range was doomed—by television.

Ain't no romance in shovelin' bullshit, they said. *Except from a distance.*

The "cow historian," Edward Everett Dale, had been wrong when he had written in *Romance of the Range* that "the fragrance of the romance" of the pioneer West would "cling" to the land, though "you may enclose the green prairies and plow up the sweet wildflowers"; for the romance he envisioned did not persist in spite of, but because of, the desecration he feared. It did not begin till the green prairies were enclosed and the wildflowers were plowed up and the old-time ranchers were gone.

In the "good old days" it had begun that way. The rancher was idealized and deprecated. He was gloried and ignored. He was no "better than an Indian," and in some ways worse. He had "half-Indian ways," wrote Constance Rourke in *The Roots of American Culture*. He was too backward and too radical. "You can hardly find a group of ranch men, or miners, from Colorado to the Pacific who will not have on their tongues' ends the labor slang of Denis Kearney, the infidel ribaldry of Robert Ingersoll, the socialistic theories of Karl Marx," cried the Reverend Josiah Strong, a kind of Billy Graham of the 1880s who was the leader of the Congressional Home Missionary Society. Strong sent his missionaries "to save" these "White Injuns" much as they did the "inferior tribes" of "aborigines"—for the ranchers were just as "beastly."

In his *Trails Plowed Under*, the Montana cowboy artist Charlie Russell parodied this view of the Wild West and the wilder Westerner in a delicious dialogue:

"Ma," says he, "do cowboys eat grass?"

"No, dear," says the old lady, "they're part human."

It was an old Indian joke, told by whites. Just the names had been changed, for "cowboy" was a dirty word, as bad as "savage," in the pioneer West. The cowboys preferred to be known as "buckaroos," a gringoizing of the Spanish *vaqueros*. "Cowboy" was an insult; it was "one name for many crimes," wrote a Texas chronicler of the word in the 1850s; it meant "outlaw," or "*banditi*," or "uncivilized."

So much of the heritage of the Western rancher and cowboy has been forgotten. Or it has been expurgated and mocked by the ironies of history.

In the myths of the West, farmers and ranchers have been romanticized for so long in the idolatry of political oratory, in novels and filmed Westerns, that they, too, have believed they were the salt of the earth. In reality, they have always been second-class citizens, the "White Injuns." The needs of the rural West have been secondary to the demands of the railroads, the land speculators, and the mine owners.

Sometimes ridiculed, sometimes humored, the ranchers and farmers were often ignored by the Congress until they howled and cursed in the "farm rebellions" that became as common on the prairies as the old "Indian uprisings." Even then, the government in the East tended to consider rural angers archaic and exotic. "Whenever American farmers leave their plows en masse and race threateningly after the regular politicians they are called wild jackasses, or worse," commented farm historian Dale Kramer in his chronicle *The Wild Jackasses*.

In the heyday of the farm rebellions, when the people were still largely rural, it was this way. One of the pioneer Masters of the Grange, Dudley W. Adams, admonished the prairie farmers and ranchers in the noble Order of Patrons of Husbandry, in 1872, to forget the "pastoral myth" about themselves: "Politicians laud in stentorian tones the 'honest yeomanry,' the 'sinews of the land,' and deluge us with equally fulsome and nauseating stuff. . . . We have heard enough of this professional blarney," he raged. "We must do something to dispel old prejudices. . . . That the farmer is a mere animal is an ancient, but abominable, heresy."

And yet at the time, when the land was deeply agrarian, rural people had little more influence than now. "Look at our State and National governments," said Adams, "to whom we entrust this great responsibility . . . a lawyer, doctor, preacher, student, merchant, or, in fact, almost anybody but a farmer. . . .

"My brother tillers of the soil," he exhorted. "What we want in agriculture is a new Declaration of Independence." Let us proclaim that our farms need not be "the abodes of overworked slaves." Slaves of whom? It was "Wall Street" that had mortgaged the lives of "widows and orphaned children," declared a Grange broadside in 1873. The "money interests" were the enemy.

In this oratory there was the echo of that popular ballad of the early Grangers:

> Brothers of the plow, the power is with you.
> Oppression stalks around; monopolies abound.
> Their great hands already clutch the tiller of the ground.

> Awake; then Awake! the great world must be fed.
> And Heaven gives the power to the hand that holds the bread.

Still, the Grangers, Populists, Greenbackers, Farm Unionists were never more than dissident groups in politics. Their rural rebellions did not come to much. They did not last. They did not succeed in halting the urbanization of the countryside. Ever since Shay's Rebellion, in 1787, uprisings of farmers had been losing battles, unable to stem the tide of concentration of power in the cities.

So were they still. . . .

On the prairie of Laramie, Wyoming, ranchers protested the building of high-power electric lines across their land "without their consent." The Bureau of Reclamation simply had "condemned" the land. Once before, ten years ago, they had fought and lost that battle, and now they were adamant. But they lost again. . . . Ranchers up near Gillette had got together to protest the railroad being built to haul forty-eight trainloads of strip-mined coal through some of their best pastures every day. They vowed no one would sell out until a majority agreed. "We don't want to sell anything," said Earl Scott. But he was reconciled: "Somebody is going to get hurt by this thing." And they were. They couldn't halt the railroad. . . .

In the burning deserts of New Mexico, a seventy-one-year-old widow sought to protect her cattle ranch from a highway interchange. "It doesn't provide access to anything but my pasture," complained Rita Hill. She built a shack in its path and resolved to face the bulldozers, in her bonnet, until "they drag me off by force." They did. She was arrested. . . .

On the Rosebud, the Tongue-Yellowstone Sugar Beet Growers, the Buffalo Rapids Irrigation Project, the Custer Rod and Gun Club, and Trout Unlimited filed a petition in court to request the Federal Power Commission to assume jurisdiction over water use by the Colstrip power projects. They did not win. . . . In the valley of Sarpy Creek, ranchers asked for a court injunction to halt a Westmoreland Coal Company's strip mine. They lost. . . .

Everywhere in the West it was much the same. If the ranchers and townspeople did stop the desecration of the land, it was usually because the decision had been made in the board room of a federal bureaucracy or a corporate energy company that the project would not be economically profitable enough. Not because of the land, or people.

And when the old-fashioned ranchers reluctantly joined hands with their ecology-minded sons and daughters in the city, they were faced with ugly bumper stickers that said: "LET THE BASTARDS FREEZE IN THE DARK."

"In Al Capp's play *Li'l Abner*, it was decided by the federal government that Dogpatch was the most unnecessary community in the U.S.A.," said rancher Wallace McRae. "There is a Dogpatch stigma attached to rural areas, which says that since there are few people in the ranching areas, they are relatively unimportant."

No one listened to rural people. And it was at their own peril that they did not. "You can't raise beef in our urban centers," McRae said. "And I think you'd better not preclude our ability to raise beef and wheat and corn and pine trees in rural areas."

In these words there was a sense of loss, as inevitable as the evening's twilight, that muted his angers.

"After nearly one hundred years of honest endeavor, I have begun to discover that my family's effort does not amount to much," McRae said. Still, he fought for his ancestral land. "I think if these plants are completed, all of us in Montana are going to look someday at a scarred landscape under a filthy sky, cut by dry riverbeds, populated by a callous, socially chaotic population, and we will say what fools we were for not stopping this exploitation when we had the chance. A French philosopher named Raynal once said: 'There is an infinity of political errors, which, being once adopted, become principles.'"

The philosophy of Wallace McRae was that of old "Sockless" Jerry Simpson, a Populist congressman from Medicine Lodge, Kansas, who long ago said, "The man who owns the earth owns the people." He was remembered, too, for saying, "Man must have access to land or be a slave." In the valley of the Rosebud, ranchers knew that without knowing. They knew the meaning of

Ralph Waldo Emerson's darker wisdom: "If a man owns the land, the land owns him."

"In the language of my neighbors the Cheyenne Indians, the name of the white man is the same as the name for spider— *veho*," McRae said. "As I see the webs of the high-voltage lines, the webs of railroads and strip mines and the poisons we exude from our activities, the rivers sucked dry of their life-giving juices, I am reminded of the wisdom of the Indian, exhibited by his prophetic name for us. Truly, we exhibit all the characteristics of a *veho*, or spider.

"Perhaps I feel this way because my ranch and my way of life are threatened. Perhaps I am selfish in wanting the world to pass me by," he said.

In the memories of America, the ideal of democracy had been the town meeting in a small farm town. Once it was believed that the nature of our land and our democratic beliefs were wedded, and that democracy itself had arisen from our closeness to the earth. Frederick Jackson Turner wrote: "American democracy is fundamentally the outcome of the experience of the American [white] people in dealing with the West." Democracy was not, he said, an urban idea.

Those who dreamed of a human and individual democracy grew fewer every year. It was not easy to have faith in a Jeffersonian idea of rural democracy when the country yearly became more darkly urbanized and desolate. One of the few men who had kept that faith was Dr. Paul Taylor, a white-haired emeritus "Dean of Land Reform" in the Economics Department at Berkeley, and the oracle of the small and democratic family farm.

"Who owns the land is not something trivial to the nation," Taylor said. "It is central to our society, to our economy, and to our political system. Our New England ancestors were committed to a belief that widespread distribution of land ownership was necessary for the kind of society they wanted to create.

"This is what this country is all about," he said.

Most people no longer knew anything about the land, the old

man acknowledged. But, he said, "They will. They'll come to it. They are beginning to wake up now. This issue isn't as remote as some think from urban problems. Much of the population pressure and discontent which disturbs our cities" is due to our having "fostered an agricultural system which has driven the modest family man off his farm. And we reap the social consequences in our cities." Once again, he said, the land had "to be culti-vated by people who live on it," or the meaning of America would be lost.

The paradox was clear. If the energy hunger of the cities meant inflicting urban problems on the rural countryside, then the problems of the countryside would migrate to the cities. And urban problems and energy hunger would be intensified. In a peculiar way, the solution was the problem.

On the plains and in the mountains of the West there was a murmur of dissent, like a whisper in the grass. The West would not be a "colony" of the Easterners, said Governor Thomas Judge of Montana. Colorado would not be "the Congo," said Governor Richard Lamm of that state. The rhetoric almost sounded real.

There was a growing "climate of hostility" to the East, which might "result in delay, or possibly prevent development of new sources of energy," the Office of Budget Management reported to the President. And the Federal Energy Administration said in quiet apprehension: "Some feel the Western States are being 'colonized' for the rest of the Nation's energy supply." This West-ern attitude could result in "delaying the achievement of, or even subverting, our national energy goals."

In an unusual confrontation with Undersecretary of the In-terior William Lyons, the governor of Colorado charged, at a meeting of the Western Governors' Conference: "You are plan-ning the West! Your decisions do plan the West! Where the new towns will arise, where the old towns will die! You are planning the West!" And Governor Ed Herschler of Wyoming agreed: "The dialogue [with us] is after you [in Washington] make the decision." And Governor Judge added slyly: "What if we say no!"

Sadly a Western governor asked: "How much time will you give us?"

It was too late for many ranchers and farmers. The feeling of despair that clouded the prairie and mountain states was typified by J. Homer Jackson, a small-town banker who specialized in farm loans in Rifle, Colorado. "There never has been a time in the history of this nation," he said, "when the economic survival of America's farm families has been more critical than it is today." Economically and politically, the rural people were facing extinction. "We can't go on," he said simply.

"Farmers and small-town businessmen have made this a strong nation," the banker continued. "But when the wealth is concentrated in Wall Street, and the Populists aren't making any money, then this will break the nation."

He had been born in a sod dugout on the prairie seventy years ago. "I've seen a lot of changes," he said. But this seemed to be the end of the road for the descendants of the pioneers of the West. They knew it. "When they can't go any further, they sell out," he said. "Many of them will have to move."

The new migrations of refugees from the dying cities of the East to the lands of the West were a further portent of death. If anything, they came as mourners, bearing urban coffins. Almost all of them were urban people who brought urban needs and urban thinking. So naturally they settled in urban areas. "The sunnier regions will have to wrestle with the boom—pollution, transportation snarls, social tensions, risng crime," commented the Washington *Post.* For "the last frontiers are getting crowded" with city dwellers who are "heading for the hills." Rather than a revival of the West, these new migrations were to be its funeral procession.

One by one the small farm and ranch towns closed down, like country fairs on dirt roads, moving on. In the prairies the Main Streets stood silent and empty. The old general store was boarded up with signs advertising the new supermarket at a shopping center miles away, the old town bank was a musty antique shop, and the old Bijou movie theater had long ago been torn down to pave the way for a parking lot.

Even the old depots were locked. Who needed them when so many people had left and did not come back?

In the Feed Bag Café in the ranch town of Ashland, Montana, in the midst of the strip mines, a radio was whining a country Western lament sung by a musical non sequitur known as The Fifth Dimension.

> They're tearin' down the street where I grew up
> Like pourin' brandy in a Dixie cup
> They're pavin' concrete on part of me
> No trial for killin' a memory.

A cowhand looked up sourly from his cup of coffee. He squinted at the radio as if it were his mortal enemy. But he hunched over his coffee, his head bent, knowing that even if he got up and smashed the jukebox the words would still be there, in the air.

> Ashes to ashes, dust to dust,
> It's the way the West was won.

When We Die, America Dies

❦ TESTAMENT OF Boyd Charter, Montana Rancher

Old Boyd Charter was ornery. He was one of the last of the old-time ranchers, who owned his place on earth and knew his own mind. He was one of those men who are so independent they seem unreal, but he was real enough. The sort of wiry, resilient, honest, straight-faced, outspoken, tough, boyishly polite, and shy man who had made the West what it once was.

He was the breed of man who always seemed to have a four-day-old growth of beard.

Some would call him a relic of the impossible past, conservative as hell, his ideas as hard as nails, his face lined as an old leather saddle, the breeder of rodeo horses and American dreams, with vinegar on his tongue and flint in his eyes. And it was true that just a few years ago he was still a "Theodore Roosevelt Republican." Until he found out that the "damned, if you forgive my language, Republicans aren't real conservatives. Not really; they believe ripping up the land and destroying our country by strip mining, is *progress*—just like everyone else."

"If you talked to that old so-and-so, hope his words were not too salty and if they were that you had an ample supply of water," Cliff Hansen had said to me. Senator Clifford P. Hansen, of Wyoming, had ridden the range in his youth as a cowhand with his old neighbor Boyd Charter.

His words were not salty. They were acid.

This is what he told me:

My father hitched up the six horses to our wagons. And he and my uncle drove them down the middle of the river, with our herd coming up behind us. There were no roads then. There were no good wagon trails either. There were hardly any real towns. We were one of the first families, *white* families, to settle there in that part of western Wyoming now known as Jackson Hole.

When we came there that land was just as the Indians had left it. No one had time to ruin it.

Now, I am not the oldest, but I am one of the oldest people living in this vicinity. So I know how it really was. I remember how the land was when the Indians left it.

The grass was tall. The towns was mostly cow towns. The cowhands mostly worked on the open range. It was beautiful country, more beautiful than you can imagine. We had clean atmosphere. We had clean people. We had clean politics. In those days a man's word was his bond. [His wife whispered across the kitchen table, "That is, among friends."] Say a man did not live up to his word. They would not go and argue with him. No. They would go and shoot him. I think that was a damned sight better, and more honest. Some of the politicians we have in Washington wouldn't have lasted one afternoon out here in the West.

If a man lived close to the land, he had to be as honest as the land.

When I was a young man, I remember how I rounded up wild horses all over Wyoming. There was herds, big herds, everywhere. There isn't hardly a rancher in the whole state I don't know personally from those days. There is no valley, no mountain, no canyon that I don't know. I rode through it on horseback when it was as free as the day it was born and created. Every mile of this land, I have known it.

That's all gone!

When I think of what they've done to Wyoming, I feel like

crying. The land is all fenced in. The land is covered with interstate highways, and gas stations, and shopping centers and fancy
hotels for the dudes and tourists, and those high-rise condominiums.

I can't hardly talk no more about it. I feel like crying for
a lost one.

They plowed up our plains. They cut down our trees. They
cemented over our grass. They polluted our water. It grieves
me to see the way our country is today, and the way they ruined
Jackson Hole, the Rockefellers and them. It just grieves me to
see that. So I sold out my father's ranches. He left me three good
ranches down in Jackson Hole. Well, I sold out and moved to
Montana, to be left alone. But they won't leave you alone.

Now the strip mining is coming to Montana. Everyone is
fearful of the coal.

In the old days, when a neighbor came to visit, or maybe
you met a rancher you knew in town, you sat down and talked
of all kind of different things—the price of calves in Chicago, a
horse you bought, or what the wind did to the roof, and the
family—you know, family things. They were good things to talk
about. Nowadays when ranchers get together all we talk about
is the coal.

Coal! The damned coal! The Goddamned coal! I get so sick
of talking about the coal and strip mining and power plants!

One afternoon I was sitting here, in my own house, and this
fellow came to the door from one of the coal companies. He
knew I was opposed to the strip mines. And he said to me: How
much do you want to keep your mouth shut?

They think they can buy just everyone and everything with
their money. So much money is involved in this coal that the
average citizen can't comprehend it.

Such as on my ranch, which consists of several sections. One
section—that is 640 acres. And I own quite a few sections. It is
known as a large ranch. Well, under each section there is a ten-
foot coal seam, which is not a big seam as Western seams go.
Well, I hired some people who know their weights and figures

to see what the coal under one section would be worth to the coal companies. And they figured out that the coal under that one section was worth about $170 million.

That is $170 million for each section. And as I say, I own quite a few sections.

Now, you multiply $170 million by millions of sections of ranches that lie within Montana, Wyoming, Nebraska, and the Dakotas, and you'll get billions on billions of dollars.

That is exactly the point of Watergate, I say.

If someone had the resources to go and find out just how much Haldeman and Ehrlichman and Nixon and the whole outfit had to do with the strip-mining coal leases! The energy crisis may turn out to be the biggest political plum ever heard of— for making millionaires. I think we would find that the Watergate outfit was in over its neck in this coal and energy dealing. I think that the giving of government land away, for subdividers and developers and resorts, may be mixed up in what they are really covering up in Watergate.

You know, compared to this, the Teapot Dome scandal was just an anthill. That was millions, but this is billions.

Some of the coal people say we ranchers are against strip mines because we don't own the mineral rights to our land. Well, in respect to that, I say they are the biggest liars the United States has ever produced.

It wouldn't make one hour of difference to me if I had the mineral rights, or not. No one is going to tear up my land for the damned dollar. Anyone who thinks otherwise doesn't know how we ranchers think. Lots of ranchers have turned down offers. I myself turned down an oil lease just this year.

Now, I will admit many ranchers in Montana and Wyoming may be fakes. What they are is big Eastern corporations who bought up the land and have no regard for it. The one thing they have regard for is money. But the real dyed-in-the-wool rancher, who makes his living out of the ground, who runs sheep or cattle, or who is growing wheat, or whatever he does, is anything but a fake. He is trying to save his way of life. He is trying to save his land.

Always, in the past, when we exploited the land, it had a chance to come back. It may sometime take centuries to bring the land back, but we could do it. We could have brought the buffalo back, if we had wanted to. If we wanted to, we could have got this country back to the way the Indians left it.

But I wonder now. . . .

If they go through with what they have proposed—the strip mining of the whole eastern plains of the Rockies, and the cutting off of all our timber, for export mostly, and the using up of all our water for power plants, and the polluting of all our mountain air—then I say this is our last chance to preserve America. This land is going to be torn up to such an extent there will not be anything left to preserve.

For God's sake, why can't we as citizens at least put the brakes on it! Before it is too late! Before America is in ruins!

On my ranch things are just the way they was. Ever see that picture *Little Big Man*? Well, they made some of it on my ranch. The director told me he was looking all over Montana for a place that was just the way it was one hundred years ago, when Custer came through. Someplace where the buffalo grass was waist high, where nothing was fake, where everything was authentic. My ranch was the only place he found. I am proud of that.

We live in a log cabin. Now, you may think that's pretty primitive. But I say we got to learn how to live again, doing for ourselves, controlling our own lives, living on the land and respecting the land.

Sometimes people ask me: Are you going Indian?

I say: What's wrong with that! The Indians had the right ideas, and we had the wrong ideas!

Listen, give me that pack of cigarettes. I don't know if you're going to want to hear this. When I say what I'm about to say, before I finish up my talk, you may not want to hear this. But I am going to say it: I am as loyal an American as there is anywhere in these United States. But when anything is ruined and exploited as our country has been by crooked politicians, I think the government, as it is run today, should be overthrown.

Now, when you say the word "overthrown," that is a pretty strong word. Well, I am anything but a Communist. I do not say overthrow it and make it communist, or socialist, or anything like that. I just say overthrow it as it is today and bring it back to the way the Constitution was written.

I say the Constitution was the greatest document written in the history of our country. But the government of the United States is run every way in the world but according to the Constitution of the United States. And so when I say overthrow the government and the people who are running it, I say let's get people in there to run it the way the Constitution says.

I say we have to stand still. And fight to preserve America. We have no choice at all. We have our backs against the wall. We are going to be the last generation of Western men if we lose. There's noplace to pioneer any more. Nowhere to go. Nowhere to run to. Nowhere to hide.

When we die, America dies.

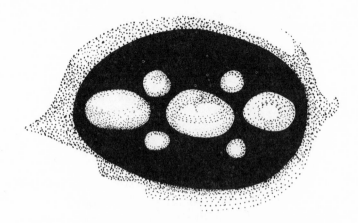

THE END OF THE BEGINNING

Man does not travel in space. It is space that travels in man.

What does that mean?

The space flight of man is very dangerous.

Why?

Man cannot conquer the space he is in. He is space. And if he enters the sky, then the sky will enter him. And he will be a different man.

Who will he be?

Man has lived in different worlds and in different forms. Your scientists do not understand these things, I think. They cannot see these changes are happening.

Why not?

Man does not know that he is growing older until he has grown old.

The old man seemed old. Maybe he seemed older than he was because of what he was saying. It was the year that the first Sputnik was launched, and everyone was talking about it and wondering what it meant. In his quiet way the Hopi was troubled; he had read about it on his trip to town and the more he thought about it, the more worried he became.

Are you very worried?

Man, the white man, will go to the moon. And if he does, will he dig up the moon as he has the earth? And if he does, will the moon fall out of the sky and burn up? Man might do that.

But why?

Man knows too little to do so much.

In those days the road to the villages of the Hopi was not paved. There had been a rainstorm in the mountains and the bridge at one of the big washes had been swept away. So the cars had to go down into the wash, across the sand, to get to the far side. Some did. It was like that in those days. Not that it mattered too much. There were few cars. On the high mesa of the Hopi there was no electricity, no telephones, no water pipes, no television, few radios. There was endless space and endless time.

So we squatted under a cottonwood tree in the summer heat and dust of the village and talked of the cosmic space that the NASA and Soviet physicists were entering and what it would do to them when it entered them.

The old man said:

Man should not go onto the moon. And if he does, that may mean his civilization may be ended.

He was silent for a moment, or longer.

And maybe, he said, then another will begin.

I have thought about that often since: Man, in his need to conquer the worlds of others, loses his harmony with his own. And with himself. He may have thought he conquered the world, but the world may have conquered him.

Man in his conceited ignorance went so far beyond the limits of his meager knowledge of life that he unleashed forces that he could neither understand nor control. In the end his own arrogance humbled him. And so the glory and triumph of his civilizations were what destroyed them.

The Circle of Life—man has one moment in it.

Is that enough?
Man is a small animal.

Civilizations rise and fall every few hundred years. The creations of man are very fragile. No matter how majestic his empires and sublime his visions of eternal cities and godly his sciences and religions, the works of man seem no more lasting than those of the smallest insects. Perhaps less so. The grasshoppers and butterflies of Rome have outlived the Caesars.

And yet, though everyone knows that civilizations come and go, Western man seems to believe it will never happen to him. He will last forever. He will be as eternal as the grasshopper.

The ruins of the Roman Empire, and the Mayan and Byzantine and Ottoman and Inca and Islamic and Egyptian and Ghanaian and Nigerian and Spanish and Aztec and English and Grecian and Persian, and the Mongolian civilization of the great khans, are visible for all to see. Is it heresy to say that the civilization of the white man of Western Europe, which has dominated much of the earth for four hundred years, is about to become just one more magnificent ruin? Not because it has failed to accomplish its goals, but because it has succeeded so well, its time on earth may be done.

Although it seems that most civilizations know when their end has come, few of them seem to understand what they know. Of those who do, fewer still accept what they understand.

In the uncut mountains of the harsh deserts of Chihuahua in northern Mexico, that land of Gran Chichimeca, there was a monument to the unwillingness of man to know what he sees— the city-states of Casa Grandes. One of these was built in about the year 900 by the merchant princes of the Toltec or Aztec. It lasted for four hundred years, until about 1340, when its rulers abandoned the city, the people fled to the countryside, the downtown area decayed, the factories went bankrupt, and the civilization ended with a suddenness that is not wholly understood to this day.

The *puchteca*, the Nahuatl word for merchants, had enticed rural and tribal peoples into the city, where they had lived in multistory urban housing projects, an unnatural environment for them. The master architects designed apartments for the people with built-in beds, stoves, windows, doors. So for these people who had always built their own environment, there was little to do but work. And this they did. It has been said that their way of working seemed to destroy their family and moral structures. But while the merchant civilization grew so the city grew.

And then the odd phenomenon began. The merchant city was an efficient and prosperous civilization that disintegrated because of its success.

On the great plaza the three-story houses collapsed. The people, who were mere tenants, no longer even attempted to clean up the debris or the dead. Instead, they "lived on the top of the destruction."

So said the anthropologist Charles DiPeso, director of the Amerind Foundation in the Dragoon Mountains not far from Tucson, Arizona. His archaeological teams had investigated the ruins of Casa Grandes. "The physical pressure should have caused mass psychological pressures, leading to self-destruction," he said, but it seems they did not. "Pure physical collapse did not disrupt the continuation of the [merchant] art tradition." In fact, "There was no drop in art style."

It was as if the technologists and workers, the intellectuals and rulers of Casa Grandes blithely went on working until the last moment. No one knew that one morning in 1340 the city would be abandoned.

That often happened at the end of a civilization. In the fourteenth century, when Europe's feudal era was about to end in the Black Death and the Hundred Years' War, there was a similar phenomenon, as noted by the historian Barbara Tuchman: "In decadence chivalry threw its brightest light; never were its ceremonies more brilliant; its jousts and tournaments so brave; its apparel so splendid; its manners so gay and amorous; its entertainments so festive its self-glorification so eloquent. The gentry elaborated the forms of chivalry *because* institutions around them were crumbling." And so the feudal knights of Europe, like the artisans of Casa Grandes, may have been celebrating the birth of a new civilization on the ruins of a dying one, with ancestral rites of renewal.

It was curious that the Black Death doomed European feudalism in the 1340s, at the very time Casa Grandes collapsed in America. While halfway across the world, in China, the famine of 1342 began the death pangs of the empire of the great Kublai Khan.

So it may be that when a civilization dies it does so not with a whimper, nor with a bang, but in a blaze of glory. The wake for a civilization, in lamentations of its death, may not be so different from that for a family member. It renews birth out of death, with a spiritual exorcism and an ecstasy of sensuality.

Men have often written of times such as these in the Domesday Book, which depicted the end of their way of life as though it were the end of the world. They see the death not of a civilization but of civilization itself. In these conceits the optimists and pessimists are mirror images; for both see man as a god, either creator or destroyer of life. He is neither. The common people may be humbler and wiser, but they have not written the Domesday Books. Nor do I know of any Domesday Book that was written by a woman.

In our time the cry of Armageddon is once more heard in the world. Gory scenes of apocalyptic disaster have become popular entertainments in which the deus ex machina of doom is more and more often not a natural catastrophe, but a man-made creation—a skyscraper, an ocean liner, a huge passenger jet. And the Domesday Book proliferated not in religious prophecy but in the fertile imaginations of white Malthusians and the unfrocked scientists, who had lost faith in the man gods of science and in man himself.

"Man alone is a beautiful thing, but put him in a car, in a B-52 bomber, and the proportion of brain, to brawn, is very small," said George Wald, a Nobel Prize laureate in medicine and physiology and a Harvard professor of biology. "Man's lost control of brawn, you see, and he's sinking lower and lower at a phenomenal speed." In despairing of man's lost control Wald despaired for life. "We are on the brink of physical disaster. Things are going down the drain, fast."

In the *Bulletin of Atomic Scientists*, a physicist, Bernard Feld, echoed the litany that had begun to sound like a eulogy for man's faith in his own accomplishments: "The world is entering upon perilous times, perhaps the most dangerous period in its entire history"—for man would probably use his scientific technology to destroy his own civilization.

Some thought he had begun to do so. "Civilization is going downhill," said Lewis Mumford. "Our technology, which we always hoped would be the means to make men happy and prosperous and give them more material possessions, is in imminent danger of doing just the opposite." Even so persevering an optimist as Norman Cousins, editor of the *Saturday Review*, expressed fears: "The evidence is strong that human society is in a stage of comprehensive breakdown." That was nothing less than the "breakdown of industrial civilization on the planet," said the author of *Future Shock*, Alvin Toffler. No wonder anthropologist Leslie White believed: "We're on the brink of chaos, *now.*"

In the fourteenth century it had been the monks and priests who led the rebellion against feudal religions, which they believed had failed God. And in the twentieth century it was the scientists and intellectuals who led the rebellion against science, which they knew had betrayed them. In dismay, the president of the National Academy of Sciences, Philip Handler, proclaimed with a tone of disbelief befitting an indignant Renaissance pope: "We find science and technology under attack." There had been a "drastic decline in our national scientific endeavor," he said. And it was the scientists who were leading this "attack." He was mistaken. It was not science as a way of learning that was under attack, but the arrogance of men, among them the men of science, who thought they were as gods, beyond all earthly laws. And who, in attempting to control the earth, had broken the Circle of Life. It was their conceit that was threatening humanity.

Once a civilization that is built on a belief in man's ability to control life loses its faith in man's godliness, it has no other. "There is a feeling of helplessness," said George Wald, "for man controls the existence of all things," and man had "lost control." If there was no faith in the sun, the earth, the sky, the spirit, but faith in man alone, what happened when that was gone?

"If then, by the question: 'Is there hope for man?' we ask whether it is possible to meet the challenges of the future without the payment of a fearful price," the historian Robert Heilbroner wrote in *An Inquiry into the Human Prospect*, "the answer must be 'There is no such hope.'"

The prophecies of these men were strangely like those of the Old People. But there was one crucial difference. In the Old People's prophecies there was some sorrow, but no sense of doom. There was always the knowledge of rebirth. When the council of the Creek Nation met "way before 1500," they told how the "four-legged" man, the white man, "would come out of the sea, his eyes made of gold, his heart made of gunpowder, his veins full of whiskey." And he would destroy the People, "almost." When he "had done all the damage, he would return back to the sea. And the People would come back. And they would live forever."

And the Eskimo William Willoya told in the prophecy of *The Warriors of the Rainbow* how the People were "physically conquered by the white people," but, "Like the joyful Indians of old, the new Indians shall bring back to their own people and spread to other races the joy of good-fellowship and kindness and courtesy. How they danced together. How they ate together in loving harmony! How they prayed together and sang together in joy! It shall come again and better in the new world."

And the Lakota wise man Lame Deer, after telling of all the sorrows the white man had brought his People, said this: "We Indians hold the pipe of peace. We must try to use the pipe for mankind, which is on the road to self-destruction. We must try to save the white man from himself."

And the Hopi elders wrote to President Harry Truman, after

he sanctioned the holocaust of Hiroshima: "What has become of your religion?" In spite of the "murderers and destroyers" the white man had become, and his "wild and reckless adventure, which we know will lead us to total ruin," they appealed to him. "We have no enemy." All humans were one. Though the civilization of the white man was too warlike—"What nation who has taken up arms ever brought peace and happiness to his people," the elders said—nonetheless he was "the white brother." If he blew up his civilization, he might destroy others. So, the elders said, "Let us make haste and set our house in order before it is too late."

And in New York City, an Iroquois woman, Doris Melliadis, said: "Now they come to gather for the coming disaster and destruction of the white man *by his own hands,* with his own progressive, advanced, technological devices, that only the American Indian can avert. Now the time is near. And it is only the Indian who knows the cure. It is only the Indian who can stop this plague. And this time the invisible will be visible. And the unheard will be heard. And we will be seen and we will be remembered."

None of the prophecies told of a battle between the native People and these white people. There was no biblical war of Armageddon in which the technological and tribal societies slaughtered each other. There was no vengeance of the tribes, but only the vengeance of nature in restoring the harmony and balance of the Circle of Life. In this way the rise and fall of civilizations were more wisely understood, it seemed to me, than in all the history books, in which civilizations were chronicled by conquest or defeat in the monotonous and inhuman wars of men.

On the earth, there were some People who knew the turn of the Circle of Life was welcome, as it was inevitable, for they knew the civilizations of man were not eternal. They knew this because they had not forgotten the emergence of their ancestors from the earth. And so they remembered that they were part of the earth.

So they knew: The end of a civilization was not the end of

life. Merely of a way of life. The many civilizations of humans had risen and fallen often, as did the cycles of the earth and universe. The new ways of life developed new forms of life, and the new forms of life developed new ways of living. And they had no fear of this.

The four worlds and the four directions where the Old People had journeyed before becoming human had once been dismissed as emergence myths. Now the famous white archaeologists the Leakeys, by the use of what was called scientific analysis, had confirmed what the Old People had said: The human animal had emerged from the mud of the earth not in one line of evolution, but in four directions. "Man's family tree has had four branches," it was now thought by the white man; and three of these, the Robustus, Africanus, and Ancestral, had never become really human, as the emergence myths had so scientifically and patiently known for so long.

In the past, scientists were often "tempted to think patronizingly of the old philosophers and tribal wise men," Dorothy Vitaliano of the U.S. Geological Survey has written in *Legends of the Earth, Their Geological Origins.* The time has come to give "credit to the powers of observation of long gone people," she said; for it may be that geology and mythology were more "interrelated" than white scientists had imagined. And the so-called myths of the Old People could be understood as "actual geological events that may have been witnessed by various groups of people."

Not merely was this true of biblical floods, the creation of oceans, and volcanic upheavals. The memory of tribal people went beyond the limits of the minuscule knowledge of the science of detribalized people, who had extirpated the root of their history and no longer remembered their ancestors, nor knew their ancestral land.

To some it may have seemed as though the Circle of Life was the perfect circle, easily knowable. It appeared neat and orderly. The processes of life seemed to fit perfectly into one another, as in a chemical formula. And so the scientists imagined it as a food chain, a helix, a double helix, a spiral, the linear path of evolution where everything fit together, with a beginning and an end. It was seen rising from the primeval swamps, from the fishes of the slimy seas, from the lowly skulls of apes, to nature's "greatest achievement," man himself.

Was this so? The elders knew it differently.

Once the Circle of Life was endless. It began nowhere and it ended everywhere and it had no beginning and no ending. Where it turned, there it went. People, too, were that way; they went wherever life did. In the Gran Chichimeca, anthropologist Charles DiPeso had seen it in the ruins: Civilizations rose and fell "in fits and starts, but seldom, if ever, in natural phase cycles," and "an historical approach should never postulate a pure society, or unmixed culture"; for all life was part of all life. That meant, DiPeso said, "There was no break in the historical continuum, merely a change in exploitable actors" in "man's passage through time" and space.

And as it was in people, so it was with all things. The life of everything was shared by everything. Even the stones knew this.

Banyacya, the Hopi, said it this way: "Many of our Old People have told us that we received some gift or power that is in the animals or birds." He himself had been given the name of corn and water. So these were part of him. "All living things of nature —birds, animals, plant life—are sisters and brothers. We are taught we are related to everything around us. And when you become initiated into some of the ceremonies, you become a father to everything—people, family, birth, animal—they're all part of you.

"I'm sure that our spiritual People are right in saying that somewhere all races of mankind are going to come back to spiritual things. And here we have that. We are ready to impart that knowledge to many nations and races of people in the hope that somebody in this world will understand—maybe. Our white brothers who are with us, they don't understand it now. But later, something's going to happen.

"So we follow the spiritual circle," he said.

The enduring wisdom of the Old People, with the serenity and humanity of its peaceful Armageddon, has become more and more sought after as the technology of modern man seems less and less wise, and his deeds have become more and more violent and futile. A profound search has begun for the knowledge of the ancients. The seekers come in larger pilgrimages every year.

These seekers have sensed not the end of civilization, but a new beginning. In their search there is humility, and in their despair there is hope. In seeking to chart the future, the historian of *The Myth of the Machine*, Lewis Mumford, forecast a new "dark age." But "Under the surface a new life may be knitting together," he said, "struggling still to find its way."

Where would it lead? He thought our time "must be very much like what happened during the transition from the Roman civilization, which was highly organized and bent on the same ends as our civilization, power! productivity! prestige!, to the Christian era. The Christians formed into little bands. They began to withdraw from society and accepted poverty. They built a spiritual foundation for their life which gave them the internal strength to take over the Roman Empire."

Nowadays, too, there were little bands and tribes which were "the seedbed of the future," Mumford said. They were learning to live without destroying life. And by giving back to the earth the energy they had taken from the earth. It was "embarrassingly simple," Mumford said, to solve the "energy crisis" and then "save the earth."

The new quest was most surprisingly expressed by the honored historian of Western Civilization, Lord Arnold Toynbee. In his monumental *Study of History*, he had chronicled the rise and fall of twenty-one civilizations, in ten volumes. All these had died, or were dying, but one, his own Western Civilization, which he hinted might be spiritually eternal. In a pontifical work, *Civilization on Trial*, Toynbee wrote: "If our secular Western Civilization perishes, Christianity may be expected not only to endure but to grow in wisdom and stature as the result of a fresh experience of secular catastrophe."

And so, though Western Civilization may indeed end, that would intensify its spiritual strength. Such was the faith of a generation ago.

People who might doubt this euphoric belief in white civilization, as did the "Appalachian 'mountain people,' " who offered "the melancholy spectacle of a people who have acquired civilization and then lost it," such people, said Toynbee, were "no better than barbarians." And if they were white, they were "latter-day white barbarians."

That had been written in 1948. By 1974, Toynbee no longer exalted the spiritual strength of Western Civilization, nor did he foresee hope of its eternity. The "modern world's malady," he now declared, "is spiritual. We are suffering from having sold our souls to the pursuit of an objective that is both spiritually wrong and practically unattainable"—the "continuous increase in material wealth."

In words that had that sage tone of old men, the historian of Western Civilization spoke of all that he had seen, and all that he had learned, in the modern world. Toynbee said:

"Mankind is now waging what is, in effect, a third World War. The belligerents, as usual, trying to justify to themselves their inhuman treatment of their fellow human beings by hoisting ideological banners. The professed ideologies of opposing sides are intentionally incompatible with each other, but they are shams: There is no difference between the combatants' objectives and no difference, either, in their behavior.

"The common objective is a continuous increase in material wealth. . . ."

And it was this that was "spiritually wrong and practically unattainable." It was a "deliberate rejection of the precepts of mankind's greatest seers, from the Buddha to Saint Francis of Assisi. These precepts are unanimous. The seers have declared that the maximization of material wealth is not right, and therefore is not a satisfying objective for human beings."

On earth there was one place and one people that offered hope, Toynbee thought. These were in America:

There is one surviving people, the Pueblo Indians, whose way of life is the antithesis of modern mechanized man. The Pueblo people, like the rest of us, are concerned to secure the material subsistence, but they are not concerned to maximize either their collective, or their individual wealth. The nonindigenous Americans and the Europeans, and the Russians and the Japanese ought now to ask themselves which of these two ways of life is the happier and the better way: The Pueblo people's or modern mechanized man's? In the modern world, who is free?

Mankind's habitat is limited to the thin film of earth, air and water that coats the surface of our native planet. If mankind is to secure its survival on earth for as long as the earth's surface is going to remain habitable, we shall have to reduce our material life to a Pueblo-like stability. We shall have to renounce our present objective of maximizing material wealth.

The Pueblo people have invested [the earth's treasure] more providently, as the Buddha and Saint Francis would say. Man does not live by bread alone. The simpletons and the seers are surely going to have the last word.

One could say that Toynbee, by his own definition, had become a "white barbarian."

On the mountains of the Hopi it was evening. The sky had come nearer the earth. And the sun had come down from the sky. It clothed the mountains with the evening and closed the eyes of the day.

In the tribal office of Alvin Dashee, the young ex-Marine and member of the Sun and Eagle Clan who was vice-president of the Hopi, it was becoming dark. He switched on a fluorescent light. He talked of how the prophecy of the Old People might end:

"The elders say: There is a time to be born, a time to learn, a time to be loved. And then, the elders say: There is a time to be married, a time to have children, a time to teach and enjoy the children. And then, the elders say: There is a time to live a full life, a time to be old, a time to be taken care of and to enjoy your grandchildren, when you have done your part. And then, the elders say: There is a time to die.

"And these are the four paths of life. It is what each of us will live. These are the plans for life on this earth. These things are sacred.

"And what I am saying is that is what this world is going through. It was born. It has had its youthful days. It has had its productive days. She is old. Mother Earth has had its time. It is dying, in a way.

"In the Prophecy of the Elders they say: At the end the white man is going to be coming to us. To ask us things so he can go and try to educate other white men. So he can try to save them. A few of the white men will be chosen to do this.

"Even as among us only a few will be chosen.

"These white men will be trying to be Hopi. We have been seeing that already. We have to be very careful with them. We have to criticize the white men who behave the way some of them do when they come.

"And we know what is happening. When that time comes, it will be near the end.

"So in the prophecy they say: Our religion will become a show-case. When that time comes, we will not allow it. Sometimes we feel as though we are becoming a zoo. That is why, I think, some Hopi do not allow some white men to come to see our religious ceremonies any more.

"In the prophecy they say: We are the most chosen. We are to be great again.

"And I think they mean all ethnic People. In the Hopi way of talking, they talk about the brown People—the People of the Sun—those with brown skins. The prophecy is talking about being one family, I think. We are coming closer to being one family.

"One family is the way we have to be."

And so in the end there was the beginning. It was the end of the beginning.

Where Are We Going?

🦷 TESTAMENT OF Gerald Wilkinson, Director,
National Indian Youth Council

*Not by words alone will people learn to understand the meaning
of their lives.*

*That may be why Western man studies so much but knows
so little. That may be why his civilization has to collapse before
he knows what's happening to it. That may be why he cannot,
or will not, change his ways of life until his ways of life change
him. He thinks he can change his life by changing his words.
That may be his real forked tongue.*

Some wise old man musing about the meaning of life? No.
These were the thoughts of a young man. He wore an old army
jacket. He once attended the Sorbonne, in Paris. He drove an un-
tamed and lamed Mustang, the kind manufactured in Detroit
by the descendants of Henry Ford. He was Gerald Wilkinson,
executive director of the National Indian Youth Council. He was
a Cherokee.

In the coffee shop of a motel on Central Avenue in Albuquerque, New Mexico, he sat in a plastic booth and philosophized
as he sipped his iced tea. He had come from another trip to
Washington, D.C., where he had testified before Congress once
more. He wondered what, if anything, his words meant to those
"strangers."

We are not gods. That is what Western man likes to think about his words. That may be why the earth has rejected him.

The man who came from Europe is a stranger in this land. He thought that he had created America. He did not. He thought he was America. He was not. He is still searching for the meaning of America. He has not found it. He will not find it.

In this land he will be a stranger forever.

Many times we had talked of this—so many times it was impossible to remember which of these words were his and which were mine. For so many years, in so many conversations, we had shared our words and our thoughts, together and with so many others, that it no longer mattered too much who said what to whom.

On that day in the coffee shop one of us said to the other:

It is strange that the white man from Europe is still so nervous on this earth. Why is he so lonely? So rootless? So lost? So violent? Why is he this way?

That had been talked of for five hundred years by the native People. Ever since the white strangers had come, they had asked themselves why they acted as they did. In the beginning these things were talked of quietly, among themselves. Now they were said to the face of the whites.

That began after the end of World War II. Hopi philosophers and religious wise men had decided that the white men might be destroying their own civilization. And the sign of that was the atomic bomb, they thought.

Since then the new Indian movements had been bolder and louder in voicing fear of the white man's self-destruction. And their hope of tribal rebirth. Among the first to speak out were the young people of the National Indian Youth Council, who gathered on a hot desert day in August 1960, in a dusty room of the Gallup Indian Center in New Mexico, behind the railroad tracks. And it was there that a quiet, scholarly young Navajo, Herbert Blatchford, a descendant of Manuelito (a great leader of his People), was the first who'd said they might become "a remnant of the Warrior Society." And if that was to be, Blatchford said, "Well, then, rise up, make haste. Our people need us." He was too modest. America needed them, too. America listened, too.

Some did become a new Warrior Society. Some went on to defend Wounded Knee again. Some went to Washington, D.C., to use the tactics of technology to build tribal society, or to try. And some tried to do all these things, to fight for the rights of modern life even as they renewed the ties to their ancestral tribes.

One of the many who had tried to do all these things was Gerald Wilkinson. And so I asked him:

Where is America going? Where are we going? Where are you going?

This is what he told me:

When the Europeans came to this country, something happened. There was a splitting off, a cutting off, of the white people's roots to their cultures. A final detribalization that was going on in Europe was completed here. The roots of the white people were just snapped in two.

And that is a cruel thing, to cut yourself off from your culture.

In America the European people began to look for something else. That document, that piece of paper, that "Bill of Rights," became their concept of themselves. It is their life. It is a weird concept for people to have of themselves as a people.

So in a basic sense, America is not a real country to most whites. America is not a nation in a cultural sense to them. To most whites America is an idea. Some kind of concept, a document, a piece of paper, the Constitution of the United States. Perhaps it's the idea of material advancement, an ideology of *things.*

Now, Indian people have a different view. They don't look at themselves as an idea. They see themselves as a People who live in a certain space, on land where their ancestors are buried. On that space there is something that takes place, a culture takes place, because the People live there. And that is America to them.

People who see themselves as an idea, well, it is very hard for them to know where America really is. Or for us to tell them what the Grand Canyon *means*.

Now, suppose I wiped out the idea of the United States so the country no longer existed! Then the white Americans would look upon themselves as no longer having any country. Because the piece of paper that guided them would be gone. The idea would be destroyed.

On an Indian reservation we would survive that. We have tribal chairmen who are close to being communists, and chairmen who are close to being fascists, and all the shades of ideology in between. That doesn't sustain us or destroy us. What sustains us is our culture. And what sustains our culture is it is part of the land, it comes from the land. It *is* America.

And the whites don't have that strength; it is a weakness of the whites. So we're dealing with people who are frightened, who are paranoid, because they have no country, no real country. In a way we're dealing with a nation of juveniles, who have never grown up, who have great power but no real strength, who pretend they are men but are really children. That's sad. It worries me. It's very strange.

The detribalization of Europeans was the final negation of 99 percent of mankind's past. Most people here call that good. And that's what makes them so dangerous. To destroy your tribal past is the same thing as going out and destroying all the books in all the libraries, all the records and documents. It is a gut fear of their birth, of their ancestors, that the whites have.

Once you have destroyed your roots can you learn how to replant them from an ideology?

No.

No one can make a culture. You don't make a culture. You don't make a nation. You don't make a tribe. The Great Spirit makes them. It happens because people live together, because they have to survive. That's what makes a culture, a nation, a tribe. That's something that's given to you. And you just accept it; you don't make it. What is a tribe? It's not rituals and customs. It's the relationships of human beings who share their lives, who are together in the way they express themselves. And if you are nothing, you can be anything.

Th communities of tribal people are not organized to progress. They are organized *to be*. And that is something that is absent in Western man—the ability *to be*. Perhaps the Indian People who have survived spiritually have created a way of saving the earth in this way, by simply *being*.

And *to be* is a hard, hard way. . . .

The "Indian way" is the hard way. Even if you eliminated all the poverty and the oppression, the "Indian way" would be hard.

Some of the whites who say that they want to live the "Indian way" might be able to; but very few. To most whites it's a romantic idea.

All the white people who come into the Indian community have a basic continuity in their visions of the world. They are basically the same people.

It seems to me that the Indian People have been the victims of versions of Western man for hundreds of years. First, the conquistadors came. And stole everything. Then the missionaries came behind them. And they said they would save the Indian People if they gave up their religion. Then the U.S. Army and the Bureau of Indian Affairs came and said they would save us by setting up a colonial system. And today white people come to the reservation and tell us they will save us by this program or that program, if we will become socialist, or capitalist.

So often in the past we got mixed up in other people's ideological fights. We are coming to look less and less for Western ideologies. We always have had to bear the brunt of these ideologies, whether of the left or of the right. Now, as we look at the world in our struggle for survival, we are beginning to see that for us capitalism and communism are just the left and the right hand of the same European beast.

One time, I remember, we were holding a protest on the

White Mountain Apache Reservation, at Cibique. And I had got up pretty early and walked down to the café there. And the Jehovah's Witnesses were broadcasting a Sunday service on a loudspeaker. And there were two guys in the café arguing with each other in Apache. It got to be pretty heated. They got up and went outside. A few minutes later there was a huge fight, a terrible fight.

So I asked this Apache girl: What are those guys fighting about?

Oh, they had a religious argument, she told me. They were fighting over the merits of salvation by faith or salvation by works!

Two Apaches!

And that brought home to me how outside ideologies divide us. And our people end up fighting each other. That's how it is in a lot of these militant actions when the outsiders rush in to provide their own ideological viewpoint and expertise in a struggle that we are conducting. Sometimes it's hard to bring these people to realize that we are not lumpenproletarians or some other ideological category that they have in their minds. It's the same idea of Western superiority as the conquistadors had.

Now they are hitting us over the head with the ecology movement. We have survived all the others, but I don't know if we can survive this one.

Why?

They have tried in every way to destroy us. They tried to use hatred. And genocide. And slavery. But we survived that. So the only thing they've got left to try is love. The ecology movement may do us in by loving us to death. And love is very difficult to fight against.

But it has occurred to me that the ecology movement has no spiritual base. Well, how can anyone save the earth who has no spiritual relationship with the earth? They can't really love the earth. Even though they talk about saving this or that, like saving the Grand Canyon, they don't really know why the Grand Canyon should be saved. And this is very disconcerting. It is rhetoric. There is a kind of intellectual abstraction about the earth, but no visceral participation in the earth.

To me, saving the earth is like putting out a fire in your house. The earth isn't an abstraction: the earth is simply your house.

One of the strange things about this country is that it still doesn't see itself as a place, a space on the earth. It doesn't see itself as a people who are living on some place, on some land.

Even so, the Old People tell us that we shouldn't hate these whites. Because if you hate someone, you are controlled by him. It's a funny kind of control.

And they also tell us we should not love them. Because if you love someone, the same kind of control exists.

So what the Old People tell us is that we should be indifferent. Because if we have no relationship, we can't be controlled by them. And there are a great many Indian communities who have survived in that way. Indifference is perhaps one of the greatest of insults.

One thing Indian People now see is that the white man has no perspective on his own world. He doesn't see that it is coming to an end. To see the end coming, you have to be able to step back, to not be part of it, to see the whole cycle.

Most people have chosen to be part of the white man's world. Even the nationalists want to be part of it, to have a piece of it. They just want to have a separate piece of it. Whereas the Indian People have never accepted the basic premises of the white man's world. Even when they take part in it, they are not part of it. That gives them the kind of perspective to see the white man's world as it is.

In Mexico, a native Maya priest said to me: Everything is a cycle. The Toltecs came, and that was a cycle. The Aztecs came, and that was a cycle. The conquistadors came, and that was a cycle.

Now they are waiting for the next cycle to come, he said. The cycle is coming back. So the white man will go just the way the Toltecs did. In Mayan, they say, no one has a name any more for the Toltecs. So maybe the white man will have no name to be remembered by. Except as a bird that is extinct is remembered by a scientific name.

Now we are on the edge of the world. The tribal People know that. Because we know these things are going to happen. It's like a tribe that has died a thousand times. That is not supposed to exist. But it does. If you are living on the verge of extinction for a long time you become toughened to the idea of death. And that's helped us deal with our death. And our rebirth.

Now the whole thing is coming to an end. It may be a holocaust, or not. And how the people deal with it will decide how the world will be put back together again.

Now, when you talk about the destruction of the earth, you are talking about political states and social systems and psychological attitudes. You are not talking about the end of life. There will be some people left, who will learn to live again.

Who will survive? People who are close to the earth, who are the custodians of the soil, who have learned from the earth, who have the earth's wisdom, who have learned how to survive. They will survive.

It is meaningless to talk of the destruction of the earth as an abstraction. The peasant in the fields won't buy that; he can't buy that. He will go on planting his corn.

On their soil, for thousands of years, the Maya have always grown corn. It is inconceivable to them that there won't always be some corn to grow somewhere, sometime. That's the beauty of life, that it continues. That's not a prison, as the white man says; it's a very satisfying way of life for the Maya, it's the knowledge of life that has made it possible for them to survive.

Now, it seems as if the white man's concept of his world is different. It is self-destructive. It is a self-fulfilling prophecy. And when we talk about living in this time when the world is coming to an end, we have to see what kind of world is coming to an end. It's a perversion of life that's being ended; a cancer. Sometimes, to save the earth, some things—that are destroying the earth—have to be destroyed. That's a natural process. That's nothing you, nor I, can do anything about.

When societies become too sick or tired to live, they die. The way a plant does.

Now, no one can know what is going to happen after this whole thing falls apart. Even in the prophecies. It is not as if anyone can just stand here and watch it. All we can know is that at that time the People will return, as People.

And maybe, through that, we will be able to create a new world, a world of human beings. There is another world. Another world is coming.

Index